MW00454125

STARRY
FIELD

STARRY FIELD

A Memoir of Lost History

MARGARET JUHAE LEE

MELVILLE HOUSE
BROOKLYN · LONDON

STARRY FIELD: A MEMOIR OF LOST HISTORY

First published in 2024 by Melville House
Copyright © 2023 by Margaret Juhae Lee

First Melville House Printing: January 2024

Melville House Publishing
46 John Street
Brooklyn, NY 11201

and

Melville House UK
Suite 2000
16/18 Woodford Road
London E7 0HA

mhpbooks.com
@melvillehouse

ISBN: 978-1-68589-093-3
ISBN: 978-1-68589-094-0 (eBook)

Library of Congress Control Number: 2023949062

Designed by Beste M. Doğan

Cover photo courtesy of the National Institute of Korean History collection

Printed in the United States of America
10 9 8 7 6 5 4 3 2 1

A catalog record for this book is available from the Library of Congress

For my family

TABLE OF CONTENTS

TIMELINE

1894	Tonghak Peasant Rebellion
1894	Sino-Japanese War breaks out between China and Japan in Korea.
1905	Korea becomes a protectorate of Japan.
1908	Min Kum Soon (Halmoni) born in Chongju, Korea
1909	Lee Chul Ha born in Kongju, Korea
1910	Korea becomes a colony of Japan.
1934	Eun Sul Lee is born in Kongju, Korea; Chong Mahn Lee is born in Seoul.
1936	Lee Chul Ha dies.
1945	Korea is divided in two after the Allied victory in World War II, ending Japanese rule. The United States and Soviet Union occupy the country, with the boundary between South and North at the 38th parallel.
1950–53	Korean War
1953–Pres.	South Korea and North Korea exist independently.

1958	Eun Sul is diagnosed with tuberculosis and recovers in a sanitarium.
1962	Eun Sul and Chong Mahn move to the United States for graduate school.
1963–79	Park Chung Hee serves as President of Korea until his assassination.
1966	Margaret Juhae Lee is born in Raleigh, North Carolina.
1969	The Lee family moves to Houston, Texas.
1972	Edward Tongju Lee is born.
1984	Margaret graduates from high school and attends college at the University of Texas at Austin.
1992	Margaret moves to San Francisco.
1995	Lee Chul Ha reburial service, Taejon National Cemetery, South Korea
1996	Margaret moves to New York to attend NYU; Eun Sul undergoes lung surgery.
1999	Margaret moves to Arlington, MA, for a Bunting Fellowship at Harvard.
2000	Margaret travels to Korea.
2018	Eun Sul Lee dies.
2019	Chong Mahn Lee dies.
End of 2019	The Lee family scatters Eun Sul and Chong Mahn's ashes in Korea.

LEE FAMILY TREE

PATERNAL SIDE

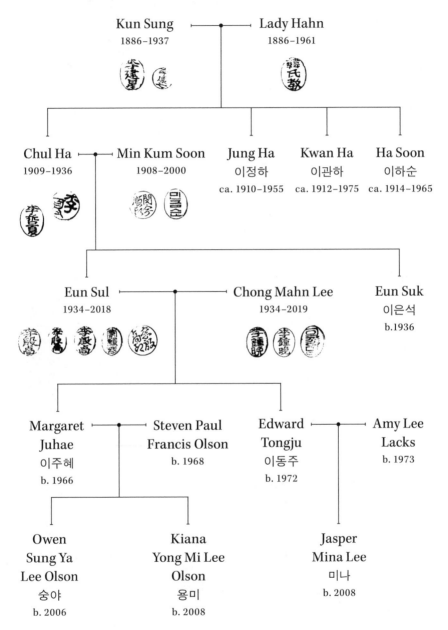

The oval stamps are dojang, signature seals. For family members
without dojang, their names have been indicated in Korean characters.

AUTHOR'S NOTE

This is a memoir of lost history, a story that has taken me over twenty years to write.

The story is rooted in my family's memories and the complicated history of Korea in the twentieth century. It employs a variety of methods to uncover the truth of my family's past—investigative journalism, oral history, archival research, and the reconstruction of scenes based upon the testimony of family members. I have changed some names to protect the identity of subjects and rebuilt conversations between people. Any speculation of events on my part is indicated in the text.

In the chapter "Defiance," I imagined my grandfather's interrogation by a Japanese police investigator, the one that took place on September 18, 1928, at the West Gate Police Station in Seoul. My grandfather's responses are verbatim from my mother's translation of the report.

ORIGIN STORY

Once upon a time there was a girl who was born in a country where she didn't feel at home. She looked different than everyone else, she ate different foods. People asked her questions like "Where are you from?" When she answered "Houston," they would ask, "No, where are you really from?"

Ten years old, and the girl traveled to the country of her parents' birth—she didn't feel at home there, either. She could understand some of what people were saying, but she could only speak in phrases, like a toddler. Her grandmother had taught her the language of her forebearers when she was little, but her parents spoke English to her at home, at the advice of the pediatrician who said, "She will fall behind in school if you don't."

The girl grew up, forgot her grandmother's language, went to college, tried a couple of careers, and settled on journalism. She decided to investigate the mystery of the grandfather she never knew, the one who went to prison and died when her father was a baby. She started by asking her grandmother questions, questions her grandmother didn't want to answer.

The girl decided to visit the country of her parents' birth again, this time alone. She wanted to solve the mystery of who her grandfather had been by finding the police and interrogation records her grandmother burned during the Korean War. The records that branded him as a teenage Communist revolutionary who protested Japanese rule.

After years of classes, the girl could now read and speak a bit of her parents' language. However, she realized that she needed to hire a translator and speak English to be taken seriously by the men who could help her find her grandfather's records.

The girl eventually found her grandfather's records, even though they were not where they were supposed to be. She brought them back to her father in the United States. They were the best present she could ever give him—except for grandchildren. She began to write a book about her search for lost history but put it down when life intervened. She picked it up again but was unable to finish it before her parents died.

WHEN OUR DAUGHTER KIKI WAS in kindergarten, I'd climb into her loft bed to do bedtime. My husband Steve exceeded the weight limit, so I would snuggle in with Kiki while he read to our son Owen, whose bed was closer to the ground. Most of the time I forgot to bring a book, so I made up stories to tell her.

There were tales of the Wonder Twins, siblings I remembered from childhood cartoons who harnessed their superpowers by touching their rings together. The twins rescued cats from trees, walked old ladies across the street. They cooperated instead of bickered, unlike Kiki and Owen.

"The Ten Thousand Bears" was a clear rip-off of Goldilocks and the Three Bears, my favorite childhood story, except in my telling Goldilocks had dark hair and wandered off from home to discover an enormous cave with ten thousand beds to choose from instead of three. In the end, Goldilocks decided to leave her birth family and live among the community of bears since she was so lonely at home.

They all lived happily ever after.

WHEN THE KIDS WERE IN preschool, I started again on my book about my grandfather. The one I abandoned when I got pregnant. I rewrote the whole thing off the top of my head during a generative writing workshop that met once a week—no notes, research, or outlines to guide me. I just wrote what flowed out from my hand to the pen and onto the lined paper of my giant spiral-bound notebook. All that material had soaked in since 2000, the year I traveled to Korea in search of my grandfather's prison records. Back then, I uncovered facts about my grandfather Lee Chul Ha's short life—his interrogation transcripts, the list of books he read while imprisoned, the secret code he devised to communicate with his Communist comrades—but what permeated my very being were the stories my grandmother Halmoni told me before she died. They embedded themselves into my body and became part of who I was—a granddaughter, a daughter, and finally, a mother.

I needed to release them from my body.

SO HERE IT IS, KIKI and Owen, here's my origin story. The one that took me over twenty years to write. There were, of course, interruptions. I moved back to the Bay Area after returning from Korea. My first agent left the publishing business. I met your father. We got married, had Owen and then, two years later, Kiki. Then came busy family life—thousands of Lego pieces, hundreds of soccer practices, long drives to Portland to visit Grandma and Grandpa, trips to Korea, lingering sicknesses, untimely deaths, crash courses in finance and estate law, and the almost unbearable gravity of grief.

My story is one I hope you can let seep into your being. For my story is our story, and involves the reclamation of the lives forgotten and seemingly buried forever in our ancestral homeland.

MY STORY BEGINS LIKE THIS:

ASHES

We arrive in Seoul the last week of 2019. Brother Ed and family meet us from Portland, via Seattle. I feel comfortable in Seoul, even though I can barely speak the language. Seoul was my home for four months in the year 2000, when I was single and carefree but still burdened with sorrow. My grandmother, Halmoni, had died two months before.

My Korean language skills have deteriorated in the last twenty years from disuse, but I'm still able to understand or at least get the gist of conversations if they involve food, bath time, school, or some subject familiar to toddlers. I can even read hangul at a snail's pace, which is handy when trying to pick a restaurant.

The type A members of my family need lots of interpretation and explanation. At the dumpling restaurant around the corner from the hotel, I explain that mandoo comes in six iterations—six dumpling servings, either pan fried, steamed, or in soup—in two varieties: veggie or pork. My brother's kid wants half pan-fried veggie and half steamed pork. I tell him that you can't special order at neighborhood restaurants in Korea. You must pick from the clearly delineated choices on the menu. His mother requests that I ask the server if a special order is possible, just this once. I take a deep breath and go find the young man with the BTS bowl cut who handed us the menus. I ask as politely as I can in my broken Korean if he can make an exception to the choices on the menu. He shakes his head, "anneyo," and in English, "just pick one." We have better luck at the hotel buffet the next morning, where there's a variety of mediocre American breakfast food to satisfy everyone.

The day after, we take two taxis to Seoul Station, one for each family. I ask the nice concierge who speaks perfect English to write down the address for my brother and family to give to their driver since they know absolutely zero Korean. My kids jockey for seats—no one wants to sit in the middle. For them, each and every interaction is a competition. The red heat of irritation crawls up my neck and into my cold cheeks. My annoyed inner voice begins to yap.

Jesus Christ, just get in the car. Hurry up, it's fricking cold.

Why do we only travel to Korea in the dead of winter?

Steve—the buffer, the wingman, the wrangler of rambunctious children—booms, "Owen, Kiki, you will take turns sitting in the middle!" My dance card is already full, tour guide duties wrapped in a heavy blanket of grief.

WE ARE VIPS FOR THE first time ever. As benefactors of my father and grandfather's alma mater, Kongju High School, we are provided first-class, high-speed train tickets. Never in my life did I think our family would be benefactors of anything. We were a middle-class immigrant family with no generational wealth in the United States. My statistician father, Eun Sul, provided us with a stable existence in the low-cost Houston suburbs. All of his so-called wealth was tied to his retirement account, which he had faithfully contributed to each month for the entirety of his appointment at the School of Public Health, even if it meant cutting back on other things for the family. Each month, he sent money to my grandmother in Korea. He gave Chong, my artist mother, a weekly allowance for groceries and other sundry items. Mom earned extra cash sewing prom dresses for the neighbors' kids and silk blouses for rich River Oaks ladies she met at church. She bought all items for the family on sale or at the Blue Bird Circle consignment shop downtown.

My father saved so much and invested so wisely that, for their final years, he and my mom were able to live at Mirabella. The high-rise retirement community in Portland with the best memory care facility in the city. They died earlier than expected, almost exactly a year apart.

DURING MY CHILDHOOD, MY FATHER described himself as a country boy from Kongju, the former capital of the Paekche dynasty, who no one dreamed would be accepted to Seoul National University after the Korean War ended. He had even surprised himself. He claimed he was only an average student. What I didn't realize until I was an adult was that his family was descended from yangban landowners, just like my mother's, but ones whose fortunes did not expand during colonialism or after the war.

On my first trip to Korea in 1976 when I was ten years old, we visited members of my mother's family in their Seoul mansions and fancy high-rise apartments. My father's side still lived in the countryside. One of his cousins was a taxi driver. His brother's house didn't have indoor plumbing. Even so, my father's family still owned land in the hills between the cities of Kongju and Taejon, including various plots where our ancestors were buried and an entire mountain made of granite. It used to house my grandfather's and great-grandfather's tombs.

In 1995, my grandfather's grave was exhumed from the mountain site and moved to the National Cemetery near Taejon. There, he joined a growing number of South Korean Patriots, generals, presidents, and politicians. From obscurity to renown, almost sixty years after his death. This event changed my father and the trajectory of my family completely.

When he and my mother moved into Mirabella in 2015, I had urged my father to sell off the land that was still under his name. He was the patriarchal head of the family—the eldest son of the eldest son, the one supposedly in charge.

"Dad, I don't want to have to deal with land in Korea after you die."

My father discovered that a family member had forged his name on one of the land deeds, as did another relative from the generation before him. My father lived across the ocean—his relations were hoping he wouldn't notice. My father sued the family member for wrongful ownership in 2010 and won. For a cut of the proceeds, he asked a more trustworthy relative to help broker the sale of the granite mountain to a developer. My father wanted to donate his portion to Kongju High School to establish a scholarship in my grandfather's name, honoring my grandfather's protests against the Japanese principal when he was a second-year student in 1927. The protests that caused my grandfather to be expelled before he could graduate.

ON THE TRAIN, THE KIDS pick window seats, on opposite sides of the aisle. I sit next to Kiki and Steve next to Owen. Springy cushion, retractable footrest, glossy travel magazine in the pouch in front of us—it's a plushy, comfortable ride. As soon as the landscape changes from extreme urban density to apartment building domino pieces, my brother's wife offers to take the kids to the snack car for treats. I close my eyes and focus my attention on my breath like my grief counselor taught me.

Breathe in, breathe out. Stay calm. Don't get irritated by the children. Remember why you are here.

WE NEVER THOUGHT MY FATHER would go first. My mother was the one with dementia, the one clearly fading away. Dad had his octogenarian ills, for sure—Meniere's disease, high blood pressure, balance issues—but overall, he was healthy and physically active. At Mirabella, he attended exercise classes, joined the Foreign Affairs club, and led an origami class, folding one thousand paper cranes to display in the memory care ward where my mother lived.

He hated to go to the doctor but he did so right away when he found blood in his stool. He needed to take care of my mother when she returned from memory care: "She might get better and be herself again," he told me, knowing that dementia was degenerative. He wanted to see Owen, his firstborn grandchild, graduate high school. He had so many reasons to live.

Stomach cancer, he explained, was more prevalent in the U.S. for those of Asian descent. It was also the number-one type of cancer in South Korea. Diet and the bacteria H. pylori, which he most likely encountered as a child before the war, were to blame. He sailed through chemo with all the hair on his head. Radiation was another matter. Horrible stomach pain, no appetite, sleepless nights, loss of bladder control. Ed bought him CBD gummies to help him sleep. I saw him fall over the bedside table on a visit. He fell again after I left, trying to get up from the recliner in the living room. The falls continued—some he told us about, some he didn't.

The blows to the head showed up on his final visit to the emergency room. Here, here, and here. The young resident pointed to the CT scan, to the dark spots in the right hemisphere of my father's brain. The cerebral tissue swelled over the fissure line that used to divide it into two equal halves.

My father waited until Ed left with his family for spring break for the fall to end all falls. He could still speak when I arrived at the OHSU Hospital on the hill, dragging my jumbo wheeled bag behind me. I walked past a padded cell with a screaming woman in a straitjacket, indigent men in wheelchairs parked in the hall. My father's room was at the end of the hallway.

"Ma-ga-ret," he said. "Take this thing off of me."

He clawed at the spine-stabilizing doughnut pillow placed around his neck. Tore it off.

"Dad," I re-Velcroed the doughnut, "I'm as stubborn as you are, you might as well give up."

He glared at me with his "how dare you" face and ripped off the pillow again. I strapped it back on while looking straight into his eyes without my usual smile. He eventually got tired and dozed off before being transferred to the ICU. I didn't realize that this would be our last exchange of true emotion.

He was never himself again.

HIS NURSE TOLD ME THAT we didn't have to listen to the doctors, the ones who recommended brain surgery. "Surgeons always recommend surgery, because that's what they do." The decision was up to the family, not them. If we didn't think my eighty-four-year-old, cancer patient father could survive the cutting open of his skull and the long recovery period, where he would most likely need to relearn how to speak and walk, we didn't have to follow the surgeon's recommendation. I conferred with Ed and my father's geriatrician.

My father's identity was tied to his intellect. A life without reasoning would be a life not worth living. Dad would rather be dead. We all agreed.

April 2018, his final days. We elected to transport him back to Mirabella so he could be near my mother. She wasn't able to speak, but she could still hear and held my father's hand as he took his last labored breath.

Needless to say, my father died without dealing with the family land. As my mother's power of attorney and the executor of their estate, I was left in charge.

ON THE TRAIN TO KONGJU, the kids return from the snack bar with boxes of Chocosongii mushroom-shaped crackers and cans of Chisung cider. Vacation means they are allowed to binge on sugar. Owen devours his treats and immediately falls asleep. Kiki nibbles the chocolate cap off of each mushroom and saves the stems for last.

Forty minutes later, we arrive at an enormous deserted station beyond the Kongju city limits, near our family's ancestral land. We are the only people to exit the train. The station had been built for the 2002 World Cup, but further development never came to the area like the South Korean government expected. The economy still hadn't fully recovered from the 2008 recession.

Two English teachers from the high school, Mr. Kim and Mr. Park, meet us at the station, and we split back into two cars according to family. I put on my smiling lady face to converse with Mr. Kim.

THE DECISION TO DONATE THE granite mountain to Kongju High School came after a frenzied five months of figuring out the intricacies of Korean inheritance law as it applied to ancestral holdings. I assembled Team Family Land, which consisted of Ed; my cousin Julie, who filled out paperwork on my uncle's behalf; Sungmo, my maternal uncle's wife, who dabbled in real estate; and Mr. Lee, an estate lawyer in Seoul who I found with the help of the father of one of Owen's preschool friends. In September 2018, I traveled to Korea to meet the lawyer and haggle with my father's supposedly trustworthy relative who was quickly proving otherwise.

Ed and I wanted to honor my father's last wish to make a donation to Kongju High School in our grandfather's name. Also, to avoid brokering the sale of a huge parcel of land across the Pacific in an uncertain real estate market. Working on Project Family Land became my job and also served as my grief process. The multitude of tasks and stacks of paperwork soothed the raw wound caused by my father's sudden passing. I immersed myself in administrative duties, taking refuge in the knowledge that I was cementing my grandfather's legacy, granting my father's last wish. The gift would ensure the education of students at Kongju High School for generations to come.

After hundreds of pages of lawyer-approved paperwork, multiple trips to Sacramento and Salem for apostille authorizations, and mailing the documents to Mr. Lee in Korea for government submission, the gift of the granite mountain was made to Kongju High School in January 2019.

ALMOST A YEAR LATER, WE are escorted into the principal's office. Thick paper nameplates have been placed in front of seven padded armchairs. The children are delighted that they, too, are deemed important enough to warrant their own assigned seats. In typical thirteen-year-old-boy fashion, Owen hides his face in the hood of his red parka, cinching the drawstring tight so that only his nose and lips are showing. Steve taps Owen on the shoulder, the cue for him to unshroud his giant melon and show proper respect. I glance at Kiki, and she nods. She knows to keep it together in front of the kind-eyed principal, who we are meeting for the first time.

The principal profusely thanks us for our generous gift to the school. Mr. Kim translates. A female assistant serves us tea. The principal leads us into the makeshift history hall. It's lined with glass cabinets containing hundreds of trophies, plaques, and framed photographs. A whole section is devoted to the school's most famous alumnus, Chan Ho Park, the first South Korean–born player in Major League Baseball.

I spy the color photo of my grandfather's National Cemetery tombstone. My father had provided it to the school during his final visit. I explain to Mr. Kim that we are planning to scatter my father's ashes at the foot of the marker later that day.

Steve takes pictures of the list of school principals, including the Japanese one who kicked my grandfather out of the school, as well as the plaque memorializing my grandfather as a South Korean Patriot. Kiki bops around and marvels at the size of the trophies. Left-handed pitcher Owen is glued to the Chan Ho Park paraphernalia. The principal informs us that they planned to move the contents of the room into a more permanent location for the school's one hundredth anniversary celebration in 2022.

MY PARENTS DIDN'T WANT COFFINS, only ashes. My father died so suddenly in April 2018 that we didn't have time to ask him where he wanted to be scattered. My mother was too far gone to offer an opinion. In Oregon, where they retired? Texas, where they lived the longest? Korea, where they were born? Where did they want their remains to rest? Where was home to them?

Ed suggested the Oregon coast. Dad had talked about getting the whole family together there after his radiation treatments were done. We'd even break Mom out of memory care for the weekend. Dad loved Oregon. He transformed into Mr. Gregarious at Mirabella. He joked with the front-desk staff, greeted every resident and server by name. He was expansive, talkative, and even though he still lectured while attempting to converse, he was surrounded by people who appreciated the enormous vault of knowledge stored in his big Korean head. He even felt comfortable enough to listen and empathize.

We did end up going to the Oregon coast as a family, sans Dad. It was my mother's final trip, to Cannon Beach. Memory care lent us a wheelchair. The most difficult part of the trip was hoisting her once-petite self into and out of the car. Mom had ballooned in confinement. Her greatest pleasure each day was a bowl of chocolate ice cream after dinner.

She couldn't speak, and only nodded yes or no when I asked her questions.

Would you like some water?

Are you comfortable?

Do you need to go to the restroom?

Ed and I took turns narrating the events of the trip.

"We are driving an hour west to the coast."

"We are going to scatter half of Dad's ashes on the hill overlooking Cannon Beach."

"Do you remember coming here with Dad when you lived in Tigard?"

Mom looked confused. Sad. She only smiled when she locked eyes with one of her grandchildren. She could see the future in them.

ED IS THE BEARER OF ashes for our trip to Korea. Dad is in an environmentally friendly cardboard tube decorated with Van Gogh's *Irises*. Mom's container is similar but with a faux-wood grain. Hers is more abstract, more tied to nature, even though she was the one allergic to trees, grass, flowers—pretty much all of outside. Ed's wide shoulders can bear the weight. Mine cannot.

After Dad died, the funeral director suggested that the kids write letters to be cremated with his body. Kiki made a funeral pyre out of Legos, which Steve took a picture of and printed. Owen, in his fifth-grade handwriting, scrawled a short note. He felt my father's death the most—he had a special bond with "glam-pa." A bond cemented in math problems and pancakes.

Dad's death came as a jolt. I could no longer call my father on the phone every other day. He couldn't ask about Owen's soccer matches or Kiki's quips and walkathons. He would never meet Brownie, our Korean rescue dog. And he could never fulfill his final wish, to attend Owen's high school graduation in 2024. Dad would have been ninety years old.

With Mom, I felt seasick witnessing her decade-long demise. She rolled back and forth between lucidity and dream state, until the scale tipped. She left our world with only her body and mammalian survival instinct remaining. Maybe this was the ideal way to go for an artist. Even though she couldn't pick up a paintbrush anymore, Mom could seek refuge in the abstract watercolor landscapes in her mind that she tried to render her entire artistic life.

WHEN I WAS IN HIGH school, Dad told me that he and my mom were planning to donate their bodies to science, so their corpses could be of use somehow.

I wrinkled my nose in disgust. "Please don't," I pleaded. "I don't want some stranger cutting into your body in anatomy class. It's gross."

I never knew if he listened to me because it took so long for him to make a decision. He was maddeningly slow, weighing pros and cons, facts and figures, discounted emotion and biases, using his own version of the scientific method to come to any conclusion. Maybe my father took my teenage reaction into account for his and my mother's last will and testament. They were to be cremated. It was up to survivors if a service was held.

Half their ashes in the United States. Half in Korea. That's what Ed and I decided. Mom's head and heart were rooted in her childhood in Seoul, the place at the center of her being, the place that even her atrophying brain couldn't erase. Except for Tapgol Park and Gyeongbokgung Palace, nothing was left of the Seoul she remembered. Everything else was destroyed during the war.

Dad's ashes would be spread at his parents' graves at the National Cemetery.

ON DECEMBER 30, 2019, KIKI'S eleventh birthday, we gather at Tap-gol Park, a short walk from the hotel. A century ago, when Korea was a colony of Japan, the park was the site where the independence movement began. On March 1, 1919, Chung Jae Yong read the Korean Declaration of Independence, urging the crowd to protest the rule of the Japanese colonizers.

The kids and I snuggle into our North Face parkas bought from the outlet on Gilman Street in Berkeley. We've come prepared—long underwear, gloves, snow boots, wool socks, and hats. Steve used to camp in the Sierras before we got married and already owned the proper gear. He's already been out earlier that morning with the octogenarians, the only ones who are tough enough to handle the sub-freezing conditions. They survived the war. Cold is nothing.

Four years before, on our last family trip to Korea, we visited Tapgol Park with my parents. Mom told us it was her favorite place in Seoul. After school, she and her best friend Chung Wha would play there until dark. She was still speaking English then, but only to impart some memory of the past before 1962, the year she left Korea for the United States. We tried to find the exact location of her childhood home behind the hotel where we were staying. We walked past the metal dishware shops, pork belly restaurants, mulberry paper vendors, and a whole row of storefronts full of horsehair brushes for sumi-e painting, some as big as Kiki. Nothing looked familiar, my mother said.

WE DECIDE TO SCATTER MY mother's ashes behind a row of trees away from the main walkway of the park. I had checked earlier with Oesamchun, my mother's brother. He told us that scattering ashes in public places was technically illegal in South Korea but was done all the time.

We huddle in a circle next to a particularly beautiful pine, while Steve keeps an eye out at the edge. Ed speaks in his sonorous baritone, and I am reminded of how he used to sing Red Hot Chili Peppers songs in the shower when he was in high school. My baby brother has perfect pitch.

Owen fidgets. He'd rather be kicking a soccer ball. Kiki's eyes grow wide. In addition to her Asian pear face, she is gifted with her grandmother's nunchi—she can feel the waves of grief emanating from the adults' bodies. She never got to know the grandmother she resembles so closely. She only knew the faded grandma, the one whose outlines were fuzzed out, half erased, like the fissures of a brain that didn't receive enough blood.

We all say a few words. They immediately float away. I focus on the circle of my family members, the pine tree, my daughter's wide eyes, Owen's red parka, the cold wind tearing my lips into shards. The resounding thud as the clump of ashes hits the frozen ground. The finality.

AFTERWARD, TEA AND DESSERT AT the café at the entrance to Insadong, directly across the street from the park. I've been there dozens of times, even though the name of the establishment changes each time I visit. My mother always took me there because she loved sweets. Sweet red beans on shaved ice, honey-filled yakgwa cookies, rolled cakes with whipped cream in the middle, a crispy chocolate croissant.

We all toast Mom with bites of dessert and tales of how Chong would eat an entire box of See's Candies by herself each Christmas. See's Candies were her absolute favorite.

MR. KIM AND MR. PARK drive us about twenty minutes away to the National Cemetery on the edge of Taejon. My dad's cousin, who I call Ajeossi, his wife, and his son In Kyun meet us there. Ajeossi is the son of my father's aunt, my grandfather's only sister. I lived with him and his wife during my trip to Korea in 2000. At the same time, In Kyun stayed with my parents in Houston while attending ESL classes at Rice University. Our own family exchange program.

The Koreans all weep as Ed scatters my father's ashes at the foot of the granite marker, which is incised with the names of Patriot Lee Chul Ha and, in smaller characters, Kum Soon Min, his wife, our Halmoni. They, too, need space and time to mourn my father's death. I am thankful some members of my father's family are in attendance. The only ones I could identify who actually cared. There would be no other service, no wake, no memorial, just the people who would keep my father in their hearts.

In front of the tombstone, the cold January sun glaring in our eyes, we take dozens of pictures. Kiki chases Owen up the main stairway to the upper level of South Korean Patriots. She is almost fast enough to catch him. They have stood still for long enough. I let them run.

I SHED NO TEARS DURING the scattering of my parents' ashes. I am desiccated, arid. Back home, I cried my share during those moments I had to myself—in the car, on a walk with the dog, while pushing the cart down the aisle of Trader Joe's. My cistern has run dry.

My grandfather Lee Chul Ha's coffin, reburial service,
Oct. 12, 1995, Taejon National Cemetery

REBURIAL

My grandfather, Lee Chul Ha, is being buried again today.
October 12, 1995, in the Taejon National Cemetery in
South Korea, almost sixty years after he was buried the first
time. That time, in 1936, my great-grandfather watched as the remains of
his twenty-seven-year-old son were laid to rest in a mountain site he had
originally reserved for himself.

This time, uniformed military officers stand in salute, paying homage.

This time, Korea exists as an independent country, albeit cut in two,
and not a colony of Japan.

This time, his eldest son, daughter-in-law, granddaughter, and grandson are in attendance, fresh from a trans-Pacific flight from the United
States.

This time, my grandfather will be buried in honor and not in shame.

IN THE FUNERAL PHOTOGRAPH, THE only photograph we have of
him, the nineteen-year-old grandfather I never knew is devastated, devastated at being caught. Eyelids heavy with fatigue, hair shorn by him or his
captors, I don't know. The lack of hair accentuates his squared-off forehead,
a family trait handed all the way down to my brother Ed, recently graduated from college, who is the same age as our grandfather was in the photograph. It is Ed who carries our grandfather's framed image today under
the searing, early fall sun.

My father discovered my grandfather's photograph in 1992 with the
help of an old college mate, or, to be exact, with the help of a graduate student of an old college mate from Seoul National University. The

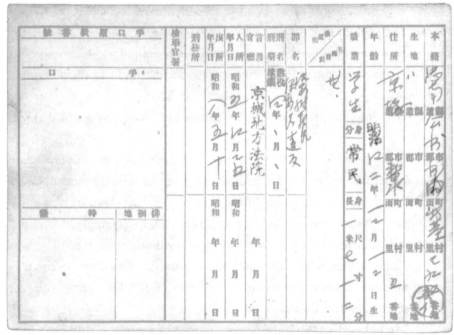

My grandfather's prison card, front and back, 1930,
Courtesy of the National Institute of Korean History collection

original black-and-white image, now blown up to portrait size, measured approximately two by three inches, the standard ID for all occupants of the Seodaemun Hyeongmuso, the prison reserved for political prisoners during the Japanese occupation.

Forlorn. Bereft. My grandfather's wide shoulders slump forward, causing his loose tunic to gape at the neck. Residual baby fat weighs down his cheeks. The corners of his closed mouth turn downward. The lettering on the sash across his chest has been erased. My father covered it with Wite-Out.

I ASK MY FATHER WHY he altered the photo as we walk up the grand staircase behind Ed to the top tier of the cemetery. "It wouldn't be proper," he whispers. I start to argue with him. Was he trying to save face in front of the relatives, to hide the fact that we were using my grandfather's mug shot as his funeral photo? Did he still feel shame about his father's prison stay and the fact that he was a Communist? My mother grabs my hand and widens her eyes, the signal for me to shut my mouth. No arguing in front of the relatives. She had already fussed at me on the car ride over for wearing the pants of my royal purple silk suit, not the skirt—which I ditched because I didn't want to wear pantyhose in the heat.

THE SOLDIERS LEAD THE PROCESSION and stop in front of the open row of grave sites to twirl their rifles in unison. Their staccato shouts drift over the valley below as they march off and allow the families to gather in front of the graves of their ancestors. I try to catch my brother's eye, to give him a silent pep talk, but his gaze is cast downward. I can tell he is nervous, tentative, worried that he might do the wrong thing and embarrass the family in some way.

My father whispers in Ed's ear. Sweating in his black wool suit, Ed places our grandfather's photograph on a low table covered in white fabric. He turns around and looks toward my father for further guidance. My father holds up two fingers. Ed lowers his six-foot-two frame to his hands and knees and bows his head in front of the picture. He stands up and bows again. My father and all of the surviving male members of the family follow his example. My mother and I, as well as the other female family members, stand behind the men, as is the custom.

Two days before, my grandfather's bones were exhumed from the family burial plot high up in the mountains surrounding the city of Kongju. The grandfather I never knew exists in the here and now as a skeleton, an archeological artifact excavated from a disintegrating wooden coffin. Resurrected, reborn—for a second chance at commemoration. A young man's bones transformed into a relic of an era no one wanted to remember, until now. His mottled skeleton is encased in a shiny silver coffin covered with the South Korean flag, which has been placed behind the low table on which his photograph rests.

THOUGH HIS WHITED-OUT SASH BRANDED him as a political prisoner, my grandfather is no longer an enemy of the state. He is not the naïve boy from the countryside who was kicked out of high school for donning traditional Korean clothing during the Japanese emperor's birthday celebration. Or the expelled youth who moved to Seoul to become involved in a student movement whose tenets he didn't fully understand. Or the criminal who got caught handing out incendiary leaflets and spent four years behind bars, which is what my father grew up believing.

On this warm October day, the grandfather I never knew is a Patriot, a nationalist, a freedom fighter who protested Japanese rule when Korea was a colony of the empire. A hero and a martyr, not the source of shame for a conservative, landowning yangban family.

ALTHOUGH I AM THE ELDEST by six years, it is my brother who is asked to speak at the ceremony. He reads Psalm 23, my grandmother's favorite passage in English. He never learned to speak Korean.

"The Lord is my shepherd; I shall not want."

Ed is the anointed heir, the first son of the first son and so on, fifteen generations into the past. I know better than to bristle over the unfairness of Korean patriarchy. We are in the old country, after all. I'm just happy I don't have to spout Bible passages I rejected long ago in front of an audience of relatives I barely know.

My father reads the poem inscribed on my grandfather's tomb marker, a poem memorializing Lee Chul Ha, aka Sung Ya, or "Starry Field," the alias his comrades gave him.

> *His will, becomes an echo in our hearts.*
> *Its ringing spreads over the mountains*
> *And across the oceans.*

The rest of the family listens and watches from behind a white ribbon, as do a dozen or so other families in front of the coffins of their own honored ancestors.

EVERY MEMBER OF THE FAMILY who is healthy enough to make it is here at the National Cemetery in the center of South Korea. My grandfather's cousins from Kongju, his big city nieces and nephews from Seoul, his sons who ended up emigrating to America, and his eldest son's children, including his grandson Ed, the heir to the patrilineal family line. But it is I, his twenty-nine-year-old American granddaughter, who takes an interest in the past.

I am the one who needs to know who my grandfather was.

EVERYONE IS HERE, THAT IS, except my grandmother Halmoni, who elected to remain in her two-bedroom apartment in the Chamsil district in Seoul.

She wants nothing to do with my grandfather. She has spent a lifetime trying to forget the handsome man in the photograph who left her with two young sons to raise by herself. In 1936, the year of her husband's death, she was left to survive the occupation, the division of her country after the

My brother Edward, at our
grandfather's reburial ceremony

Group photo with me, my parents, Edward,
my uncle Eun Suk, and other members of my
father's family at the reburial ceremony

Japanese lost the Pacific campaign of World War II, and the destruction of Seoul during the Korean War. Halmoni rebuilt her family's life through hard work and deeply embedded survival skills she didn't know she possessed. She worked as a seamstress after her husband's death. She helped run an orphanage near Taejon called Heavenly Garden, only a couple of miles from the National Cemetery, in the 1950s. Throughout it all, she was confronted with the tainted reputation of her late husband—the traitor, the Communist, the criminal.

She is not ready to remember after all these years. Even now, after her husband's reputation has been restored.

INHERITANCE

The first time I flew to Korea in 1976, a stewardess locked me in the bathroom. The lock clicked as I sat down to pee. Like a good girl, I washed my hands afterward and knocked on the door. I waited while my wire-rimmed glasses slipped down my nose. Then turbulence threw me into the wall. I banged on the door with my fist and stifled the urge to yell.

Luckily, a nice Korean man in the row closest to the bathrooms heard me and let me out. I bowed, said thank you. He sat back down—didn't meet my eyes. I pushed my glasses back up my nose.

I tried my best not to fall into anyone's lap as I stumbled to my seat at the back of the plane. Mom was busy with little brother Ed. Dad was asleep. No one noticed I was gone, so I didn't tell them about my momentary ordeal.

I was ten years old.

IT'S SEPTEMBER 2000, AND I'M on a plane to Korea. This time, I'm an adult—thirty-four and flying solo. Even though I ditched the glasses for contacts long ago, I still remember the way I felt as a ten-year-old on my first trip to my parents' homeland. It was the Bicentennial, the summer before fifth grade. We had moved into a two-story immigrant dream house located in the outer reaches of northwest Houston a couple of years before. Fourth grade had ended on a high note. The only Korean girl at Matzke Elementary—me—marched Old Glory down the main aisle of the school auditorium while my classmates sang "You're a grand old flag, you're a high-flying flag." It was perhaps the proudest moment of my life up until then.

Looking back on that first trip to Korea, I realize that I had hit some sort of developmental milestone with the bathroom incident. I existed independently from my parents. I possessed private thoughts I could choose to share or not. I didn't have to tell them I was trapped in the airplane bathroom. And I never did.

Just like I never told them that when I went to Donna's house in high school to "study physics," we drank Keller Geister wine and chased after cars of teenagers through Champions, the subdivision where all the streets were named after famous golf courses. Or that when I lived in San Francisco in my midtwenties, I spent the money they gave me for a writing course at Berkeley Extension on an amazing pair of Prince purple knee-high boots made in France. Or that two years ago, my New York boyfriend had a nervous breakdown and was committed to the state hospital, where I visited him behind locked doors.

They didn't need to know about any of these things.

FOURTEEN HOURS IN THE AIR. I have loads of time to kill. At the Hudson News at Logan Airport, I buy a stash of magazines, like I always do. *Elle* and *ARTnews*, the giant September *Vogue* to see the fall collections, and *The New Yorker*, the holy grail for all magazine journalists like myself. I had already stuffed the latest *Nation* magazine into my backpack before I left my rented room for good. My former employer provided me with a gratis subscription after I left New York.

Goodbye Boston, see you later. I promise not to miss you, since you are the city I've liked the least in the litany of places where I've lived. New York, San Francisco, Minneapolis/St. Paul, Austin, and Houston, my hometown. Boston served its purpose. I spent a year on a fellowship at Radcliffe laying the groundwork for this trip to Korea. I know I won't be back.

I've made the long flight to Seoul half a dozen times since I was ten. This time it's different. First of all, it's 2000, a new century. I'm not going to

Korea out of a sense of obligation to attend family events or to visit Halmoni, my only grandparent who has lived long enough to see the new millennium. I'm headed to Korea for the next four months—of my own volition.

I am traveling to my parents' homeland to pursue the story of a lifetime.

FIVE YEARS HAVE PASSED SINCE the reburial ceremony at the National Cemetery. Five years in which I have tried to make up for the four years I wasted at the art museum in San Francisco. The summer of 1996 brought a new career path, a new city, a new boyfriend. A second stint in grad school, this time for journalism at NYU. A rented room in an artist's live/work space on Eighth Street and Ave. B across the street from St. Brigid Catholic Church, named after the Irish patron saint of babies, chicken farmers, and scholars—all of whom are relevant to my story. I met goateed Ciaran, a friend of a friend of a friend, at a bar a month after I arrived in New York. He drove the U-Haul with me to Boston three years later, even though we were broken up by then.

In 1996, my parents moved to Korea, perhaps to stay. My father took a job at the medical school at Ajou University while on leave from his position in Houston. My mother followed like the good Korean wife she was. They rented a spacious apartment near the university and moved in Halmoni so they could be all together.

My father wanted to further his career, maybe in the country of his birth, but he also wanted to locate his father's prison and interrogation records, the ones he remembered seeing in Halmoni's wedding chest before the war. The prison and interrogation records would provide the final clues to how his father, a teenager from the countryside, became involved in the student Communist movement in Seoul. Then the reclamation of his father's short life would be complete.

Before he could investigate further, though, my father fell ill, coughing up blood after trying to move bookshelves into Halmoni's bedroom.

He underwent emergency surgery to remove the upper lobe of his right lung, which was heavily scarred from a bout of tuberculosis he suffered as a young man. After surgery, he lost entire parcels of his memory, including those concerning his livelihood as a professor of statistics. He wasn't able to answer the first problem in the textbook he wrote. He wasn't able to teach. My parents returned home to Houston. My father's search for his father's records would have to wait.

THIS IS WHERE I COME in. This is where I joined my father in his quest to discover who Lee Chul Ha was. My involvement began at my mother's request, as a means for Dad to regain his memory and to hopefully stave off a deep depression marked by his withdrawal into complete silence. In J-school, I was learning to follow leads, interview sources, and conduct research—the skills needed to uncover information on the life of a forgotten Korean patriot, the man who happened to be my paternal grandfather. I could help in my father's search.

My father couldn't remember how to solve statistics problems, but he could conjure up childhood memories. I asked him to write down anything he recalled his mother, grandmother, or any other relative saying about Lee Chul Ha. We discussed over the phone what it felt like for him to grow up fatherless as the firstborn son, the de facto head of a conservative Confucian family after both his father and grandfather died when he was only two years old. He shared stories I never heard before—of growing up during the colonial era, of speaking Korean at home and Japanese at school, of feeling like a foreign student in his own country, which was the precursor for his experience as a graduate student in the U.S. in the 1960s. He told me his Japanese name, Kunimore Zuneyoshi, which was bestowed on him in the third grade as a requirement of the Japanese colonial government. He explained that his long-standing distrust of authority figures, especially teachers, was rooted in fourth grade, when the Japanese vice principal slapped him for squirming during the emperor's birthday ceremony. Afterward, his Korean homeroom teacher called him a "fatherless bastard" while beating him in front of his classmates.

I asked him question after question, and the stories poured forth.

The stories I never grew up with. The stories that my father once thought were better left forgotten.

MY FATHER AND I WORKED together through my two years of journalism school and after, when I became the assistant literary editor at *The Nation*—the perfect place for the granddaughter of a Communist revolutionary. We reforged the close bond that was lost twenty years before, during that first trip to Korea in 1976, when I realized my life was my own and not an extension of my parents'. Slowly, as we collaborated, my father's search for the father he never knew became mine as well.

At *The Nation*, I began to comprehend the political and historical ramifications of my grandfather's story—its relation to the rise of Communism in Russia, in China, and all over the world. I knew almost nothing about the history of Korea before the Korean War, the era in which my parents grew up but never spoke about.

My grandfather's forgotten life was entwined with Korea's tumultuous twentieth century—from Japanese colonialism, World War II, division, occupation, the Korean War, reconstruction, military dictatorship—to democracy and prosperity at the end of the millennium.

THE PURSUIT OF FAMILY HISTORY offered me purpose and a means to get to know my father again. It also provided me an escape route out of New York, whose aura of possibility had dimmed to semidarkness. A prestigious yet poorly paid position in the most expensive city in the world. Another failed relationship, self-doubt, and trying to find myself again—I was nowhere near a place of stability in which to start a family because what I really wanted was to find someone with which to start one. I still ground my teeth at night until they cracked.

I left my editorial job at *The Nation* for a research fellowship at Radcliffe. There, I audited classes in modern Korean history, scoured the Yenching Library for information on Korea's colonial era, and asked my father even more questions about the years of his life I knew next to nothing about—the life he lived before immigrating to the United States.

All in preparation for this trip to Korea, where I hoped to find the paper remains of my grandfather's life—his high school transcripts, trial documents, and interrogation and prison records.

░░░░░░░░░░░░░░░░░

I KNOW ALL THIS. SLUMPED down in my cramped economy seat, I actually have time to wonder what might lie beneath.

Why are you really embarking on this journey into the past? Aside from your career ambitions, do you hope that solving a family mystery will lead to figuring out what you really want out of your own life?

Well, therapist who lives in my head, this I do know: My involvement in the search began as a way to help my father not lapse into silence. What I've learned so far is that my grandfather's erasure is part of my family's legacy that has been passed down, through the generations and across continents, from my grandmother, to my father, to me. I sense that the forgetting of his life is connected to why I have never really felt at home anywhere, not in any of those cities in which I have lived, not in the U.S., and definitely not in Korea. The only constant in my peripatetic adult life is an urge to move, to escape—to somewhere more promising, more exciting, more "better." To fill that empty space inside myself, the space that is filled by a sense of belonging in other people.

MY TEN-YEAR-OLD SELF FLOATS INTO view. She sits in silence in her airline seat after being locked in the bathroom. She has already swallowed the panic, the fear of being trapped, the prospect of dying alone in a small, enclosed space where no one can hear her. All that emotion has been squashed into a tiny, hard kernel lodged deep inside her prepubescent body.

What seemed like a feat of strength then—of asserting my independence, of holding on to an experience that was mine alone—fades into something entirely different twenty-five years later. Perhaps it manifests a pattern, a legacy, born from family history.

I

FIRST INTERVIEW

WITH HALMONI

Mom and Halmoni on Halmoni's 60th birthday, 1968

GIRL ON THE SPOT

In March 1999, I make the 3,000-mile trek from New York to visit Halmoni in Seoul, courtesy of frequent flyer miles. My parents are already in Korea, their first trip since Dad's lung surgery, to check up on Halmoni in her apartment south of the Han River. I am here for the week to lay the groundwork for the next phase of my life, a fellowship year at Radcliffe to research a book about my grandfather's life. The week is packed full of meetings with various professors, acquaintances of my father's and experts on the colonial era. A visit to my grandfather's burial place. Various meals with various relatives. I have also prepared a list of questions for Halmoni, to see what she remembers of the man she married seventy-five years before.

We finish our breakfast of seaweed soup and rice. Mom clears the dishes away from the low table. My ninety-year-old grandmother keeps her place on the floor atop her favorite gray satin cushion embossed with the Chinese characters for double happiness, which I find out later is the traditional symbol for marriage. Dad and I head to the extra bedroom—me to fetch my tape recorder, him to make some phone calls. He knows to make himself scarce while I ask Halmoni questions.

"Ma-ga-ret, Halmoni might not want to talk about your grandfather," he warns. "She got angry at me for digging into the past the last time we were here. She even forbade me to do it."

I nod. I know she is stubborn. All I can do is try. I'm hoping since I'm a generation removed, she will feel free enough to open up.

HALMONI DRIFTED IN AND OUT of my childhood every five years or so. She allowed my father to send for her across the Pacific in 1968, to our first home in Raleigh, North Carolina, to meet me, her first grandchild, and celebrate her reaching her sixtieth hwangap birthday. My father had scrimped and saved for years to afford the almost $2,000 airfare. He wrote letters to the State Department to try to get the visa application pushed through. After it was, he wrote more letters to my mother's brother, my Oesamchun, in Korea to make travel arrangements and to Northwest Airlines to take care of her on her long flight.

Her flight stopped at Haneda Airport in Tokyo for a refueling layover. But while the other passengers left the plane, she refused to move from her seat. The cleaning crew was forced to work around the stone-faced woman dressed in a stiff hanbok.

"How could I set foot on Japanese soil?" she told my parents later.

HALMONI STAYED WITH US IN the little red-brick house at the end of a tree-lined lane, a couple of blocks away from Rex Hospital, where I had been born on borrowed funds in 1966. My father's academic advisor lent him the $800 it cost for an emergency C-section since my parents didn't have health insurance. Halmoni took care of me while my mother worked at the local Presbyterian church as the education director. My father had recently finished coursework for his PhD and was employed part-time as a statistician for the North Carolina Department of Higher Education.

Halmoni taught me Korean and shooed away the other neighborhood children with a broom if they dared to knock on our back door. She mopped the kitchen floor every day. She picked weeds and raked oak leaves in the yard while I toddled around outside. She cooked doengjang jigae and rice for dinner.

MY FATHER WORKED ON HIS dissertation at the library most weekday nights, so Halmoni and my mother spent the evenings together. Halmoni wasn't talkative and rarely smiled—the complete opposite of my mother. Over time, though, she grew to trust my mother, who possessed the great gift of listening and making you feel like you were the most important person in the world. She trusted my mother enough to talk about her last wishes. She was sixty, after all, and had survived long enough to make it to a new cycle of the lunar calendar.

"When I die, I don't want to be buried next to Eun Sul's father. I know it's the custom for the wife to be buried next to her husband, but I want to be buried somewhere else. Maybe in Chongju, near my father's grave. Or at the orphanage where I worked in Taejon."

My mother started to ask why. Halmoni turned her back to her. She walked into her bedroom and closed the door.

HALMONI STAYED LONG ENOUGH TO help us move down farther south to Houston, where a tenure-track job at a new school of public health was waiting for my father. Her visa expired a couple of months after the move, so she returned to Korea. Four years later in March 1972, a week before my brother was born via another C-section, Halmoni arrived again. The intervening years had seen the birth of two more grandchildren in Kongju, the children of my father's brother Eun Suk, for whom Halmoni served as primary caretaker—and two miscarriages on the part of my mother. Halmoni stayed on in Houston after my baby brother Tongju (Ed) was born to help with the cooking and cleaning and getting me off to kindergarten, since my mother was bedridden for what seemed like months.

My childhood memories of Halmoni always involve her Korean/English Bible with the black leather cover and delicate pages, so thin that you could see the print from the opposite side. I'm not sure if she read it from front to back over and over again or if she skipped around to the juicy parts. All I know is that it was her constant companion.

When I think about Halmoni, this is what I see:

The knife-sharp hair part bisecting her head.

The pomaded hair sleek as a wet seal, pulled tightly back into a low bun at the nape of her neck.

Halmoni frozen in time in front of the three-tiered frosted Duncan Hines masterpiece my baking-challenged mother whipped up for her hwangap birthday celebration.

Halmoni tending the vegetable garden my father set up for her in the space behind the garage, walking slowly like she always did with her hands clasped behind her osteoporotic back, torso tilted forward sixty degrees from the ground.

Her plodding footsteps down the red shag–carpeted staircase after I yelled "gingejopsoosay-o" to summon her to dinner each evening when I was a child, a task transferred to me since Halmoni refused to hear my mother's call. She did not want to be answerable to anyone anymore. She was done with that part of her life.

Her rare smiles and uncomfortable displays of affection if one of her American grandchildren had somehow hurt themselves.

Me flinching away. I never got over my reaction when I first met her in North Carolina when I was a toddler. The two-year-old me ran away and hid if she tried to touch me.

NOW, AT THIRTY-THREE, EVEN THOUGH I am the journalist, the one with the tape recorder who has traveled across the ocean to interview her, it is Halmoni who asks the first question.

"Why?" she says, her unsmiling eyes staring into mine. "Why do you want to know about painful things?"

I explain to Halmoni that it's important for me to understand what happened in the past, to understand the history of our family so I can better understand myself. This is why I am asking her all these questions.

Halmoni stares at me without moving one muscle in her face.

Okay, try again. Think in practical terms.

"Halmoni, I received a fellowship to research a book about my grandfather in order to uncover lost history. You are the survivor, the person living who knew him best. It's only you and Grandpa's two cousins from Kongju. You are the only ones left who knew him."

My mother translates. Halmoni nods her head slowly. She will help her granddaughter only because it's beneficial to her career.

I glance over my shoulder and see Dad standing underneath the doorway of the guest room, just out of Halmoni's sight. His head is bowed, and his eyes are closed. He doesn't realize that I can see him. I turn on the tape recorder.

I START AT THE BEGINNING, I ask Halmoni about her childhood in Chongju, the capital of the Chungcheongbuk province, the only South Korean province that doesn't border the water.

Born in 1908, two years before the annexation of Korea by Japan, Halmoni was the first daughter of a yangban landowner named Min Yung Duk. The first in the area to employ modern farming methods in his hilly rice fields, her father was so successful that the ruling Japanese magistrate sent him to Japan, where he taught their farmers how to grow rice.

> *I remember my father cutting off his topknot before he went to Japan. I must have been four or five. You know, years later, the Japanese forced all Korean men to cut off their topknots. So they wouldn't look Korean anymore.*

Halmoni's mother died when she was eight years old and her sister was four. She didn't remember much of her mother, only that she wasn't there. She did remember hiding behind a stack of blankets in a bureau and crying for what seemed like hours after she was told of her death. Her father soon remarried.

> *I remember the moans of my first stepmother, a year after my mother died. We were both sick with diphtheria. I survived, but she didn't. I think I lived this long because of that early sickness. It made me strong.*

My father married again, soon after, to a woman who was only six years older than me. My grandmother kept me away from her. She was trying to protect me, to make sure that I wasn't mistreated by the new lady of the household. She kept me in the far end of the house, where her room was. I was her constant companion as she went through her day. My stepmother was a stranger to me. My father was away most of the time on business.

Halmoni and her younger sister were both born without formal names, as was the custom at the time. When Halmoni was seven, the local registrar visited the house to count the members of the household under orders from the Japanese colonial government, whose first major initiative was the update of family registers to reassess property values. Halmoni's father was away, so the registrar gave her the name "Kum Soon," which means "girl on the spot," the name of thousands of Korean girls at the time. Halmoni's sister brought a bowl of water for the registrar to drink, so he named her "Kum Bong" or "service on the spot."

My sister had more freedom than me because she was younger. She was allowed to play with the farmhand children outside the compound walls. My father started a school for his workers at night so they could learn to read and write. My sister got to tag along with him, but my grandmother kept me with her behind the compound walls. I was so jealous. I wanted to learn, too. But I never told anyone.

My second stepmother soon had a daughter. I only remember that baby girl crying, crying all the time. She was crying out of hunger. She died after a short illness while my stepmother was pregnant with my brother. My stepmother was so eager to produce an heir for the family that she weaned her baby girl too early.

Halmoni pauses, her eyes far away. She has drifted off into the memory of her baby stepsister. We all sit together in silence with the shared knowledge of what happened to unwanted girls at that time.

WHEN I WAS A PRETEEN, Halmoni came to live with us again. We had moved to a bigger house located beyond the border of northwest Houston and into Harris County. Her bedroom was next to mine. I would awaken most mornings to the low tones of her chanting—she sounded like she was growling incantations of brimstone and forgiveness in a language I had mostly forgotten. The couple of times I peeked into her room, I saw her kneeling on the carpet, rocking back and forth with her eyes tightly shut, her Bible sitting on the floor in front of her. Oblivious to my intrusion, she looked possessed, which scared me.

She dressed carefully every Sunday morning in her best sky-blue silk hanbok while my parents tried to wrangle their church-resistant children with bribes of doughnuts or a trip to Luby's Cafeteria after the service for Jell-O and fried fish filets. It was Halmoni's only trip away from the house for the week. She sat immobile in the back pew of Northwoods Presbyterian Church, only daring to speak when she recognized a Bible passage she had memorized in English.

As a child, I never considered whether Halmoni was happy living with us, half a world away from her friends, her family, her beloved church. If she was lonely with only my parents to talk to, since her grandchildren didn't speak Korean. If sequestered days of gardening, reading the Bible, and watching television were enough to occupy any person.

On a couple of occasions, she beckoned me into her room, opened up her Bible, and pointed to a verse she asked me to read in English. It was then I noticed that her fingernails were unusually thick, the consistency of an animal claw. I don't remember which verses I read, except for one—because it was the only one that I could actually recite by memory. I enunciated the words slowly, while Halmoni listened with her eyes closed.

> *The Lord is my shepherd; I shall not want.*
> *He maketh me lie down in green pastures: he leadeth me beside*
> *the still waters.*

Halmoni's father, Min Yung Duk (1887–1956)

Halmoni's grandmother, Lady Park (1866–1942)

He restoreth my soul: he leadeth me in the paths of righteousness for his name's sake.

Yea, though I walk through the valley of the shadow of death, I will fear no evil: for thou art with me; thy rod and thy staff they comfort me.

She silently mouthed the words of the King James Bible version of Psalm 23 with me and even smiled when I finished.

"Gamsahabnida," she said with a bow. Thank you.

HALMONI'S DEVOUTNESS WAS A MYSTERY to me. I wondered what it would feel like to believe in something so much, so completely. My parents were believers, I guess, since they forced me and Ed to attend church every Sunday. Just like they forced me to take piano lessons until I left the house to go to college. But Dad was the skeptical mathematician type who told me from the get-go that the Bible was made up of stories, of fables, almost, like the Aesop's I loved so much as a kid.

In sixth grade, one of the church elders on the confirmation committee recommended that I not be allowed to join the First Presbyterian Church as a member because I repeated my father's explanation of the Bible as literature. The other two committee members knew my parents and passed me through as a favor. Looking back, I knew I didn't really want to be a member of the church my parents forced me to go to, the church over twenty-five miles away from our house with the rich white River Oaks ladies, fancy lawyers, and their children who all went to private schools. I never considered whether I had a say in the matter and never expressed my ambivalence to my parents. Instead, I intentionally upset my mom, a graduate of two Presbyterian seminaries, by throwing her faith back in her face.

"Mom, you know I don't believe in all that resurrection stuff. There's no way Jesus rose from the dead. Why is an entire religion based on that one story? I don't believe it."

My mother stared at me in shock. She didn't say a word and turned her head to cry. My father patted her on the back. I willed myself to not feel bad for upsetting my mother.

HALMONI WAS IN A DIFFERENT league. A true-believer, speaking-in-tongues league of the fundamentalist evangelical Holiness Church, which was loosely associated with the Methodist Church of America. Religion was lifeblood, the end-all, be-all, necessary on a daily basis in order to survive.

"It gives her strength," Dad explained. "Because I don't think she started out strong as a girl. Religion gave her the will to survive after your grandfather died."

Dad told me later that Halmoni converted to Christianity only a year or so after my grandfather's death at the urging of a female evangelist, Mrs. Yu, who had also been recently widowed. Mrs. Yu became Halmoni's first true friend.

I CONTINUE WITH MY QUESTIONS even though I know we are all a bit devastated by Halmoni's recollection of her dead baby stepsister. I continue because I know Halmoni might not be amenable to imparting the events of her past again. She has kept it locked up for most of a lifetime.

I ask Halmoni about her marriage to my grandfather in February 1924 when she was teenager. How did it come about? What were the circumstances?

> *My father knew your grandfather's family in Kongju through a cousin. I think one of my second cousins had married into the Lee clan years before. When I was sixteen, my father arranged the marriage with your grandfather's father. I didn't meet your grandfather until the day of the ceremony. He and his father traveled to Chongju, driving a mule cart to our home. Your grandfather was a year younger than me. They came and left on the same day. I stayed home so my father could assemble my dowry.*
>
> *My father had gathered quite a collection of fabric from his travels. There were Chinese embroidered silks, Japanese cottons, and local fresh ramie cloth for everyday wear. Back then,*

the bride's family was responsible for providing all the linens the
bride would need for the rest of her life. A covered carriage was
packed with the fabric, futon rolls, cotton batting, quilts, head
pillows, chests of drawers, and other furniture. I left home a
month after I was married. No one went with me to Kongju,
just the driver.

When Halmoni arrived at her new home, the older female relatives took one look at her and immediately began whispering among themselves.

Have you ever seen a girl so tall?

HALMONI TELLS ME HER FATHER acquired the latest style in fabrics and furniture for her dowry to somehow make up for her motherless child-hood. Halmoni's new female relatives admired her collection, especially her mother-in-law, who nagged her husband for months to buy a modern-style dresser just like Halmoni's for her bedroom.

Your grandfather's home was much larger than mine. All of the
extended family lived in the compound. My room was at the end
of a long hallway across from the room used for ancestor worship
ceremonies, in the women's section of the house. I didn't like being
near that room. At night, I would get scared. I was afraid there
were ghosts in that room.

I had no idea how a household was to be run. No one had taught
me how to cook or sew or clean. My grandmother was so busy pro-
tecting me from my stepmother that she didn't teach me any skills
for my life as a married woman. In the Lee household, I was put in
charge of polishing all the brassware used for ancestor worship. My
father-in-law was very superstitious and followed all the ritual
dates, not just Chuseok like at our house. He sought advice from the
town's geomancer on a regular basis. The geomancer got rich off my
father-in-law. But he spent it all on parties and drink and ended
up penniless.

I was given a metal brush to wipe away all the tarnish on the brassware. There was so much to clean. Six or seven sets of bowls of different sizes that fit together. Fruit stands, chopsticks, lids for the bowls—enough to feed all the generations of Lee family ancestors. Each piece had to be washed and carefully dried so no water spots showed. If they weren't completely dry, they would rust. After they were dry, they needed to be polished and buffed with a soft cloth.

I hated polishing that brassware. My father-in-law finally replaced all of it with a stainless-steel set, but that was long after I had left the house.

Halmoni's grandmother-in-law was kind and woke her most mornings so she wouldn't be late for her breakfast duties. Halmoni was not used to working with servants, since her family didn't have any, but she learned to manage the three person–kitchen team so the meal service went smoothly. If the soup was cold or the rice too gummy, her mother-in-law would yell at her.

In her new home, men and women ate separately. Each meal was served twice. Halmoni ate after everyone in the family was finished. She ate in the kitchen with the servants.

I learned how to cook and clean and sew by just watching. No one ever taught me. I liked sewing the best. My father bought me a Singer sewing machine on one of his trips. It was made of black iron and was very heavy. When he brought it to Kongju and put it together, all my female relatives watched. I think they were jealous.

Another one of my duties was to sew socks for the women in the household. I started by tracing the women's feet on a piece of paper. Then I made patterns from the tracings and labeled each one. I used the patterns to cut the thick white muslin cloth in sets of two. Then I'd put cotton batting in between and sew the edges together. Before I got the Singer, I stitched them by hand in the

Halmoni's mother-in-law,
Han Shi Kyo (1886–1961)

evenings after dinner was put away. It took a long time. With the sewing machine, I could finish a whole batch in one afternoon. I couldn't use the sewing machine at night though, since it made too much noise.

Halmoni's cadence quickens when describing her sewing, a skill I know has served her well throughout her life. I remember the pair of quilts she stitched while she lived with us in Houston. Hexagons cut carefully from old Sears Roebuck cotton-blend sheets. She fashioned them into pastel starbursts of Dreamsicle orange, pale yellow, and a rather putrid green. All handstitched into place, with the backing made of a floral sheet. One quilt each for her American grandchildren.

HALMONI, SO FAR, HAS BARELY mentioned her husband except to note that she first met him with his father in Chongju, so I ask her, "What was your relationship like with Grandpa?"

She looks at me with mild surprise, as if she forgot about her husband's existence. As if she forgot for a minute, an hour, a year—or most of a lifetime.

After I moved to Kongju, I would see your grandfather every month or so. He was always carrying a book. He was the eldest of three sons and the most studious. He rarely spoke to me, so I didn't get to know him. He wasn't interested in me. After he was kicked out of high school, he moved to Seoul to go to school there. I only saw him when he came home to visit.

Halmoni stops speaking. She rubs her eyes and slowly unfolds herself from her seated position. This is all she can muster up about my grandfather today. The man who was her husband, whom she barely knew.

I thank Halmoni as she makes her way to the bathroom. Mom asks what I want for lunch.

"Whatever is around is fine."

I gather up my notebook and tape recorder and walk toward the extra bedroom. My father is leaning against the doorjamb in the position I left him in more than an hour before. He shakes his head.

"I never heard those stories before. I never knew she was so sick as a child or how much she wanted to learn but couldn't." He looks at me, his eyes moist. "As a kid, I asked her about the past, but she would never tell me."

GIRLHOOD

I t's the summer of 1976, and my parents buy me a blue Pan Am shoulder bag in the airport gift shop before our flight to Korea. I immediately grab my books from Mom's carry-on. Encyclopedia Brown, half of the Narnia series, and a selection from my father's collection he presented to me the month before. *Animal Farm*, some enormous book by a Russian with the word "gulag" in the title, and another unpronounceable book by some German guy named Herman. I'm ten years old.

My second trip on an airplane. I don't remember the first, from Raleigh to Pittsburgh when I was two to visit my mom's best friend. It's Ed's first flight, though, and he's four. And my parents' first trip home since moving to the U.S.

The pretty brunette stewardess with the triangular hat compliments my new bag. I smile behind gold, wire-rimmed glasses. She's the one who locks me in the bathroom six hours later.

MY AUNT'S DRIVER PICKS US up from the airport in a black sedan. We drive through a mass of tiny blue taxicabs in central Seoul, then up a hill on narrow S curves barricaded by concrete walls. It's like going through a tunnel with no roof. Up, up, up the hill to Chong Pil eemo's house. Large metal gates open to a three-story mansion built into a grassy hill.

Chong Pil's husband loved architecture, Mom tells me. His favorite architect was Frank Lloyd Wright, who designed the Guggenheim Museum, whose swirling atrium I would visit the summer afterward on my first trip to New York City. My uncle had visited the Guggenheim and other

Wright buildings on a business trip to the U.S. the decade before. He was so impressed he built his own version of the prairie style on a hill in the middle of Seoul.

Chong Pil and three of her four children are there to greet us. A somber bunch, all dressed in dark hues, since their patriarch had died six months before.

"They are still in mourning," Mom explains when I tug at her sleeve.

My entire family stays in the bedroom at the end of the hall on the second floor, next to my cousin In Young, who has a black ebony piano in her room. In Young is sixteen years old and always has tears in her eyes.

Ed quickly befriends the son of the housekeeper, who is also four and wears short pants with suspenders—shorts so short his butt cheeks hang out. They run through the sprinkler on the enormous green lawn. They play hide-and-seek behind the bushes and trees that hide the concrete walls that separate the idyllic compound from the outside world. They traipse down the hill for ice cream treats at the corner store whose wares spill out onto the street. It doesn't matter that they don't speak the same language. They are young enough not to care.

I find myself caught in between. Six years older than my brother, six years younger than my sad cousin In Young. Alone most of the time. I watch American Forces Korean Network television. Cartoons, game shows, soap operas, and even *Hee Haw*, which I never watch at home. And during the afternoon lulls, I visit my late uncle's library on the first floor, off the main entrance.

No one enters the library except for me and the housekeeper. Me to read and snoop around. She to dust all the books. Chong Pil's family thinks my uncle's ghost lingers in the library; that's why they never go in. It's the room where he spent most of his time. I don't believe in ghosts, so he never bothers me.

Dark wood everywhere. On the walls, the floors, the floor-to-ceiling bookshelves, the giant mahogany desk in the corner. Cool, like a cave, when it's too hot to venture outside.

I discover a stash of *Life* and *Look* magazines behind his desk, which I love for their black and whites of starlets and everyday people in interesting places far away from my home in Houston. Jane Fonda as Barbarella, some Italian actress with huge boobs posing in a fountain in Rome, bereted beatniks riding bikes in Greenwich Village, the Kennedy clan playing touch football on a lawn much like the one outside.

An entire half a shelf of volumes on various members of the Kennedy family—Bobby, Joe Sr., Jackie, and JFK. I read about the destruction of PT-109 and JFK's heroic actions saving members of his crew. I thumb through the picture sections of the biographies: Joe, the controlling father; Rose, the saintly mother; and so, so many children. The assassinations of two of them years later.

I discover a treasure at the bottom of a stack of Korean journals. The freckled face of Alfred E. Neuman. My dead uncle, whom I never met, who worked for the Korean government, lived in a fancy house and had a driver, read *Mad* magazine.

DOWN THE HALL FROM THE library, past the grand staircase where hollow brass rods are strung from ceiling to stair and separate the walkway from the high-ceilinged main room, is the master suite. I never venture in. I'm not allowed. I wouldn't even try to sneak a look, because I am frightened.

In front of my eemo's room is an altar. Incense sticks burn day and night. White chrysanthemums arranged in a giant vase stand underneath an oil portrait of the deceased. A man older than my father, maybe in his sixties, wearing a suit and tie, his right hand tucked into his jacket. His hair still dark.

Eemo sequesters herself in her bedroom and only allows her children and my mother to enter. She never appears at breakfast, when the housekeeper serves us fried eggs with dark yellow yolks and milk that tastes like grass. Sometimes she joins us for dinner in the formal dining room, especially if one of her two sons is in attendance. In Hyun, the eldest in his midtwenties who works at a bank, or In Hyuk, who just graduated from college. When the younger son does appear, he always has a giggly girl on his arm.

"He's a playboy," my mother whispers.

Why? I don't understand. Skinny with pockmarked skin, In Hyuk isn't cute at all. In Hyun is much more handsome.

DAD LEAVES THE HOUSE EACH morning wearing white slip-on loafers from Sears, which makes him look like Pat Boone. Mom fusses and tells him that no one wears white shoes anymore. White shoes were the fashion when he left Korea fifteen years ago.

"Someone's going to think you are a North Korean spy."

And sure enough, someone does. Dad misses dinner one evening, and everyone is worried. Mom calls the research center at the university to see if he is working late. The graduate student who answers says he left at the usual time.

Ed and I stay up late watching TV while the adults try to figure out where Dad is. He finally returns close to midnight. My mom leads him into the dining room, where his now-cold dinner waits for him. We all gather around the table, and he tells us between bites that he was stopped by the police on his walk up the steep street to eemo's house from the bus stop. They made him wait for hours while they checked his passport. After they figure out he is a professor from the U.S., they let him go.

THAT SUMMER PASSES SLOWLY. THREE whole months in a foreign country. Weekdays behind compound walls. Weekend taxi rides to some high-rise apartment building north of the Han River where all the new developments are. They all look the same to me.

I hate those trips. Long evenings at some friend of Dad's where I am rendered mute. Ed and I on view, like prized farm animals: look at them, the exotic children from the U.S.

The teenagers and young adults I meet ask questions about the particulars of American history, about my country's involvement in foreign affairs, the upheavals in South America, the Vietnam War, Korean politics. Questions I don't know the answers to. They know so much about my country. I know next to nothing about theirs, except that Park Chung Hee is president. They all speak English or some semblance of it; they have been learning the language since kindergarten.

One young man, a college student, the nephew of Dad's academic colleague, gives me a cross with beads, like a necklace, one I would never wear. He tells me to hold it while I pray. When I show it to Mom, she tells me to give it back.

"It's a rosary and not a proper gift to someone who isn't Catholic. Maybe he's trying to convert you."

I shrug my shoulders. I know even then that I'm not conversion material. I'm not a fan of church in general, not our Presbyterian one or the Baptist one I visited with my next-door neighbor. I would never consider going to a different one.

I just don't want to go.

THAT SUMMER I FAVOR DUSTY blue, the color of the gauzy cotton vest and matching gaucho set Mom sewed for me before we left for Korea. A peasant top, white knee socks, and, on my feet, wooden, white-strapped leather wedges. The outfit I wear for dressy occasions, like the celebration in honor of Sonsaengnim Lee, Mom's former professor.

After lunch, Ed and I retreat to a corner table and play tic-tac-toe over and over again on the back of a church announcement. The adults mill about and talk. I even let him win a couple of times so he doesn't get frustrated and quit. There's nothing else for us to do in this resort banquet hall in the off-season with no other kids around.

Dad in his embarrassing white shoes is listening to the woman of honor. Head bowed, chin nestled in the crook between his thumb and index finger. He lifts his head to ask a question, then lowers it down again in a pose of deep reflection.

I remember that my mother has stashed a magazine for me and a toy for Ed in her purse. I retrieve them and head back to the table.

My father started bringing home the English-language Asian editions of *Time* magazine from his office since I had read all my books. I am text-deprived and devour the magazines, but I don't understand the political articles; my grasp of current events is meager, and some pages are missing entire paragraphs. They have been cut out. One article on Park Chung Hee's regime resembles a crooked snowflake and falls apart when I open up to it. Dad explains that the Korean government doesn't agree with some of what has been written, so the offensive passages are cut out. He tells me that this is an example of censorship, a concept made concrete for me through the minced pages of *Time* magazine.

WE FINALLY LEAVE KOREA A week later. I was ready to go the month before, when we were waiting for our visa to be extended, but I didn't tell my parents. They were so busy, and they knew anyway. They could tell I wasn't happy in Korea. I just packed my bags as quickly as I could.

But afterward, when the visa was extended at the last minute, I lamented that I would be late starting school. A whole month late for fifth grade.

"You'll catch up with no problem" was the answer.

TO MAKE UP FOR MY unhappiness, my father offers us three layovers on the way home. Tokyo, Hawaii, Disneyland.

A couple of days in Japan, enough to catch some sights, like half a dozen temples and the bright-orange tower with steel latticework that looks like the Eiffel Tower but, as the placard informs us, is taller and better built. A sushi dinner so expensive Dad has to use all of our traveler's checks to pay for it.

Ed and I jump on the beds of our high-rise hotel room. Back and forth from one full size to another. Yay! No more sleeping on the floor. I am fascinated by Japanese TV, for this is the year my love affair with television has begun.

"Mom, why are there blond people in Japanese commercials?"

"Oh, those are the native people from Hokkaido, up north near Russia. Some of them look Western."

WEEKEND IN HAWAII. HOLIDAY INN on Waikiki Beach. Seemingly shallow waters, ten, fifteen, twenty yards out, then a sudden drop like walking off a cliff. In one step I am completely submerged. Gone.

I quickly scamper out, spitting out salty water. I spend the rest of the day broiling on the beach.

Yet another visit to an academic colleague of Dad's, at the University of Hawaii. Dr. Suh, who used to teach at the University of Houston, who is the primary expert on Communism in Korea. Afterward, I send my family on a mission to find a pukka shell necklace, which we purchase at a tourist stand off the scenic drive. I pick one with a shark's tooth in the middle. I wear it every day for the next year.

WE ARRIVE IN LOS ANGELES and spend the night at Dad's uncle's house in Glendale. Dad's uncle, Won Shik, who is two years younger than my father. I ask, How can this happen? Because Halmoni's father remarried when she was a teenager. He and his new wife had children after Halmoni did.

It sounds yucky and wrong to me.

Uncle Won Shik offers to take us to Disneyland, but I am too old and homesick to visit Sleeping Beauty Castle.

Even baby brother Ed shakes his head no.

PHOTOGRAPH

In 1992, my father goes on sabbatical at Seoul National University, his alma mater. He and my mom elect to stay in a guest cottage on campus instead of with Halmoni in her first-floor apartment, the apartment my dad helped purchase with his monthly dispatches over the years. Built in the early 1980s, the low-rise AID Complex occupies prime real estate between Lotte World's megamalldom and Gangnam's glass and steel edifices. Twenty-five identical, boxlike, four-story buildings whose gray concrete edges are already turning to dust due to improper pouring or truncated drying time or some other construction shortcut.

Halmoni loves her apartment. It's walking distance to the Methodist church where she is a deacon and the senior center where she takes lunch every day. Shops in between provide all the necessities. A fruit stand with fresh produce from the countryside, from her home province. The round crispy pears she peels after dinner, the chestnuts she roasts in her tiny oven, the purple-edged turnips she boils in her favorite doenjang broth.

City life suits this country girl. Halmoni enjoys living alone among the mass of humanity in the capital city. The pattering of tiny feet from the toddler who lives above makes her smile. Her much younger neighbors bow to her, and she nods back in acknowledgment. A television provides her with news of the world and a means to work on her English with the AFKN channel at night. Best of all, she has her own bedroom that she doesn't have to share with anyone. She can read her Bible there as much as she wants. And the ultimate luxury, an extra room to house an errant relative who has hit on difficult times or an occasional boarder, or even to keep empty.

She can decide.

AFTER MY FATHER COMPLETES HIS teaching duties, he and my mom move in with Halmoni for the rest of the summer. Halmoni is eager to have her firstborn visit, but that doesn't mean it is easy. She grumbles when my mom's citified food preparation deviates from her own simple dishes. She shuts herself in her room when my father answers the beckoning calls of former students, colleagues, and distant relatives. But she is most perturbed by my dad's search for information on her long-dead husband, the father he never knew and shouldn't ever know, since all that ever came from that man was disappointment and pain.

Halmoni tells my father that he shouldn't waste his time, he should concentrate on his research. That's why he's here, isn't it? To do research. Her stubborn son persists, though, like he always does, and even unearths his father's prison photograph with the help of an old friend. He tries to show it to her, but she waves it away.

"I don't want to look at it. Get it away from me."

It isn't until her nephew comes to visit a couple of weeks later that Halmoni's interest is piqued. The only child of her younger sister, Hee Sung had been spirited away from Seoul in 1945 by relatives after the Japanese surrendered at the end of World War II. His parents had died the week after liberation from some communicable disease. A medical doctor now, Hee Sung doesn't come to visit Halmoni often, even though his office is nearby. He makes a special trip, though, to see his cousin from the U.S. and the photograph of his long-lost uncle.

Halmoni shuts herself in her bedroom after a short greeting and bow from her only nephew. She opens her worn Korean/English Bible to the middle, to Psalms, and kneels on the floor pillow. She can hear the muted conversation between the cousins outside her bedroom. The slow, measured Kongju drawl of her son explaining how he found the photograph. The excited response of her nephew, who practically yells—"He looks just like your son Tongju! So handsome."

Hee Sung departs after half an hour or so. He's on his lunch break and needs to get back to his patients. Halmoni waits until he leaves to open her bedroom door. She walks slowly to her son, who is sitting by the low rosewood table she uses when guests come over.

"Let me see the photo. Let me decide if he looks like Tongju or not."

Dad hands it over. Halmoni holds the black and white in her wrinkled hand and stares at the man who died and left her a widow over sixty years before. He tries to discern what she is thinking. She stands expressionless, as usual. She clicks her tongue and gives the photo back to her son.

"Tongju is much more handsome than that man."

THE NEXT DAY, AFTER DAD leaves the apartment for an appointment, Halmoni admits to my mother that she didn't recognize the man in the photograph. The man who was her husband.

"I forgot what he looked like. I try not to think about him, you know."

Mom is stunned. How could a woman not remember what her husband looked like? The father of her children. Did she hate him so much that she willed herself to forget his face?

Halmoni's thoughtful look dissipates to irritation as she walks past my mom and into the kitchen. "I still think it's a waste of time for Eun Sul to try to dig up the past. He shouldn't bother."

HISTORY LOST

It's August 1950. My father Eun Sul is fifteen years old. He spends the morning digging a hole, an enormous hole in the dirt floor of the kitchen. He is technically too young to be conscripted into the South Korean army, but tall enough that he could be mistaken for an adult. As a result, he hasn't left the house much during the two months since the war began at the end of June. When he does, it is only under the cover of darkness.

Halmoni has been cooking all day. Barley and rice and corn kernels bubble away in the huge iron pot over the fire. Eun Sul sweats in the late summer humidity as the hole gets deeper and his horizon line descends. At dusk, his eyes are level with the ground.

His brother Eun Suk bursts through the doorway with an armful of family heirlooms. "Hurry up," Eun Suk orders.

Halmoni enters the kitchen in her slow, deliberate way, carrying a kerosene lamp. She bends over her eldest son and peers down into the hole. "Good work, now just pack down the dirt at the bottom and you will be done."

Eun Sul does what he is told and tramples the dense soil with his sandaled feet. He hoists himself out of the hole and leaves the chore of filling it with the family's belongings to his mother and younger brother.

He washes up to his brother's singsong refrain of "the North Koreans are coming, the North Koreans are coming." Everything is a game to my brother, Eun Sul thinks to himself as he shakes his head. Eun Suk is playful and mischievous, while Eun Sul is dead serious. As the first son of the first son, Eun Sul is the head of the family, a mantle he inherited as an infant after his father died. The weight of responsibility has dampened his spirit, seemingly forever.

Halmoni hands items down to Eun Suk, who has positioned himself in the hole. First the locked ebony box decorated with brass-filigreed plates that holds the family's land deeds, the family register that dates back over fifteen generations to the royal family of the Silla dynasty, and a hand-painted map of Korea the peasant Tonghak army left behind when it took over the family compound during the last years of the nineteenth century.

Her jewelry box goes in next, with its retractable foldout mirror, a gift from her in-laws on her wedding day. In it, she stores the beoseon sock patterns of all the female members of the Lee family. She allows herself to remember the only enjoyable task of young married life, when she was only a teenager—stitching the pointy, white cotton socks for her new family.

HALMONI HAS CAREFULLY WRAPPED THE remainder of her dowry of fabric in a shroud of tissue paper—the treasures from China and Japan her father gathered for her on his travels. Eun Suk places these pillowed treasures on top.

Earlier that day, Halmoni dismantled her beloved Singer sewing machine, which had been imported from the U.S. by her father at great cost. She carefully polished each black iron piece and smiled as she remembered how jealous her female in-laws were when her father unloaded the gift from his horse cart.

These pieces she saved for last. She pushes them gently down the sides of the hole, where they will provide support for the deed box and fabric parcels.

They are done. Halmoni instructs Eun Suk to push the rice chest over the hole. She doles out some of the contents of the iron pot and serves it with the leftover kongnamulguk from breakfast. The boys slurp down their dinner and head straight for bed. They will be leaving the next day for the house of the caretaker of the family burial site, deep inside the Sobaek Mountain range.

Surely, no North Korean would dare to venture to such an out-of-the-way place.

EUN SUL AWAKES IN THE middle of the night drenched in sweat. He dreamed he was floating—atop a field of fire. He reaches his arm out from the edges of his futon raft. The golden ondol floor is hot to the touch.

Why is the floor heated in the middle of summer, he wonders to himself as he drags the bedding outside to the adjoining wooden porch. He falls back asleep without an answer.

HOURS LATER, WARM ORANGE PERMEATES his closed eyelids. He blinks a couple of times and sits up. He is sweating again, but this time it's from the moist air that clings to his skin. Why is he outside? It takes him a minute to remember that he moved from the bedroom to the porch in the middle of the night.

It's Sunday morning, the day they are leaving home. The house is quiet. Halmoni and his brother must have gone to church services—up the three hundred steps to the makeshift sanctuary where the old Shinto temple stands. Eun Sul is thankful his mother let him sleep. It's his reward for all his labor the day before.

He stacks his futon on top of his brother's in the ebony blanket chest, the one decorated with an inlayed mother-of-pearl wedding procession. At night, if the moon hits it just right, the bride's face lights up from inside her palanquin. The groom, dressed in long robes, sits on his steed and looks longingly at his wife-to-be.

Eun Sul's stomach rumbles. He tromps through the courtyard to the kitchen at the side of the house in search of breakfast. He looks toward the location of yesterday's toil. The hill of dirt has been hauled away, and the rice chest stands where it always does. Halmoni has left him a bowl of something on top of the rice chest. Eun Sul doesn't bother taking his breakfast into the courtyard and eats standing up.

He notices a huge pile of ash on the hearth whose edges have spilled over onto the dirt floor. Did Halmoni cook all night? he wonders. Suddenly, he remembers the intense heat of the ondol floor.

Then he sees it. A book spine sticking out sideways from the mountain of ash. He pulls it out of its resting place. Its edges are charred. He can barely make out four embossed gold English letters: M-A-R-X.

Eun Sul stands still while his mind races. He runs to his mother's room and opens the lid of her wedding chest. He pulls out her one remaining hanbok, the one she wears for ancestor worship rituals, and throws it on the floor.

"Where are they? Where are they?" he says aloud, startling himself.

They are gone. All gone. His father's books and papers are all gone. Burned, he would soon discover, in the kitchen fire by his mother.

THROUGHOUT HIS CHILDHOOD, EUN SUL liked to sneak into his mother's room when he was alone at home. Halmoni at some prayer meeting, his brother off running around the neighborhood with his friends. He would slowly open the lid of the heavy wooden chest where she kept her formal dresses. He'd stack them to the side, careful not to crease the tissue paper casings.

She hid them there, away from view. So her sons and nosy in-laws couldn't find them.

Eun Sul had memorized all the titles and authors of the hidden objects on his secret missions. Marx, Engels, Lenin, Goethe. Thomas Hardy's *Tess of the d'Urbervilles*. Fabre's treatise on insects. A book by a Japanese author called the *Discovery of Zero*. And a thick volume swathed in black leather, a manual outlining the steps to operate a chicken hatchery, published by the Chicago Stock Exchange in the United States of America.

Carefully written in brown ink on each book's flyleaf was his father's name. Lee Chul Ha.

Deep inside one of the political tomes, Eun Sul discovered a single piece of onionskin paper, already yellowing at the edges. It was addressed to Brother Sung Ya, or "Starry Field."

Underneath the books lay his father's writings—on the tenets of Communism and other things Eun Sul didn't understand. Speeches for his study group, one that mentioned Goethe and Lord Byron. Pages upon pages of rice paper decorated in finely wrought characters, the handwriting of an upper-class yangban scholar. And official-looking records stamped with the seal of the Japanese imperial government, whose rule of Korea ceased only five years before in 1945, the year the Japanese surrendered at the end of World War II.

THE SHEATHS OF RICE PAPER must have burned quickly. His father's words transmuted by fire, traveling through the cement brick channels underneath the house, dissipated to pure heat upon which Eun Sul floated in the night.

His father's records met the same fate. As did errant pages of correspondence with his comrades in Seoul. Even the scrapbook of newspaper articles his father had written while he headed the Chongju branch of the *JoongAng Ilbo* newspaper. All gone.

Everything of his father's is gone.

ESCAPE

ll my gay friends in high school love Annie Lennox. All of them, except they don't identify as gay because "coming out" isn't even a concept in early 1980s suburban Houston. Music is what draws us together—Kevin, Kevin, Erik, Todd, Donna, Patty, Maria, and me. The Gang.

Annie sings on the soundtrack to the movie version of George Orwell's *1984*. Nineteen eighty-four is also our graduation year and the emblem of all that is wrong with Cypress Creek High School during the height of Reaganism.

"Doubleplusgood," sings Annie in her clear contralto.

"Doubleplusbad" is more like it.

Some iteration of the Gang sees the Eurythmics at the University of Houston the month before graduation. Annie is a force, strutting across the stage in her close-cropped blond hair and red lipstick. We dance the whole time in absolute euphoria.

OUR HIGH SCHOOL PRINCIPAL IS a former football coach who mispronounces the names of almost every non-white person in our graduating class of approximately 550 students—but not me, because my parents and I decided to use my English name in first grade after an uncomfortable year of kindergarten when no one, including the teacher, could pronounce Ju-hae. Mr. Equal Opportunity principal mangles some of the white students' names, too. Jose A. is "Josie." M. Abel's last name is pronounced "a bell." And that's just the As.

Even so, I still rank graduation day as one of the top ten moments of my now middle-aged life. After the birth of my two kids and my wedding day, but before seeing the Cure in the pouring rain.

I couldn't wait to get the hell out of suburban Houston.

OUR GRADUATION CEREMONY IS HELD at Hofheinz Pavilion on the University of Houston campus, where the basketball team plays. It's a forty-five-minute drive from our home in the outer northwest suburbs. Why so far away? Maybe there isn't an indoor space closer to fit all of us and our families? The Cy-Fair school district football field, which seats twenty thousand, is too hot in the June sun.

The summa cum laude students are seated alphabetically in the front two rows. Kevin B. first in line, Donna second. I am seated next to Jon L., who is a huge stoner and the smartest person I would ever meet. The rest of the Gang in the laude section, except for Kevin T., who is relegated to the plebeian portion of the name-butchering ceremony.

Todd receives the most cheers out of everyone. His entire extended family from Oklahoma is in attendance. His father died of a heart attack the week before. His relatives are all still in town after the funeral.

LIKE ALL KOREAN PARENTS, MINE want their firstborn to become a doctor. I acquiesce because I have no other plan. I am just happy to leave home and head to UT Austin. Biology, calculus, organic chemistry—I take them all while going out to New Wave clubs four nights a week. I wake up drunk each Tuesday for chemistry lab, which starts at 8:00 a.m. Luckily, Jill L. from high school is my lab partner. She is responsible and diligent and does everything, thank God. I just stand around and try not to throw up. Jill's a doctor now in the Woodlands, near where we grew up. She has two elementary school kids. She had kids even later than me.

I drink vodka tonics because they are refreshing and taste the least like liquor. I like how clean they feel on my tongue. A faint hint of lime infused with the antiseptic nature of the cheapest vodka known to man. Sparkling tonic water as clear as Annie Lennox's voice. The drinks are watered down, of course, but after four or five, I still get all Asian red-faced and my lips go numb. Only then can I be at one with the pulsing bass on the dance floor.

Reverberations in my solar plexus as the strobes shine pink and purple, as gravity disappears. I shed my skin of self-consciousness and forget to check what I look like in the eyes of those moving their bodies next to mine. I flail pieces of my outer layer off with each downbeat. I spin round and round as confetti spills from the heavens and the Weather Girls sing hallelujah because it's always raining men at the Boathouse. Afrika Bambaataa merges into Frankie Goes to Hollywood and back into Book of Love and Ministry. Time stops until last call for alcohol. At precisely 2:00 a.m., the lights go up and I fall back to earth like David Bowie in that movie where he's an alien. Runny mascara, deflated hairspray, sore knees. Kevin T. is always soaked, his too-loud shirt stuck to his chest. We all look a mess and scamper out of the formerly pulsing den and into the car. We head to Katz's Never Closes to eat knishes and dill pickles and slow our heartbeats before collapsing into bed.

Even with my club-kid lifestyle, I am still a child of immigrants who has been taught to achieve at all costs, even if it involves subsuming your true personality under a cavalcade of straight As, which I maintain for the most part except for a glaring C the second semester of organic chemistry when I dance so much I forget to eat. It takes me until junior year to drop out of premed. I go so far as to sign up for the MCAT. I hate all the premed students, except Jill, of course, who takes care of me, and our friend Kathleen V. who looks like a beauty pageant contestant and laughs at all my jokes.

I hate them all—the entitled sons of surgeons who cheat on exams and get away with it, the overachieving blond private school girls from Dallas who wear only Ralph Lauren, the Asian American kids who try their darndest to be as preppy as possible and also bear the weight of their parents' hopes and dreams. But they choose not to act out. Not like me.

I don't want to be any of them. I tell myself that I am probably the only one out of all of them who didn't vote for Ronald Reagan.

SECOND SEMESTER JUNIOR YEAR, I announce to my parents that I
plan to switch from premed to art history. My favorite class is an interdis-
ciplinary seminar on the concept of zeitgeist across cultural fields—from
architecture to painting to music.

I seek refuge on a weekly basis in the university gallery, where it's quiet
and cool and I can sit and stare at paintings when the Texas sun is at its
highest. My favorite is *Cadmium Red Above Black* by Adolf Gottlieb. A red
lipstick slash seeps into the canvas over a furious black explosion, all brushstrokes and chaos. Nine by seven feet, big enough so I am totally subsumed
into the elemental. The painting represents the absolute distillation of what
I feel deep inside.

Seeping blood over internal combustion.

WHEN I TELL MY PARENTS about my decision, this is what they say:

My father: "You know, art history is an M.R.S. degree."

My mom, the painter: "Why don't you become a doctor and then you
can afford to buy art?"

Which makes sense, but I know I'm not cut out to be a doctor. And
I'm the only one of two people on my floor in the girls' dorm—the one my
mother forces me to live in—whose primary goal in college isn't to find a
husband. The other is my friend Jordan, who's androgynous, and always
wants to talk about which U2 album is the best. My vote is *War*. Hers is *Boy*.

NEW BEGINNINGS

I open the blinds after I change to go to bed in my borrowed apartment. In the glow of the city lights, Anita's room never gets quite dark, even in the middle of the night. I want to see the shining silver spire of the Empire State Building poking above the apartment buildings before I take off my glasses and fall asleep. I love that building, with its needle top gleaming from the reflected light of the city below. It's sharp enough to prick all of Andy Warhol's silver balloon clouds that were kicked around the bright white walls of the Leo Castelli Gallery. Pop, pop, pop. I bask in the spire's circular waves of electromagnetism, 103 floors down and 17 blocks over, while I fall asleep on a futon on the floor of a friend's apartment in Chelsea.

I'm in New York City in the summer of 1996 to start my new life. The early 1990s' foray out west to pursue a dream museum job didn't work out; neither did any of my San Francisco romances. The City by the Bay never felt like home, no matter how hard I tried to put down roots. So, at age thirty, I'm back in grad school, this time at NYU.

I am happy and a little buzzed after an evening at the Temple Bar. Anita's friend Sofia put me in the hands of her friend Jim, a fast-moving attorney who knows everyone and every place, while she and Anita embarked to Florence, teaching Italian to privileged NYU students. They left me behind in the big city to face my new life without close friends.

I MET JIM AND HIS posse at the unmarked establishment on Lafayette and moved from the hot stinky sidewalk to a red curtain–swathed cocoon of Marrakesh lamps and royal-hued pillows. Jim holding court, quoting

the Smashing Pumpkins—*despite all his rage, he is still just a rat in a cage*—
the cage being the ESPN headquarters across the river in Jersey.

Included in Jim's entourage was a college pal from University of
Michigan, a former male model who designs furniture from his DUMBO
studio; some law school friends, including a bald shiny one who I later find
out is the ex-boyfriend of a friend in San Francisco; maybe a date or two,
including the bald one's two pretty-boy groupies who hang on every word
he says; and me, soaking it all in on a stool at the end of the curvilinear bar.

The male model's high school friend arrived late. Ruddy and goateed,
Ciaran had just driven back from California, from the Bay Area. Literally.
His dusty Good Times van parked out front.

We talked Bay Area—Ciaran worked at Yoshi's, the jazz bar and sushi
restaurant. I worked at SFMOMA. He ferried around jazz musicians. I
helped hang Matisses on gallery walls.

"I liked the job at first," I told him. "Until I figured out that my job
wasn't about art, even though I was in the curatorial department." It was
about making rich people happy—the Fishers, the Schwabs, the Haases.
They were more important than the art.

Ciaran was returning home. He was a local boy, went to college at St.
Mary's. I was making a new start in the only way I knew how, by going
back to school—for a second master's degree, but the right degree this
time, in journalism. We talked and I sipped my frothy cocktail. He drank
Coca-Cola.

I realized that Sofia sent me there for her friend Jim when he shot me
a disappointed look from the other end of the bar. I should have told her
that lawyers were not my type—they talked too much—even though I had
been dating one before I moved to New York. Maybe that's where she got
the idea. I hadn't explained that it had been a last fling before moving on.

Ciaran flashed a full-faced grin, stood with his arm around his childhood pal, and put him in a mock headlock. He talked about wanting to
check out bands at his favorite venues. I told him I was a former college
radio DJ. We talked about Faith No More, John Zorn, Yoko Ono, the
Velvet Underground.

"Have you been to CBGB?"

"No, but I want to go."

Hours passed, and the rest of the group faded into the background. Everyone was packing up. Ciaran offered me a ride to Chelsea, since he was apartment sitting there for his younger brother. I climbed into his van, a '70s original, complete with a rainbow painted on the side above a bubble window. I spied Hefty bags full of clothing in the back. A Marshall amp, a guitar case.

I was intrigued.

THE PHONE RINGS. I SQUINT and make out the LED numbers on the clock: 3:15. I answer the phone not waiting for the person on the other end to speak.

"It's three o'clock in the morning. New York is thirteen hours behind you."

I know it's my mother. Her weekly calls from Korea come at the same time in the dead of night. She never remembers the time difference, no matter how many times I explain it to her.

"Juhae, Juhae," she says softly.

Something is wrong. She's using my Korean name.

"Juhae, I'm at the hospital. Your father was overdoing it and started coughing up blood. The doctor said that one of the lobes of his lung needs to be removed."

I sit up and grab my glasses so I can think. "They have to take out part of his lung?"

My mom, uncharacteristically calm, explains the doctor's words. "The scar tissue is from the TB he had after the war. It finally gave way after all these years. He was feeling weak and short of breath. The lung expert at the medical school where Daddy is teaching told him to take it easy and not exert himself. He didn't listen and decided to put up some bookshelves in Halmoni's room."

I let the words sink in. "Do you think he should have surgery there? Shouldn't he come back home and have it in Houston?"

"Well, your father already asked the doctor about that, and he said that more doctors in Korea are skilled in doing this type of surgery, since there were so many TB patients after the war."

I start to cry.

"It'll be okay, Juhae, don't worry," my mom says in her best soothing voice. "He'll be okay. He's a faculty member here, so he will get the best care."

She pauses and guesses what I am thinking.

"You don't need to come. He'll be fine."

I grab a tissue. "Are you sure?"

"Yes, I've already discussed it with Daddy. You shouldn't interrupt school."

"Have you called Ed?" I ask.

"No, I was going to call him next."

MY FATHER'S RECOVERY FROM SURGERY is long and difficult. He convalesces for a couple of months in the double bed of the furnished apartment in Suwon, south of Seoul, while my mother hands him warm tea to sip and freshly peeled fruit to nibble. I call every couple of days, but my father immediately hands the phone over to my mother, not wanting to speak, not even to say hello.

My mother tells me of long days she spent shuttling dishes and linens back and forth from the apartment to the hospital. There's no room or cleaning service in Korean hospitals. Family members are responsible for providing meals, fresh sheets, and clothing. Even cups and pitchers of water.

"Your father's a horrible patient. He wouldn't listen to the doctor and insisted on coming home a week before he was supposed to."

When my father can finally manage a slow shuffle, he and my mother set forth back over the Pacific. He's forbidden from carrying anything, so my five-foot-tall mother somehow manages two immigrant bags and two carry-ons by herself—through Kimpo, LAX, and finally home to Houston.

She laughs as she relays the story over the phone. "People were giving your father dirty looks, but he didn't notice. They looked at me with pity, but no one offered to help."

MY FATHER EMERGES FROM THE house and ventures outside, finding solace amid the ginkgo trees he originally planted in the front yard when our family moved in twenty-five years before. He remembers the warnings he gave to my brother and me so we wouldn't trample the tiny saplings as we bolted across the prickly St. Augustine grass. My father moved the fragile trees to the side of the house, away from the bare feet of his children and the neighborhood kids. There, they thrived. The only ginkgo trees in all of northwest Houston.

The trees rain their sunshine-variegated leaves, which prettify the drab, late-fall harvest of Lakewood Forest, the planned community of cul-de-sacs and no sidewalks that I escaped when I moved away to college. I vowed then to my parents and whoever else would listen that I would never live in suburbia again. No way. I was destined for somewhere beyond the outskirts. I wanted to live in a real city.

My calls from New York continue, but my father still won't stay on the line. My mother assures me that he's glad that I called.

"Maybe you could email him?" she offers. "He spends so much time in front of the computer anyway."

SCAR TISSUE

Christmases at the Lee household are a four-person affair—me, my brother, Mom, and Dad in a two-story at Houston's edge. No other relatives in the country, save for my father's brother and family in Salt Lake City. We never see them. In fact, the only time I have ever come into contact with them is during our trips to Korea. Never in the United States.

The artificial tree from Sears is decorated with ornaments made by the Lee children during elementary school and dozens of origami animals folded by Dad in his cushy La-Z-Boy. It's his meditation, folding origami animals. The hobby Mom picked out for him to help him bide his time. The perfect hobby for a mathematician. Square, rectangle, triangle, hexagon. Geometry exploded into three dimensions from colorful square sheets of paper imported from Japan.

My father shows me his scar during the Christmas of 1996—a dark pinkish arc, stark against the pale skin of his chest. A quarter of a circle whose full shape would encircle his heart, from throat to navel.

Full circle. The final journey of a bacterial infection has come full circle. My father tells me that according to Halmoni, it was my grandfather who exposed him to tuberculosis when he was an infant. The tuberculosis my grandfather most likely contracted in prison. The bacteria lay dormant for over two decades and bloomed into full-blown TB in 1958 after my father graduated from college in Seoul. TB became an epidemic after the war.

He spent six months in a sanitarium and recovered. The scar tissue on his right lung held throughout adulthood, for almost forty years—long enough for a new life in a new country, only to give way on a trip back to the homeland.

The legacy of the father he never knew was an infectious disease that most likely was the cause or at least a major contributor to his father's death. Dormancy to bloom, to scar tissue, and then the opening of a wound that never quite healed.

The wound of growing up without a father. The wound of not knowing who his father was. The wound passed down to me.

MY FATHER'S TWO-YEAR SABBATICAL IN Korea has been cut short a year. He spends the rest of it convalescing back home in Houston, straining to regain what was lost during his four-hour surgery.

He lost a mass of scar tissue almost forty years old where tuberculosis had ravaged his lung. He lost the top lobe of his right lung where the tissue gave way. But worst of all, my father lost his livelihood. Maybe the anesthesia fuzzed over the surface of his brain. Or maybe when he was cut open, his problem-solving ability escaped from deep inside his chest. He doesn't know.

What he does know is that he can't remember numbers, which he has relied upon since childhood to lend certainty to his life. What's his home phone number? His zip code? His bank balance? His TOEFL score, which led him to graduate school in the United States?

He can't recall. That's the most difficult thing. Not the pain in his chest that keeps him up at night. Or the slowness in his limbs as he meanders through the house during the day. Even the increased reliance on his faithful wife, who in addition to cooking and cleaning must do all the heavy lifting and outdoor chores that running a household requires.

MY QUIET FATHER HAS GROWN absolutely silent. The familiar lectures on the greatest moments in the history of public health are absent from our dinnertime gatherings this Christmas. No Irish potato famine. No black death—"It wasn't the rats that caused all those deaths, it was the fleas on the rats." No mercury poisoning in Japanese coastal towns in the 1950s.

Mom tries to fill the air with idle talk of relatives in Korea or the crazy born-again neighbors next door who are homeschooling their three boys in fear that public schoolteachers will somehow turn their sons gay.

Ed talks about his new apartment in the basement of a mansion in DC near the zoo. I gush about my first semester at J-school at NYU, how I know I have finally picked the right career. And my undying love for the City, the real City, not the fake one out west where I lost my way. Dad sits and gnaws the kalbi ribs of all their gristle, leaving behind glistening nubs on his plate.

Mom takes me aside after Dad trundles up the shag-carpeted stairs after dinner.

"He goes to bed so early these days."

Ed clears the table and loads the dishwasher while we talk.

"Your father needs something to do. Something not related to work. He putters around in the garden, but it's so hard for him to bend over and pull weeds."

MY FATHER WAS THE ONE who wanted to write it all down, the story of the uncovering of my grandfather's life. He already laid the groundwork—gathering newspaper articles that chronicled my grandfather's arrest and trial in 1930 and conferring with Dr. Shin to apply for a Patriot's Medal in his honor. But his grand plans of unearthing my grandfather's prison and interrogation records during his sabbatical had to be abandoned.

I take my mother's entreaty to heart. I share her capacity to empathize—sometimes to excess. I can't ignore the vibrations of pain or anger emitted by friends, strangers, and especially family members. They echo inside of me. And I know a little about what it feels like to flail and sputter, to feel at a loss, not exactly like my father does but enough. In his eyes, he failed. He was on the verge of discovering who his father really was, but then his lung wept.

If my father needs something to fill his days, then I will give it to him. One semester down in journalism school, I know what has to be done, what questions need to be asked.

LATER IN THE WEEK, OVER breakfast, I ask Dad to write down any memories he has of his father. Anything he remembers Halmoni or his relatives having said about him.

What did it feel like to grow up fatherless? Do you remember seeing any pictures of your father? Did Halmoni keep any of his belongings?

"Dad, just write down anything that pops into your head."

My father nods. He looks a little less glazed than usual. After I return to New York for the spring semester, he responds with determination. I know he is stubborn. Maddeningly so, since he has passed down that trait to me. Faced with a challenge, he will attack it in his slow, methodical way. Ten minutes at first, then half an hour, soon an hour at a time. Every day, at the same time, after he makes an attempt at the daily crossword puzzle and eats breakfast. Upstairs in his study, in front of his less than state of the art Dell computer, typing anything he can remember.

He emails me his remembrances, and I ask him for more. He begins somewhere in the middle, when he was a teenager, when history was lost in the early days of the Korean War. He will circle back to childhood and arc outward to adulthood afterward.

PROTEST

BRIEF SKETCH OF FAMILY HISTORY
Prepared by Eun Sul Lee for Margaret Lee, 8/22/1998

SECTION 1: EARLY HISTORY
The Lee family was made up of well-to-do yangban landown-ers whose family compound was taken over by peasants during the Tonghak uprising in October 1894. The peasants used the compound as their headquarters in the final battle against the Japanese-backed government forces, a battle which they lost.

I KNOW FROM MY VOLUME of *A New History of Korea* that Tong-hak means "eastern learning," as opposed to "western learning." "Western learning" refers to the infiltration of foreign ideas into Korea, from Christian missionaries from Europe and the U.S. in the latter half of the nineteenth century and from Japanese businessmen who saw Korea as a market to conquer, as well as a source for raw materials and rice. Tonghak was an indigenous religious and social movement popular among the peasant class that opposed the yangban landowning elite and foreign interests.

At the beginning of the Tonghak rebellion, the Korean government panicked and called in Chinese troops, since Korea was then a tributary of China. Japan called its troops as well—it had an eye toward annexing the peninsula. With both opposing countries' troops in Korea, the Sino-Japanese War broke out in July 1894. The victor, Japan, won control of Korea.

DURING OUR WEEKLY CALL, MOM tells me that Dad works each morning on our family history project. Compiling all he remembers of my grandfather, and all he uncovered on his aborted trip to Korea years before, before his lung surgery.

"It helps him remember . . . It gives him something to focus on . . . It's good for him."

My mother acts as my father's emotional mouthpiece since he is unable to give voice to his own feelings. My father interacts with me through a written document, through a recitation of facts. These are roles we are all comfortable with. This is the way it's always been in my family.

"He has more to show you. He's just waiting until you read the first part."

I AMBLE INTO THE OFFICE at ten or ten thirty, taking my time through the mostly deserted streets of the East Village. Down five flights to the stoop and smelly garbage, past the lemon-yellow Catholic church on the corner where I hear children playing. Around the corner to Avenue B and on the lookout for Iggy Pop, since he lives in the Cristadora half a block down. I never see him, but my aspiring stand-up comedian roommate does at the photoshop where he works. He says that Mr. Pop waits his turn and is always polite, which proves the old adage that punk rockers are nice people.

I walk down B to 14th and Stuyvesant Town and envy those who are descendants of New York Life employees or somehow lucky enough to snag one of those rent-controlled apartments. If I am feeling lazy or too hot, I take the bus the five or six long blocks to Irving Place. Then it's up eight stories into the brand-new offices of *The Nation*.

It's the summer of the great transition and the great move. John and Sue decide to leave their shared literary editor post that spring, and Art takes over. The landlord on Fifth Avenue raised the rent out of reach of the perpetually in-the-red publication, so we move to new offices on the other side of Union Square. My cubicle digs of sleek white Formica and other man-made materials offer stark contrast to the former dusty closet that barely fit a chair, a slab of plywood/desk, and my five-foot-two-and-a-half self. I joked to John that the real reason he and Sue hired me as the assistant literary editor was because I was the only candidate who was small enough to fit in the closet.

I finally get around to downloading the latest of my father's remembrances of the past, which arrived during the whirlwind of serial commas, Facts on File runs, and last-minute changes that accompany each issue's closing. I glance at the title on the computer screen and smile. Dad writes like he's preparing a term paper or an academic article, even though his document is for my eyes only. I print the file and stand up to tend to the pile of boxes dumped in the vicinity of the bookshelf next to my desk.

Small stash today. I rip cardboard casings with my atrophying arm muscles. Some academic treatise on the future of the Arab state—put it with the others; a stack of review copies from Knopf's fall releases—better save those; and an errant romance novel—straight to the giveaway shelf. The interns start filing in. I wave to each as they make their way to their desks in the "intern pen," as they like to call it.

It's August 1998 and the last week of the summer schedule—two whole weeks to prepare an issue instead of one. A relief after a year of the relentless weekly grind, plus two special "Books & the Arts" issues, double sized and triple the work. A year of filling in the gaps of my supposed comprehensive liberal arts education—the trials of the Lincoln Brigade, the aging red diaper baby population, the blacklisting of Paul Robeson, and more than I ever want to know about the Rosenbergs and Alger Hiss.

Where else does the granddaughter of a student revolutionary belong?

NOT THAT I PLANNED IT this way. I answered the ad in *The New York Times* just like all the left-leaning members of my graduate journalism program at NYU. I read *The Nation* enough to know that its politics fit mine. My Austin boyfriend was an avid reader who would pore over issues after late nights of studying. He would spend the rest of the evening railing against Reagan and/or Bush, even when my head hit the pillow. My old roomie Kristin in St. Paul subscribed. I nibbled bites—mostly the culture stuff from the back of the book—on the ratty couch in the front room underneath the bone-arch sculpture her friend Nina made.

I told Ellen, my mentor and head of the Cultural Reporting & Criticism program at NYU, I was applying for the *Nation* job. She immediately offered to call up John and put in a good word. The lefty New York intellectual elites all knew each other, it seemed. I got an interview and impressed John and Sue with my ability to think on my feet, exemplary office skills, and vast knowledge of art history, especially in relation to social and political movements. With the added bonus of fitting in the closet, I was in.

WHAT DO I NEED TO tackle today? I compile a list in my mind. Make sure the interns have control of the fact-checking. Answer email and phone messages so the red light on my phone stops flashing. Order review copies and fax over the requests to the publishers. Input articles into the Quark system, no prob. Check, check, check. Most under control, so there's actually time to take a deep breath.

I walk over to Art's office, where stacks of books cover almost the entirety of the floor. He's on the phone, like always. He lifts his ear from the receiver and covers the mouthpiece.

"What do you need?"

"Can I take a look at the short story collections?"

He nods and points to the stack nearest the window behind his desk. *The Nation* rarely reviews short story collections, but Art's on the board of the National Book Critics Circle, so he receives everything. One day, I need to help him clean his office. Not today, though. Maybe over Christmas.

I snatch Lorrie Moore's new collection from the top of the pile. The one about birds. I will savor one story at a time right before bedtime, which is my habit. Something tightly constructed with an epiphany at the end, but not too well-crafted so as to be sterile. The epiphany is crucial since I want to learn how to identify them in my own life.

The section lineup is set for the week so I wait for Stuart's film review, which almost never needs editing. He's that good. Art wants to do all the line editing since he's just starting, so my duties lighten and the skies open up to more opportunities past my paper-strewn desk. Like time to nurture my freelance career. Another book review, maybe an art article or two. If I could snag another gig from *Elle*, I could avoid running out of cash at the end of the month like I usually do, maybe for the rest of the year.

I have time to consider my landlord Barb's suggestion to apply for that fellowship at Radcliffe, where she completed her Opium Wars art installation. "You get an office," she said, "and access to the Harvard libraries, free classes, and even your own research assistant. They love projects like yours," she added. "You're a perfect fit."

Barb's words ring through my head, but my stomach rumbles. Listen to your body, I remind myself. Wait too long and your blood sugar levels will plummet. Your eyes will dilate. Your brain will stall. Remember, you're borderline hypoglycemic.

SUMMER MEANS I CAN TAKE a real lunch, outside in the sun. And the usual crowd in the park will have dissipated. It's August—the city is as vacated as it ever will be. Those who can have already decamped to the Hamptons or Jones Beach or even the Rockaways for some surfing. Not that I've been to any of those places. Rockaway Beach is a Ramones song, and I don't like to swim, let alone surf. The Hamptons are out of reach on an assistant editor's salary, even if I wanted to go, and I'm not really a beach fan, either. Too hot. Too sandy.

Two years in, I'm not ready to escape the city yet, even if I could afford to. Granted, I need to decompress most evenings with a bubble bath and that week's copy of *The New Yorker*. All traces of my healthy California lifestyle have melted away into vats of mediocre coffee. Chinese takeout instead of fresh vegetables. Peeling fingernails instead of regular manicures. Walks to work in stylish yet painful shoes instead of a regular exercise program. My lower back aches from a fall down half a flight of concrete

stairs in my apartment building. New Beatle boots with no traction were
to blame—that's why they were on sale! A mysterious rash appears on my
belly. Allergies are in full bloom, without offending trees in view. Maybe
I'm allergic to dirt? Or pollution?

Someone at the museum told me before I left San Francisco that New
York is good for the mind but bad for the body. And San Francisco is the
opposite. She's right. I had been as healthy as I ever was during my four
years in SF. My mind, not so much, since the most valued part of my curatorial job was to procure pics of new acquisitions to present to the board.
I didn't go to grad school to become a glorified slide librarian, but that's
what I became.

Here, amid the tight grid of numbered streets and avenues, my mind
veers and reels with new sights and thoughts and ideas. I finally have an
intellectually fulfilling job, even though I'm still the only person of color in
my department like I was at the museum, but at least my boss is supportive
and actually cares about me as a person. If I could only prevent my body
from falling apart, I'd truly be happy. Really.

BOOKS OPENED, I RETURN TO my desk to check what's going on in
the world. "North Korea fires ballistic missile into the Sea of Japan," shouts
a headline. Good God, what are those pesky North Koreans doing now?
Just when they decided to meet with U.S. diplomats. They must be desperate for something—like food for their starving people. I remember some
magazine article quoting some expert who said that an entire generation
of North Korean children would be stunted, physically and mentally, for
lack of nutrition.

The *Los Angeles Times* agrees with my assessment. North Korea was "us-
ing the threat of nuclear and missile programs to try to extract aid from its
Asian neighbors and the U.S.—a policy termed as 'militant mendicancy.'"
Military begging. I shake my head. Not again.

My father's pages wait in the printer. I gather them up and shove
them into my purse. It's noon, I'm hungry, and I did some work, so
I'm warranted in leaving the office only an hour and a half after I

arrived. Buy a sandwich and Diet Coke at the bodega downstairs. Find a bench near the southern entrance of Union Square away from the Greenmarket.

SECTION 2: ABOUT YOUR GRANDPA, LEE CHUL HA

Lee Chul Ha was born on December 11, 1909, in a remote village outside of Kongju. He was homeschooled until 1921, when the family moved closer to the city. He started his formal education at fifth grade. According to his younger brother, your grandfather liked to read and loved to debate. On their hour-long walks to and from school in downtown Kongju, he and his two brothers had plenty of time to discuss the state of the country, which became an official colony of Japan in 1910. He and his brothers scribbled "Long Live Korea" and "Japanese Go Home" on the stone mileage posts along the road. Sometimes they even pasted these slogans on trees. The police looked for the offenders but never caught them.

My eyes crinkle at my grandfather's foray into graffiti. You go, Grandpa. I glance across the walkway to where some wayward youth has emblazoned a curlicue tag on the concrete planter wall. I know the tag won't last until sundown. On the way to the park bench, I spied a city worker with a pail of bleach water in his hand. Which reminds me of a story my friend Annabeth from my art history program told me, about her bicycle mechanic boyfriend who lived in New York in the early 1980s. He took the subway down from the Bronx to Manhattan every morning and saw Keith Haring's original radiant babies emanating from atop black placards on the subway walls. The glowing infants, too, disappeared by the evening rush hour. Later, after Haring became famous, subway riders ripped the now-valuable placards off and took them home before the cleaning crew could get to them.

Your grandfather was married to Kum Soon Min (Halmoni) on February 20, 1924, when he was fifteen. They were married in

Halmoni's hometown of Chongju. She didn't come to live with him until October of that year because his grandfather had died in the interim and the family was in mourning.

Your grandfather's mother (my paternal grandmother) told me this story about my father when I was young. She said, "Your father was born to be a leader." In the summer of 1925, a year after they were married, he and Halmoni traveled to Chongju to visit her family. He accompanied her grandmother to the city's center on a bus, and on a busy market street, the bus hit a cow and tore off one of its horns. Blood was everywhere, and people on the street and the bus were screaming and shouting. My father walked off the bus, quieted the crowd, and directed the bus away from the dead animal. My grandmother told me, "Your father was a tall, handsome young man, and nobody dared to disobey him." He was sixteen years old.

I love this story so much. I can easily see it as a scene from the movie version of my grandfather's life in my head. An overhead pan of the main thoroughfare of a bustling Korean town crowded with men on bicycles, women walking with wrapped loads balanced on their heads, donkey carts, farmers leading their cattle to market, and the lone city bus. Cut to the bus driver's view of the impending crash between his vehicle and a large cow. Close up on the cow's right eye, open wide with fear, like the calf's in Luis Buñuel and Salvador Dali's *Un Chien Andalou* before it gets slashed by a razor. Brakes screech, the standing passengers lurch forward, some hit the floor.

Focus in on a tall, handsome young passenger (who looks like Chow Yun Fat with his squared-off forehead, but younger and Korean). He regains his balance and makes sure his grandmother-in-law in the seat next to him is okay. He makes his way to the front of the bus, careful not to step on fallen passengers, and jumps down the steps. Outside, close-up on his squinting eyes and strong jaw as he takes in the chaos and decides to act. He clears the gathering crowd from the dead cow, whose right eye is still open, with the look of fear forever imprinted—jump cut a la Buñuel—and starts directing traffic.

Pan up and out to the restored movement of the street. An empty mule cart is rolled into view. Half a dozen men gather around the cow and lift it into the cart. The gawkers stop gawking and return to whatever they were doing. The handsome young man boards the bus. The passengers clap. Focus in on his grandmother-in-law. She looks up at her grandson-in-law, who has resumed his spot next to her, and squeezes his hand.

> *During the winter recess from high school in 1926, the Japanese emperor Yoshihito died. The first order of business when school started in January was a memorial service for the deceased emperor. Your grandpa helped organize a resistance demonstration. Instead of wearing a black armband, which was prescribed by the principal, the protestors wore traditional Korean funeral robes. School officials stripped off their robes before the ceremony, and the students were beaten. After that, the entire student body was punished for the protest. Some classes were replaced with disciplinary chores, and all privileges were revoked.*
>
> *Six months later, your grandfather was severely beaten and kicked out of school by the Japanese principal. He had sent a protest letter to the principal's office demanding a formal apology for his imperialistic attitude and harassment of Korean students. The fourth-year class responded to his expulsion by boycotting school six days later. Students from the three other classes decided to join them. A group of parents decided to mediate and persuaded the students to resume classes a week later.*

My grandfather's anti-Japanese graffiti evolved into donning Korean funeral robes and penning a protest letter, offenses punishable by expulsion. Then by corporal punishment and public humiliation in front of his peers. Such strong beliefs and courage were formed when my grandfather was only a teenager. I'm in awe.

I can't help comparing his political acts of defiance to my own measly demonstration experience. None until college at the University of Texas, but a deep, abiding hatred of President Reagan and my schoolmates' parroting of their parents' conservative ethos in high school. The future lawyer

in government class proclaiming that only English speakers should be allowed to vote. And poor people should be put in cages. Yes, he really said
that, and most of the class started yelling at him afterward.

In college, a march here, a rally there. Chants of "UT out of South
Africa" and "Divest now" freshman year. Yelling "L-I-A-R" in anger and
a nice skirt and heels from the top section of Memorial Stadium when
President Bush gave the commencement address for my *Nation*-reading
boyfriend's graduation. Calls to my senator's office to protest cuts to the
NEA. Ready signing of most any liberal petition.

Would I have done any of those things if I knew that there was a possibility that I would be punished? With a beating or expulsion or public
humiliation?

Probably not.

THE NIGHT OPERATION DESERT STORM begins in January 1991, I
can't pry myself off the couch while my roommates march down Sum-
mit Avenue to the Minnesota State Capitol in protest. Instead, I bask in
the green glow emitted from CNN's night-vision coverage of the lights
illuminating the Baghdad sky. Lights from a real-life video game, where
real bombs are bursting in air killing who knows how many below. I don't
budge until my roommates return. I am frozen.

I know my strong embrace of leftist politics stems from my reaction to
the lily-white childhood surroundings where I was treated like a foreigner,
even though I was born in this country—or even like an alien, the extrater-
restrial kind. My closest friends then, and now, are gay, even though they
didn't dare come out in high school lest they be beaten up on a weekly basis
by the Skoal-dipping, football-playing contingent. As a result, I am good
at reacting against, of being the naysayer, the contrarian, albeit in a polite,
smiling way, because that's how my proper Korean mother raised me. Do
I believe in something or want to be part of a group so much that I would
risk bodily harm?

I'm kidding myself. The real answer is: certainly not.

That fall your grandpa went up to Seoul to finish up high school. Halmoni's father was there, managing a pharmaceutical store for a relative, Min Kang, who had been active in the anti-Japanese movement and financed many activities. Because of the Japanese crackdown on the nationalist movement, Min Kang had moved to China in exile.

Your grandpa lived with his father-in-law in Min Kang's house in Seoul and enrolled at Bae Jae High School, a private school started by Methodist missionaries. Syngman Rhee, who would become the first president of the Republic of Korea in 1948, had studied there previously. After a semester, your grandfather transferred to the High School for Electrical Engineering and later to Joongdong High School. The reason for the frequent transfers is not clear, but I suspect that your grandpa tried to run from police surveillance. He must have been more active in extracurricular activities than in schoolwork.

"He must have been more active in extracurricular activities than in schoolwork." Indeed. His extracurricular activities were political in nature. Mine? At his age? Not so much.

Grandpa and I did share the feeling of getting the hell out of the provinces, though. Suburban Houston being my province. I spent the summer after high school trawling downtown record stores for imported extended singles during the day, attending concerts or going to Numbers, the only New Wave club in Houston, to dance to extended mixes at night. These were my extracurricular activities as a teenager.

I longed to escape the dead-end cul-de-sacs of Lakewood Forest as soon as I hit puberty. Through books, television, movies, magazines, music—whatever form of mass media I could get my hands on. The back issues of *Vogue* for the beautiful clothes and people, the rock 'n' roll excesses of *CREEM* in the downtown branch of the Houston Public Library, where my parents deposited Ed and me on Sunday afternoons while they enjoyed the symphony. Patti Hansen, Christie Brinkley, Cheryl Tiegs—all blond, all on the cover of *Vogue*. Iggy Pop pressing beer bottle shards into his bare chest. David Bowie in Kabuki makeup anchoring his face in the vicinity of Mick Ronson's crotch. All fascinating fodder for a suburban preteen mind.

Channel 13's after-school movie marathons. Godzilla week. Elvis week. Academy Award–winner week, with all the offending scenes cut out. I watched them all. It took me a decade to figure out that Dustin Hoffman took Katharine Ross to a strip joint on their first date in *The Graduate*. That in *Midnight Cowboy*, Jon Voigt was a male prostitute and not just some Texas bumpkin fresh off the bus in New York City.

I yearned to be at the center of cultural activity, where movements were born and artists gathered, where I didn't feel at a remove. I was tired of being the obedient daughter and stifling my true self to fit into my parents' immigrant dreams of upper-middle-class professional security.

Big city life suited my grandfather, just like me. Still, my struggles—with identity, with figuring out what I really want out of life—seem frivolous in comparison to his. He was a teenage revolutionary fighting for the independence of his country who was imprisoned for his activities and dead at age twenty-seven. He never had the luxury of time to "find himself" like his granddaughter, the thirty-two-year-old single woman on her second career in the big city who sits on this park bench in 1996, sixty years after his death.

HERE I AM IN NEW York City, maybe a decade after I really wanted to be, a decade after the East Village was truly decrepit and vibrant with a bastion of artist and writer squats. Where my advisor Ellen lived when she first started writing for *The Village Voice* in a crumbling tenement across the street from my renovated one. Where my landlord Barb and other artists took over an abandoned building and bought it from the city with the promise of helping to revitalize the neighborhood. Where during the Tompkins Square Park riots, Barb and her neighbor tried to block the SWAT team who swarmed into her building and clambered to the roof to point their weapons at protestors in the park.

Today, if I wake up early enough, I might spy an errant investment banker passed out on a bench in Tompkins Square Park, disheveled in his navy-blue suit.

Even so, I got here, didn't I? Working for a political magazine that existed during my grandfather's lifetime, one that espoused something close to his beliefs, albeit half a world away. This counts for something.

I can't ignore the gaps in understanding about my family, about myself, that the revelations about my grandfather's activities fill. Can family legacy help explain why my parents left Korea in the first place? Why they were some of the only liberals in all of Houston's Harris County? Why my first job out of J-school is at *The Nation* and not some glossy women's magazine?

THE NOONTIME RAYS BEAT DOWN. A tiny pool of sweat gathers in my earlobe. I glance at my watch. It's time to get back to the air conditioning and work.

Stand and stretch.

I spy the willowy intern from Yale yelling at the haggard guy who catcalled her at the park's entrance. The guy whom I avoided eye contact with when I sat down for lunch. I giggle and cover my mouth, Asian girl–style. He wasn't expecting to be publicly berated, but he deserves it. All the catcallers that seem to inhabit each and every street corner in the city deserve it.

FABLE

I t starts out innocently enough. It's the summer of 1996. Two people in their early thirties, fresh from the Bay Area and broken relationships, without a permanent place to live, meet at a bar in New York City, talk, flirt, and exchange cell phone numbers. A home-cooked Italian meal coaxes a slosh on the waterbed of an apartment-sit. The New York native/former bass guitarist tours the newbie gal to all the best music venues—Mercury Lounge, CBGB, Knitting Factory, Village Vanguard. He introduces her to Mingus, Pastorius, Art Tatum, and Charlie Parker, whose last residence is a basement apartment off of Tompkins Square Park emblazoned with a historical marker.

The summer fling morphs into an autumn romance with no effort at all.

It's easy to tell the story of our relationship in the third person, like a fable. He is Ciaran. She is me. And everything falls into place with only a couple of hiccups.

CIARAN GETS INTO A FIGHT at a Stereolab concert at NYU. He goes off to find the bathroom and next thing I know, I hear men yelling over the tinklings of the electronic keyboard and monotone French lyrics. I wonder who the hell gets into a fight at a Stereolab concert but keep my eyes on the stage and bop my head to the beat. Then I hear the whistles of the university police and look toward the back of the auditorium.

There's Ciaran cocking his arm back, his chin jutting out in anger in a stop-motion flash under the strobe light. Momentary blackness. His fist hits the chin of a huge guy in a black trench coat. It goes dark again. Two guys hold back my much-smaller boyfriend while the big guy socks him in the ribs. Next scene: The cops grab the big guy and escort him out. The big guy yells, "I didn't start the fight, he did."

The band never stops playing. Ciaran limps over to me. I'm worried, hysterical, and angry, all at the same time.

Are you hurt?

Let me see your ribs.

What the hell were you doing?

What's wrong with you?

This isn't a punk rock concert. It's Stereolab!

Did you rip your leather jacket?

If you get into a fight again, I'm leaving.

I'm serious.

Ciaran looks past me and doesn't hear anything I say. "That guy was a jerk. He bumped into me on purpose when I walked by. When I stopped to ask what's up, he bumped into me again. He deserved it."

Maybe Ciaran has anger issues. He did go through basic training for the Marines right out of college. But he dropped out after training was over. He doesn't drink alcohol anymore, he explained. Only Coca-Cola. Back in the Bay Area, he attended AA meetings.

I FORGIVE HIM ONCE, BUT maybe not twice. As winter approaches, we spend almost every night together, after my days at NYU and his as an IT guy at a midtown firm.

I remind myself that Ciaran's open heart and easy laugh are so different from the icy veneer of the Roman-numeraled WASP prince back in San Francisco. The self-involved, recently divorced, post-Minimalist sculptor. The history grad student who hated Robert Ryman's white paintings and thought they were a willful sham. The collection of my most recent exes.

Ciaran introduces me to his Irish-Catholic family, who are as warm and inviting as he is. But they are broken in places. Two of his four siblings aren't speaking. And even though the divorce was final over a decade ago, his dad still waits patiently in front of the TV for Ciaran's mom to walk through the front door. She never does. She left the minute after their youngest child went off to college, just like she planned.

I bring Ciaran home to Houston for Christmas. My parents welcome him but insist that we sleep in separate bedrooms. Ciaran doesn't understand—we sleep together when we visit his dad up the MetroNorth line. I tell him that my parents are Korean, they're from the old country, that's why we can't sleep together.

My parents can't pronounce his name. So they just call him Key. Ciaran asks if we can go to Christmas Eve services at the local Catholic church—Prince of Peace. To be nice, I accompany him and sit in the pew while he kneels and grasps the crucifix around his neck, the one he got in Peru. He buys my parents a fancy Waterford Crystal ornament for their artificial tree. He sneaks into my bedroom in the middle of the night. My parents don't notice since their room is on the opposite side of the house. I can tell my parents don't dislike him, that he has charmed them at least a little, but I know they wish he were Korean. Or at least a doctor or a lawyer or someone with an advanced degree.

BACK IN NEW YORK, I joke with a friend visiting from Minneapolis that in five years I picture myself living in a big house in Westchester with a baby on my hip. I mean to be ironic, because that's how I always am, but he can sense the truth beneath the admission and looks at me with an expression that I interpret as light amusement tinged with a smattering of disdain.

In my semi-ironic vision of the future, I can see the farmhouse sink, butcher-block island, the view from the kitchen window onto a verdant backyard full of old-growth maples. I'm barefoot, clad in a Marimekko print dress and holding a cute chubby baby with a mop of black hair to match mine. It's my cute chubby baby, that I am sure of.

But who is the father?

He's not in the picture. It's just me with my happy baby.

Is the father Ciaran?

More questions follow: It seems like my house, because I'm standing in my dream kitchen in a dress I'd like to wear, but how can I afford a home in Westchester as a journalist?

Did someone else pay for the house?

Did I win the lottery? Oh yeah, I don't believe in the lottery because I'm the daughter of a statistician and know the real odds of winning, which are next to nil.

Did I get married?

Did I marry Ciaran?

Do I want to marry him?

Ciaran can't afford a home in Westchester as an IT guy. Even with both our salaries, we could never even hope to buy a house in the tristate area. Never. In a million years.

And neither of us want to live with his dad up the Hudson.

THERAPY

Anita has raved about her therapist Bob for months. How she loves his office in the West Village brownstone with the wide red staircase and dark patina molding, the kind you see in movies; how he is omniscient and wise; how he is finally making her deal with the coma-inducing car accident she suffered the week after college graduation.

She gives me his number and I call. I know the instant I hear his deep, gravelly voice that Bob is the guy for me. I could listen to his voice forever.

Kind Bob extends a sliding scale payment plan to a fellow progressive, even though he complains that *The Nation* has been way too soft on President Clinton. Only one session in the brownstone; that space is reserved for full-paying clients. I meet him at his academic office across town.

I tell Bob that my boyfriend Ciaran had a nervous breakdown a year into our relationship. And that I didn't see it coming. I visited him at a mental hospital facility. Soon after he got out, he stopped taking his meds and seeing his therapist. I tell Bob the whole saga. He is the only person who gets the entire story.

At the next session he asks about my former boyfriends. I tell him about them, too. How almost all of them had substance abuse issues.

After that, he asks, "What do you want?"

"In general, or in a boyfriend?"

"In general."

A long pause.

"I want to be a writer, and I want a family."

There, I say it.

"Do you think Ciaran would make a good father?"

"Well, if he wasn't depressed. He's great with kids."

"Do you think he'll not be depressed?"

"No, not without some help."

"Do you think he'll get help?"

"No."

Everything seems so clear sitting on the blue plastic chair in Bob's office, where I can look up and see all of Shakespeare's plays on the bookshelf behind his desk. Outside, where the warm dusk breeze whips my skirt around my legs, things cloud over a bit, and by the time I take the bus home, my hard resolve has softened to a molten mass in the pit of my stomach.

THE FIRST TIME I WENT to therapy was three years before in San Francisco, in 1994. I was miserable. I hated my job at the museum. An intense, six-month relationship with someone whose values totally diverged with mine flamed and collapsed in short order. My parents were living in Korea and left me, the eldest daughter, to deal with Ed, recently graduated from Carnegie Mellon and engaged to his college girlfriend, who had grand plans for a huge wedding and condo ownership, both of which I knew my little brother didn't want.

Straight off, the therapist offered to write me a Prozac prescription. I refused. She looked surprised, as if no one had ever refused meds before. Or maybe she was taken aback at my vehemence in refusing. Instead, I talked and cried and talked and blew my nose.

I asked Dad for financial help, since I couldn't afford the weekly sessions on my curatorial assistant salary. When I called him on the phone in Korea, he agreed. But when I came home to Houston for Christmas, he lectured me about ethics violations of therapists who crossed personal boundaries with their patients. Didn't I read about the therapist in Massachusetts who had an affair with one of her clients, who ended up killing himself? He didn't think therapists could be trusted. They had too much control. How could my therapist really understand me and offer relevant advice if I only saw her once a week for an hour? Dad went on and on, since he was in professorial mode and it wasn't time for the question-and-answer period.

I knew where this was headed.

He wasn't going to pay anymore.

I wasn't surprised, really. Just sad. Dad worked at the School of Public Health and was a longtime consultant to the National Institute of Mental Health, but he hated to go to the doctor, any doctor, let alone a therapist. He would never go to a therapist. What stubborn Korean immigrant man would go to a therapist? In his mind, seeing a therapist meant asking for help, and asking for help meant ceding control, and ceding control was a fate worse than any illness.

Then there was the issue of the lack of trust. Who did my father trust? Not a doctor or a therapist. Or his colleagues at school, especially the dean, who repeatedly passed him over for tenure, even though he consulted regularly for the NIMH, NIH, and WHO, and published more than those who were bestowed with lifetime job security.

Who could my father trust? Who had his back? Who could he rely on? Not his family back in Korea, that's for sure. Maybe my mother. But ultimately, he had learned to only trust himself.

I TOLD MY THERAPIST ABOUT the entreaty my mother repeated throughout my adolescence: "Don't let a man try to control you with money." My mother didn't have to add "like your father."

I told her how I used to accompany my mother as a child on her weekend trips to the fabric store. The one closest to our house in the strip mall at Jones Road and FM1960. The fancy one on Westheimer in River Oaks, where the salespeople knew Mom by name and offered us cold cans of Coke when we entered from the steaming parking lot. I'd head to the *Vogue* pattern books to see what the designers had come up with for the current season; she'd walk straight back to the remnants section and finger the Japanese silks, the Swiss cottons, the Scottish woolens. Each remnant was a treasure—a dress for me, a blouse for her, a smart suit for when my mother got a real job, maybe as an assistant in a law office, since she had always wanted to go to law school.

After the war was over, Mom was accepted to Seoul National University's law program, the most difficult program to get into at the best school in the country. She didn't go because her father refused to pay. It was more important for her two younger brothers to go to college instead of her. She was better off just getting married.

After we returned from our outing, Mom would stash the Gallery Fabrics shopping bags in the wet bar by the back door, where we stored the family's shoes. "Don't tell Daddy," she'd whisper to me. But if she waited too long to hide the bags in the closet upstairs, Dad would find them. And get angry.

MY THERAPIST IN SAN FRANCISCO was motherly, encouraging. Each Tuesday afternoon I'd take the MUNI from the museum to an overwhelmingly beige office off of Jackson Street in Pacific Heights. I was tempted to lie down on the overstuffed couch and pretend I was in a Woody Allen movie but never did. Instead, I sat in the cushy chair opposite her cushy chair with a Kleenex box on the coffee table between us.

"Do you think you are wary of men trying to control you because of how your father tried to control your mother with money?"

Check.

"Which is a difficulty since you really want to find a partner to share your life and start a family with?"

Yup.

"And do you think you pick men who need mothering, since you have such a strong urge to nurture and have a child of your own?"

Totally spot on. You got it.

"And do you think you resent the boyfriend who needs mothering because the effort to nurture distracts you from dealing with your own issues?"

How did you know?

Each session was filled with probing insights posed as questions. There was the additional insight of how my parents were passing on parenting duties for my younger brother Ed, who was drifting along in the wake of a fiancée who knew exactly what she wanted while he had absolutely no idea.

I had just accepted that it was my job as the first child, the big sister, to take care of my younger sibling because that's what I was supposed to do. I never thought to ponder where my outsized sense of duty originated, that my role as a surrogate mother to my brother, the son, the male, the heir, was rooted in a culture rife in patriarchal tenets—it was Korean.

The push/pull between cultures, between my own desires and my family's, between ego and id, explained my ambivalence about so many things. The mixed messages about marriage from my mother. She was a good Korean wife who cooked and cleaned and sewed her American children nice outfits. She made prom dresses for the neighbors' daughters, hemmed suit pants, became the personal tailor for an enormous woman who went to our church. She told me that when I was a baby, she wanted to enroll in a computer-programming course sponsored by IBM, but my dad didn't let her.

"Juhae, you make your own money. You make lots of money."

I chose a low-paying career in the arts and was now pursuing another nonlucrative career in journalism. I couldn't bear to be a doctor or lawyer or investment consultant, which was a job I interviewed for at Smith Barney my senior year in college. Why? Because my parents wanted me to. Did I get the job? No.

After all of these realizations and more, the money ran out. During our last weeks together, my therapist and I discussed my plans to attend graduate school in New York, where I really wanted to live, where I could pursue a new career in journalism, where everything could be different and better and I could be happy, fulfilled.

My therapist gave me a warm hug but left me with a warning: "Even if you move away, your issues will follow you."

I LOVE THE WAY BOB says Ciaran's name. The bass tone gravity, the rolling of the R. We talk about Ciaran at every session, so Bob says his name a lot. He asks when I noticed Ciaran unraveling.

We drove up to Woodstock for a long weekend. Ciaran had been acting paranoid for a couple of days. Asking where I'd been, who was there, what time I'd be home, trying to keep tabs on me hour by hour. He'd never acted like that before. He picked me up from my apartment late that Friday night to drive up north. We stopped at the all-hours Israeli place near NYU to grab some food. I had a falafel sandwich. He had chicken schwarma. He started in on me, accusing me of sleeping with an old boyfriend who was a sculptor. I threw up out the window. I thought I had food poisoning because I never vomit. I hate to vomit.

We got to the motel in Woodstock, a crappy one, with water stains on the ceiling. Ciaran wouldn't let me sleep. He yelled and then jabbed my side with his finger if my eyes drooped. I didn't throw up again but I wanted to. I wanted to vomit all over him so he would shut up.

After that night, he closed up on himself. He could speak, but only in niceties. What do you want for breakfast? Isn't the weather great? Do you want to get a cappuccino? You look nice today. His eyes glassed over. It was like the night before never happened. We walked down Main Street, peered into the head shops, saw every variety of tie-dye imaginable. We picked up bagels with lox and cream cheese. He ate his. I barely touched mine.

I asked him about the night before. Why he was acting so paranoid. He couldn't look me in the eye. I couldn't reach him. He wasn't there anymore. I lost him. It was worse than when he was berating me.

BOB ASKS ME ALL THE questions. The questions my girlfriends ask:
    "Why do you stay with him?"
    "Why is it so hard to let go?"
    And more questions about why I don't tell my family about Ciaran's breakdown.

"You say you don't want them to worry, but is that the real reason?"

"Is it because it represents failure?"

"Did you think you will disappoint your parents?"

"Is keeping them out of your personal life a means to assert your independence from their influence, from their culture?"

I have some answers: I can't let go because Ciaran needs me. He needs help. I can't leave him to face the breakdown alone. Like his ex-fiancée. She left him. I can't in good conscience do that. It's cruel. He can't even accept he has a problem. That's why he went to AA back in California. He can accept alcoholism but not mental illness.

"But what about you?" ask Bob and my girlfriends. "How is this affecting you?"

"Why do you feel responsible?"

My father, Eun Sul Lee, on a Christian Children's Fund outing, ca. 1961

TUBERCULOSIS

It is spring, 1958. My father Eun Sul misses the date of his required induction into the South Korean military. He doesn't get the notice in August like his classmates from Seoul National University since it was sent to his home address in Kongju. Eun Sul forgot to update it after Halmoni moved to live with him in Seoul. Eun Sul is officially a draft dodger.

He knew to expect the call to duty. All male college graduates are required to be drafted after commencement. His graduating class was called up the previous fall, but Eun Sul was left behind because his birthday was nineteen days past the cutoff date of September 1.

So, instead of enlisting, he applied for a translation job at the Christian Children's Fund and, to his surprise, got it. It's a good job with the U.S.-based agency that places orphans from the Korean War with families abroad. He translates letters between the Korean orphans and their American sponsors. His English gets much, much better and he learns to type.

That fall, after a couple all-nighters working on speeches for the organization's director, Eun Sul contracts a severe flu. He is sick for an entire month, but he doesn't bother to go to the doctor. The flu symptoms finally subside, but the cough persists.

Eun Sul's draft dodger status weighs heavily on him. He tries to be inconspicuous as he goes about his days, especially when he walks by the police checkpoint near the office. Head down, hands in pockets. No eye contact. In a rush like everyone else in the capital city. He is afraid he will be stopped and taken in.

In 1958, Syngman Rhee is still the president of the Republic of Korea, an office he was elected to a decade earlier with the backing of the U.S. His tenure was extended by an amendment to the Constitution in late 1954, but he hasn't brought any semblance of economic or political stability to the country after the war, in Eun Sul's opinion. South Korea continues to be dependent on international economic aid. And under the cover of anti-Communism, the Rhee regime targets opposition groups and routinely arrests individuals at police checkpoints all around Seoul.

Eun Sul is effectively living in a police state.

EUN SUL SEES THE ANNOUNCEMENT from the Air Force in the newspaper for a special officer training corps made up of college graduates to serve at the Academy as instructors. This is how he can resolve his draft status. He applies and takes the required written test and an oral examination before a table of officers. One thousand applicants, then a hundred finalists, of which Eun Sul is one.

Summoned to the Air Force Training Center in Taejon for a physical examination, fitness test, and interview with the superintendent of the Academy, Eun Sul takes the train down from Seoul Station with a carful of anxious young men. He is confident he can prevail and finally fulfill his obligatory duty.

The morning of the first day: physical exam. Shirt off, cold stethoscope on his chest. Breathe in, breathe out. Obligatory TB chest x-ray. On the second day, the superintendent conducts an interview with him in English, since the Air Force needs officers proficient in the language to deal with the Americans who still occupy the country.

Eun Sul is certain his performance is exemplary.

Afterward: "Lee Eun Sul, return to the doctor's office."

A second, larger x-ray is ordered, because something suspicious was found in the first. The second shows a dark spot on his right lung. The attending physician makes an on-the-spot diagnosis: tuberculosis, early stage.

Needs immediate treatment, he writes on Eun Sul's chart.

EUN SUL REMEMBERS TAKING THE skin test for TB in the sixth grade, shortly after the establishment of the American military government in 1947. A pinprick on the underside of his wrist. A red welt erupted before his eyes, the size of his pinky fingernail. Perhaps a third of his classmates, as well as his brother, tested positive for exposure to the bacterial infection. Eun Sul's reaction was tame in comparison to some. He and his brother required no treatment, but Halmoni made an extra effort to feed them a healthy diet afterward.

Halmoni was clear in her explanation of how her sons were exposed to the disease. Their father was desperately ill when he was released from prison. Pale, wasted away—that's how he looked in the photograph displayed at his funeral, the photograph Eun Sul remembered hanging on the wall of his house when he was a child. Halmoni worried about Eun Sul's complexion—he was noticeably paler than his brother. She fed him deer-horn tonic every spring to fend off sickness. Eun Sul had been exposed to his father's tuberculosis a year longer than his younger brother.

EUN SUL ARRIVES AT THE tuberculosis sanitarium in a shiny jeep emblazoned with the Christian Children's Fund logo on the side. He is accompanied by a nurse and the head of the facility, Miss Beard, a Presbyterian missionary. They have driven up from Taejon and into the rolling hills north of the city where grapevines ripple up and down like waves. Half a dozen pairs of eyes stare through the tiny windows of the white plywood barracks as they head up the gravel drive.

Immediately taken to his cubicle, the second one from the left in the row reserved for male patients, Eun Sul unpacks. Three sets of clothing, half a dozen English-language books (fiction, philosophy, sociology), and a Philips radio he places on the table beside a long, wide shelf, on top of which lies a thick cotton futon. His bed for the next six months. He stores his battered leather suitcase underneath. All the furniture, the walls, the floor are painted white, just like the outside of the buildings, of which there are three to house patients and two for staff.

Eun Sul is prepared to rest and does so without difficulty. He is determined to rehabilitate himself. On the second day he feels better than he has in a long time. For the first time in months, he doesn't have to rush off somewhere. After lunch, rose blooms arise on both cheeks. He has a mild fever, one of the symptoms of TB. He realizes he must have run a fever for weeks. He was too busy to notice.

Every day is the same. Breakfast in bed. Reading for the rest of the morning with only one interruption by the young female nurse who takes his temperature and dispenses medication—tiny isoniazid pills. If the weather is nice, a male staff member opens the mosquito-netted window from the outside. After lunch, which is also served in bed, all patients are expected to rest. Reading is discouraged during this time. Even so, Eun Sul sneaks a look at his book. Footsteps echo loudly down the wooden plank hallway, so he has ample time to stash the book under his futon when the orderly makes his rounds. Patients are forbidden to venture outside, save for fifteen minutes after the evening meal.

On his after-dinner strolls, Eun Sul looks up to where the grapevines give way to pine trees, to the north, where Seoul lies and his mother lives—and beyond, to North Korea. Sometimes, after midnight with his Philips radio turned down low, he listens to North Korean music, mostly military marches. The rest of the day the radio signal from the North is scrambled by South Korean authorities.

Eun Sul enjoys listening to the radio. He learns to appreciate light operas by von Suppé, Smetana, Borodin. He becomes well versed in the different eras of the Western classical music tradition. The high school graduate four cubicles away teaches him about the history of music. Baroque, High Classical, Early Romantic, Romantic. He doesn't get to the Modern era. The music lover has been at the sanitarium for a long time and remains, even though he seems to have recovered. Another patient tells Eun Sul, "He hasn't left because he's the only one of his family alive. He's poor and has nowhere to go."

It takes Eun Sul three months to finish reading his first book. He picked the longest novel he could find at the English-language bookstore in Seoul, the one on the main boulevard leading to Gyeongbokgung Palace. *War and Peace*. He sails through the war portions quite easily, to his surprise. The peace parts are the ones he has trouble with. He is forced to consult his English/Korean dictionary every other sentence to understand the particulars of Russian high society. He draws an elaborate chart on the frontispiece to help him keep the members of the five aristocratic families straight. Even so, the details of courtship between members of the nobility seem beyond his mental grasp.

Eun Sul is glad he finishes *War and Peace* before winter arrives. Frigid temperatures prevent his hands from venturing out from underneath the thick covers to turn the pages of any book. No heat, no hot water. Doctor's orders. The crippled veteran in the last cubicle requests hot water at each sponge bath, but Miss Beard is firm in her refusal. The cranky patient makes his displeasure heard as he rat-a-tat-tats his peg leg down the hallway, scaring the orderlies on his way to the bathroom.

Eun Sul meditates and thinks about his future during the winter months. First and foremost, how can he resolve his draft dodger status? After his sanitarium stay, should he return to his job at the Christian Children's Fund or find another one? He considers his long-term plans. He's only twenty-four. What does he want to do with the rest of his life? Does he want to continue his studies? And how will he continue to help support Halmoni and his brother?

EUN SUL RECEIVES THREE VISITORS during his stay, which is extended two months, since it takes him longer to recover than expected. Halmoni visits only once on a hot summer day, a couple of weeks after he is admitted. Visitors usually arrive by bus from Taejon and walk the twenty minutes to the sanitarium from the nearest stop. Unfamiliar with the bus route, Halmoni ends up walking an hour and a half all the way from the city. She arrives, exhausted, in the late afternoon, carrying a big sack on her head. Eun Sul meets her on the bench underneath one of the looming pines up the hill. She opens her package and pulls out some chapssal-tteok cakes to share.

"I decided to give up on living in Seoul and opening a sewing shop. With you sick and not working, I can't afford to do it. I really wanted to start a business with your auntie there since we are both without husbands, but it wasn't meant to be. It's because I'm cursed, cursed by that man who was your father. He ruined my life, you know, leaving me to deal with his family and raise you and your brother by myself."

Halmoni continues her lament without looking her son in the eye.

"Why did you get sick now? You bought me that new sewing machine, and I was about to sign a lease on a space for the shop. It's been my dream to live in Seoul ever since I was there when your father was in prison. I tried to return right before the war started, so you and your brother could go to school in Seoul.

Your father ruined my life before and you are ruining it now. You might never recover from TB and leave me, too."

The bell for the evening meal rings before Eun Sul can respond. Not that he knows what to say. He has never seen his mother so bitter or defeated. Or so angry at him and the father he never knew.

"It's time for me to go," Halmoni tells him.

She quickly gathers her things and leaves the sack for him—it's filled with clothing and linens to last him the rest of his stay. Eun Sul watches as she makes her way down the gravel driveway to the bus stop. She never once looks back. She doesn't give him the chance to wave goodbye.

Eun Sul stares at his plate at dinnertime. He has lost his appetite. He can't sleep that evening, either. He lies awake wondering why his mother harbors so much resentment toward his father. And now, why it's pointed toward him.

IN THE FALL, HIS BROTHER Eun Suk visits him with two of his college friends. They arrive in a whirlwind, during the early afternoon rest period, waking most of the patients, alarming the staff. The nice nurse advises the trio to leave and return during visiting hours later in the afternoon or the next morning. The two friends stand outside the patient barracks and argue with her. Eun Suk sneaks around the corner and peeks into his brother's cubicle. He waves at Eun Sul through the open window with a grin. He and his friends leave and never return.

Eun Sul's childhood friend is his most devoted visitor. Jong Min makes the trek to the sanitarium three times from Taejon, where he is teaching high school. He feels indebted to Eun Sul, since he tutored him for his second try at the Seoul National University entrance exam. Jong Min entered Seoul National a year after Eun Sul, and they have kept in close touch ever since.

The friends have known each other since 1945—fifth grade, when Korea was liberated from the Japanese. In high school Jong Min moved to a seaside town. When school was canceled because of the war, Eun Sul and three other friends hitchhiked the seventy-five kilometers from Kongju to the ocean on the back of a flatbed truck whose only other cargo was a corpse. Jong Min had arranged for them to stay at an empty beach house owned by some missionaries and gave them a sack of rice so they could eat for the week. The boys supplemented the rice with fish they caught at the beach.

With Jong Min's help, Eun Sul devises a plan to resolve his draft dodger status. Jong Min consults a former classmate, who is a military lawyer in Taejon. The lawyer makes the necessary arrangements. Eun Sul should report for duty with no mention of his tuberculosis. After his legal induction, he should request a physical exam. After the doctor discovers his disease, Eun Sul will be officially discharged from military duty for medical reasons.

Eun Sul asks the sanitarium for a two week–long home leave. His request is accepted. Instead of visiting Halmoni, he enters the military training center at the Nonsan base nearby, according to plan. After a week of basic training, he complains of tightness in his chest, shortness of breath. A physical examination is scheduled, and sure enough, his TB is discovered. He is dismissed from military duty within a few days.

Eun Sul returns to the sanitarium and doesn't tell anyone where he has been. Not the nurses nor the patients. Not even his own mother. He's already disappointed her enough.

HE FORWARDS HIS MILITARY DISMISSAL papers to the draft board in Seoul. In due time, Eun Sul is reclassified from draft dodger to draft exemptee. Even with his reclassification, he knows he will have difficulty landing a good job in the future, since most employers give priority to those who have completed military service.

What are his prospects now? He's not sure that the Christian Children's Fund will hold his job through such a long absence. He would like to continue his studies in sociology and maybe teach someday. After four years at Seoul National, Eun Sul knows that a comprehensive understanding of the subject can only occur outside the country, since so few resources are available in Korea. His most rewarding learning experiences occurred outside the classroom—with his own reading and conversations with visiting lecturers who had studied in the United States. Maybe he could apply for a scholarship to attend graduate school abroad.

After getting his degree, he would return home.

DICTATORSHIP

My father Eun Sul is glad to go home. For Korea is still home, even after almost fifteen years in the U.S. He has talked it over with Chong, my mom—he will look for a job while we are in Seoul this summer, the summer of 1976. His journey back to the homeland had been delayed by lack of funds and an unexpected offer from a new school of public health in Houston. An offer he couldn't refuse. Throughout the years of struggle, the hope of returning home persists.

His former advisor at Seoul National University offers the bait. A semester-long residency funded by the United Nations Fund for Population Activity. All expenses paid, including plane tickets for the entire family. His advisor wanted him to come the previous fall, but Eun Sul asked if he could postpone until the summer so as to not interfere with my schooling and his own teaching schedule.

Then there's the issue of Halmoni. She arrived in Houston to stay with us the previous November on a permanent visa, with the option of applying for naturalization after five years. She does not want to return to Korea after just arriving in the United States. Luckily, a cousin in New Jersey offers to host her for the summer.

The airline tickets arrive from the UN in the aftermath of an enormous thunderstorm, the season's worst. Horizontal sheets of rain penetrate each crevice of the newly constructed School of Public Health building. Windows and doors are rendered useless. Burnt-orange upholstered furniture floats in knee-high water in the lobby.

The DHL courier can't even make it to the parking lot, so he delivers the envelope to the president's office, which is safely perched on a mini hill in the heart of the Medical Center. A kind secretary drives the package to our three-bedroom house in Alief. The package is accompanied by a note from the president: We are proud that you are representing the University of Texas Health Science Center on a UN-funded research project.

EUN SUL AND HIS FAMILY arrive at Kimpo Airport late in the evening. A delegation is waiting. Four of Chong's siblings, his brother, and half a dozen graduate students from his alma mater. The homecoming ceremony is cut short, though. They need to hurry. They must make it to Chong's sister's house before midnight. The nationwide curfew has been in effect since the American occupation troops instated it after the end of World War II.

A few weeks pass; everyone seems to settle into Korean life quite nicely. Eun Sul with his research and catching up with former classmates who are now professors. Chong reunited with her siblings. Ed and I discover for the first time what it's like to have cousins. Eun Sul is most pleased with how quickly Ed is picking up the language with the help of the housekeeper's son. I'm not as interested in learning Korean.

Eun Sul reconnects with most of his old colleagues, except one. Where is Dr. Han, his friend from the sociology department, the one who went to Emory University in Atlanta to get his PhD? Isn't he teaching at Seoul National?

"He was dismissed," the department chair whispers.

"Why?"

"We can't talk about it," is the answer.

Behind closed doors, Eun Sul discovers that Dr. Han was fired for advising a study group, for trying to protect his students from the heavy hand of Park Chung Hee's regime.

"Dr. Han now heads a Christian church journal. I would advise you not to visit him," the chair warns.

But Eun Sul does. When he arrives at the journal office, his old friend starts to cry.

"You are the first person from the university to visit," he says.

After Eun Sul leaves, he notices two men in dark suits lurking outside the door of the building. They follow him through the alleyway and onto the main avenue. They follow him until he gets sucked into the crowd making its way down the stairs into the subway.

Eun Sul is more careful after that visit. He learns to look and listen. On his way home one evening he notices professors from his department surveying the student protests in the park near the bus stop. He realizes his colleagues are keeping tabs on their students during summer break because someone has asked them to. Perhaps they file reports later, perhaps to other men in dark suits.

Eun Sul realizes that he doesn't want to teach in such an environment, even though his dream was to secure a professorship at his alma mater. He decides to look elsewhere. USAID has established an Institute of Public Health in conjunction with the South Korean government. Eun Sul is acquainted with the newly appointed director, who sets up a meeting with the American advisor, a longtime USAID employee and engineer.

At the meeting, the American displays no understanding of what a public health initiative entails.

Data gathering?

Not essential.

Analysis of data?

Not needed.

A position at the Korea Development Institute opens up—as the research head for the development of social welfare programs, of which there are none in South Korea. Eun Sul speaks to the director and associate director, conversations that convince him it is a position worth considering. He hopes that they will make an offer soon, before his three-month visa expires.

THE VISA EXTENSION IS SUPPOSED to be a formality. Don't worry about it, says his former advisor. But Eun Sul does, and sure enough, there is a delay.

Need more information, says the Korean Ministry of Justice. Need additional supporting documents. Must submit your formal family registry, of the Deokcheon-gun branch of the Jeonju Lee family, the one that traces the family back to the son of the second king Jeongjo of the Joseon Dynasty.

The day before the visa's expiration date, we pack our bags. Ed doesn't want to return home. He is speaking Korean all the time now. He can even answer the phone at our aunt's house and direct the call to the correct family member. I don't say a word. I fold my clothes and pack them along with my books into my orange Samsonite.

Bags packed, ready to go. Then a phone call from the Seoul National University president's office. Your visa extension has been approved.

Eun Sul surmises that his visit to Dr. Han's office has caused the delay and has put him on some sort of blacklist. He tries his best to be careful after the scare. No talk of opposition politics at the university. No conversing with protesting students, even though he is interested in what they have to say.

But he is tailed once more one evening after he steps off the SNU commuter bus at the bottom of the hill near his sister-in-law's house. He is sure his brown leather briefcase is what raises suspicion. Maybe the police thought there were stolen items in the briefcase. Chong thinks it's his white loafers, a fashion faux pas that marked him as an outsider in the fancy neighborhood. In any case, on the uphill climb through the passageway made deep by ten-foot-high walls, which hide sprawling households of government officials and business magnates, a uniformed policeman stops him and asks that he accompany him to the station.

The policeman inspects the offending briefcase and removes a couple of letters as well as Eun Sul's passport. He disappears into a back room.

Eun Sul waits on a hard, wooden chair and watches while other suspects are being processed. Most are thieves dressed in dark clothing. He sits for two hours. Finally, a different policeman than the one who had taken his papers appears, a more high-ranking one, judging from the hardware on his uniform. He hands Eun Sul his American passport.

We are sorry to keep you waiting. We have learned that you are doing important work for the United Nations. Why is such a person walking the streets on foot?

Eun Sul is ushered home by two young officers. He manages to keep his legs steady for the short walk and resolves to stop carrying the leather briefcase.

EUN SUL'S LAST MONTH IN Korea goes by quickly. The week before departure, the family travels via taxi to the Academy House, a retreat affiliated with the Korean Christian Presbyterian Church. A friend organized the meeting so that Chong could see her old professor from Hankuk Presbyterian Theological Seminary, who has just been released from house arrest.

Professor Lee Oo Chung was imprisoned along with other faculty members and dissidents for opposing President Park's amendment to the constitution, the amendment he enacted so he could run for a third term. During the years they were incarcerated, Park Chung Hee dissolved Parliament and ratified a new constitution, the Yushin, a term borrowed from imperial Japan. The president had effectively turned South Korea into a legal dictatorship.

Professor Lee shows no fear. She spells out Park's abuses of power in a soft but firm voice. Prison hasn't broken this tiny woman with the low-key manner. Eun Sul realizes the political situation in his home country is much worse than what he has witnessed at the university.

BEFORE HIS DEPARTURE, EUN SUL informs the Korean Development Institute that he is interested in the open position as research head and can return to Korea the following year to fill it. Contrary to practice in the U.S., the director informs him that the Institute cannot issue a formal offer until Eun Sul presents evidence of his commitment to take the position and move back to Korea, such as a copy of a resignation letter to his current employer.

Eun Sul leaves with his family on a flight to Tokyo. He is surprised he feels relieved in leaving. He realizes he has felt short of breath, like he did when he had tuberculosis. Not because of the lack of fresh air, even though the Seoul air is polluted, but because of the stifling atmosphere in his homeland.

As soon as the plane lifts off, Ed stops speaking Korean. He reverts back to English, as if the previous four months never happened. Eun Sul wonders if his children really enjoyed living in Korea for the summer. He wonders how they would feel if they knew the family might be returning for good the following year.

DISSIDENT

I n the fall of 1977, I don't realize my parents are harboring a Korean dissident at our home in the outer reaches of suburban Houston. I don't realize this fact until much later, until I am an adult.

I guess they don't tell me because they know my attention was elsewhere—with my hair, which never looks like Farrah Fawcett's no matter how long I leave it in hot rollers; with what to wear in the era of Jordache and Gloria Vanderbilt jeans my family can't afford; with trying to figure out a way to fit into sixth grade at Bleyl Junior High, home of the Brahma Bulls, where Farrah's younger cousin Jan goes to school. She lives in Champions or Huntwick or one of those fancy developments down Farm Road 1960 whose streets are named after the world's famous golf courses.

AN ELDERLY KOREAN MAN COMES to visit that fall, a year after we return from Korea. I am instructed to call him Haraboji, which means "grandfather" in Korean.

Haraboji is a Presbyterian minister. He was the dean of Hankuk Theological Seminary in Seoul and my mother's professor when she studied there. He is also the father of Mom's high school friend and officiated my parents' engagement ceremony on June 25, 1961, the eleventh anniversary of the start of the Korean War. The year after, both my parents left Korea for graduate school in the United States.

Haraboji is visiting from Vancouver, Mom tells me. That's where he lives because he was kicked out of South Korea by President Park Chung Hee. He isn't allowed to return home, to see his wife, his children, his real grandchildren.

My parents' engagement photo
with Kim Kai Choon, 1961

Why does he live in Canada? I ask.

He lives in Canada because the American government refused to let him live here is the answer.

When I take a moment, I wonder why anyone would punish a minister. A Presbyterian minister, like Reverend Lancaster at our old church downtown whom all the white-haired ladies treated like royalty. Or like Stewart at our new church in the northwest suburbs who helps pregnant teenagers with donations to Planned Parenthood, an action which will later cause him to be fired by the church elders.

I like Haraboji. He looks like a grandfather with his wavy, silvered hair and wide smile. I guess Haraboji is the closest thing to a grandfather that I ever had, since both of mine died—Dad's father when he was a baby, Mom's shortly after I was born. Mom told me that she wanted to go to Korea when her father first fell ill. We lived in North Carolina then, but my parents decided to postpone her trip back home because we were about to move to Houston. My grandfather died a couple of weeks before the move. Mom still cries when she talks about missing the funeral. She was his favorite of twelve children.

For some reason, Haraboji reminds me of Fred Astaire in those dancing musicals I watch after school during Fred and Ginger week. Elegant, refined, dashing in an old man kind of way. His voice is soft and soothing. He's also fluent in English, unlike most of the visitors from Korea who have been shuttled through our home over the years. He speaks directly to me and asks questions—*What is your favorite subject at school? Who are your friends? What book are you reading?*—instead of asking my parents questions about me while I am standing there, like the other Koreans do. He tells my parents I don't have to accompany them on the obligatory sightseeing trips to NASA, the Battleship Texas, the San Jacinto monument, places where we take all the Koreans. For this, I am eternally grateful.

I am old enough to stay home by myself and listen to my small collection of albums in peace on my new Pioneer component stereo. *Saturday Night Fever*, the *Grease* soundtrack, *Flowing Rivers* by Andy Gibb. The stereo is my most prized possession, recently purchased with years of saved allowance and an extra cash reward from Dad after performing well at my last piano competition.

FOR EVERY YEAR I CAN remember, my uncle, Oesamchun, has sent us a Korean desk calendar at Christmastime. Its thick, creamy pages are full of color pictures of the South Korean president, his wife, his residence, his land. He is a military man, President Park Chung Hee, and stands, in most instances, with epaulets and medals and sometimes a saber at his side. He stands tall like he is trying to stretch, for he is short like most Korean men, except for my father. Maybe he is trying to tiptoe taller than his pretty wife, who is always smiling.

The president, though, never smiles. He has jet-black, slightly greasy hair, which makes me wonder if maybe he uses Brylcreem like Dad.

This man in the calendar is the one who kicked Haraboji out of Korea?

OESAMCHUN IS THE ONLY ONE of Mom's eleven siblings who has visited us in the United States. He came to visit before Ed was born, when I was five. When we lived in Alief on the other side of Houston in the tiny Spanish-style house with the attached garage.

I call him Octopus. Octopus Oesamchun, because he liked to tease me and wave eight of his stubby fingers when I walked down the dark hallway to the bathroom. He likes to tease, my Oesamchun. Tease his American niece, his older sister, even his serious brother-in-law with the country drawl.

Oesamchun works for the president of South Korea, Mom explains. He used to be a diplomat in Thailand, but the president asked him to teach him English since he speaks like a native even though he's never lived in an English-speaking country. That's why he sends us those fancy calendars every year. They're from the president's office.

PRESIDENT PARK CHUNG HEE'S NAME comes up a lot during Haraboji's stay. My father drafts letters—to the local Korean consulate, to Texas senator Lloyd Bentsen, to President Gerald Ford—letters to protest

Park's oppressive regime. He shows them to Haraboji. Haraboji makes suggestions for wording changes. My mother cuts up crisp Asian pears into perfect wedges and edits my father's grammar with a red pen.

"Her English is so much better than mine," my father explains. "Your mom is good at languages. She's still fluent in Japanese. I remember almost none of the Japanese I was forced to learn as a child."

Haraboji also advises my parents not to return to Korea because of the political situation. "You are better off staying here," he says in Korean.

I sit on the floor of the living room and watch television, half listening to the grown-ups at the kitchen table. Excited that my parents are too occupied to tell me to go to bed. I don't realize that my father has been considering moving the family to Korea since he received a job offer from the Korean Development Institute the summer we were in Korea. Or that upon our return, he was promoted to associate professor and received tenure from his school. Or that it was always his intention to move back to Korea after getting his PhD. I have no idea. I just want to watch *Charlie's Angels*.

IN A HARVARD CLASSROOM ALMOST twenty-five years later, I hear an audio recording of one of President Park Chung Hee's speeches from 1974. August 15. Korean Independence Day. The National Theater, Seoul. The president, a former army general who seized power over the country in a military coup in 1961, is droning on about how far South Korea has advanced, especially during his tenure as president. He is the one who transformed the country from a third-world nation into an economic powerhouse.

Then a pop and screams. The sound of chairs tumbling, a scuffle, more pops. Mild chaos. A minute or two later, applause from the audience as the president resumes his speech and drones on again.

The professor tells us that a North Korean secret agent in the front row stood up with a pistol and shot at the president. The well-trained military man ducked, just in time, behind the wooden lectern. A bullet hit the

First Lady, who was sitting in a chair in the middle of the stage. She was shot in the head. Her husband resumed his speech as her body was carried out of the theater and to the hospital. She died there an hour later.

AROUND THE SAME TIME, I discover that Haraboji, whose name is Kim Chai Choon (1901–1987), is considered one of the founders of Korean liberalist theology and led the Christian opposition against President Park Chung Hee's dissolution of Parliament and suspension of the Constitution in October 1972. He directed the Korean committee of Amnesty International and held other posts to protest human rights abuses. During this time, President Park declared martial law. Human rights abuses abounded. Freedom of the press and freedom of speech meant little. Park Chung Hee tolerated no dissent—from students, from academics, from ministers, from anyone. They would all be punished.

In 1974, three years before he came to visit us in Houston, Haraboji was forced into exile in Canada under Park's military dictatorship. During that time, he acted as the chairman of the North American Council for Korean Human Rights and the North American Committee of the People's Coalition for Korean Democracy and Reunification. While in Houston, he spoke about the political situation in South Korea under Park's regime and the Christian opposition movement to my parents' Korean Fellowship Group. After the event, my parents were labeled as anti-government dissidents within the conservative Korean community. The Korean Consulate stopped inviting them to social events for years to come.

After Haraboji leaves, my father informs the KDI that he will not be accepting their job offer and his dean that he will remain in Houston.

My 9:00 p.m. bedtime is enforced once again, and I am not allowed to watch *Charlie's Angels* until school lets out.

II

SECOND INTERVIEW

WITH HALMONI

TASTE OF FREEDOM

I t's March 1999, and I'm interviewing Halmoni for the second time in her apartment in Seoul. "Just girls today," my mother says to me in her cheerful voice. "I think it will be easier for Halmoni to speak about the past without your father here."

She stops talking when Halmoni steps into the room. Halmoni plops down on her cushion, I fetch my tape recorder, and my mother sits in between us so she can translate. It's the day after our first interview.

I gently goad Halmoni into talking about her late husband. She has been much more forthcoming and comfortable relating her own story. She asks again why I need to know. I explain, repeating my words from before.

My mother translates in her gentle way, with a beseeching look to convey, *Do it for your granddaughter.* Halmoni nods her slow nod. She will do it for me, because I have asked. She will do it for her first grandchild, because Juhae is a journalist, because it's her profession and livelihood.

I ASK HALMONI ABOUT HER husband. About his prison sentence. Halmoni tells me he was placed in solitary confinement after his first interrogation session, as punishment for not revealing the information the Japanese wanted to hear.

> *It was the first time we really talked to each other. It was the first time I really got to know your grandfather, on my trips to the prison.*
> *After your grandfather was sentenced in 1929, it was decided I would go to Seoul. My father had a business acquaintance who owned pharmacies there, and he let me stay in a room off the base-*

ment, where they stored supplies. The family made their money sell-
ing tonics to cure any illness. You can still buy them today. I think
they are called energy drinks.

I helped the family with household chores during the day and
sewed for them in the evenings. Their house was near the southwest
gate, near the vice president's residence. Later, I did some extra
mending for a distant cousin who worked for a sewing machine
company. My father gave me money to live, so I saved most of what
I earned.

I visited your grandfather every two months on a fixed day, al-
ways in the morning. We talked mostly about family—about his
family in Kongju, about mine in Chongju. Our visits would last
ten or fifteen minutes. He never talked about his time in prison, or
what had gotten him there, but that was to be expected since there
was always a guard in the room and another stationed outside.

He did tell me to get an education. To take classes while I was
living in Seoul. He said getting an education was the most impor-
tant thing a person could do.

"Did the family you stayed with ever talk about politics?" I ask. "Or did
they ever mention their patriarch, Min Kang, who had escaped to China?"

Halmoni shakes her head no. "No one talked about politics around me,
and I never heard them mention Min Kang. I didn't even know why the
Japanese were in Korea in the first place. That's just the way it was."

"What did you know about the student group Grandpa was involved in
before he went to prison?"

Another shake of the head. "I remember his father complaining that
your grandpa was involved with the wrong people when he moved to Seoul.
That's the reason he was in prison. He had dangerous friends."

Halmoni knew almost nothing about his political activities. I had
guessed as much. Time to switch gears. I ask about her own education.

I never went to school as a child, but that was normal for girls at
the time. The first time I went to school was in Seoul when your

grandpa was in prison. I took a night class to learn to read and write. It was only a short distance away from the house. I was one of a handful of girls in the class and the oldest one. I was already in my twenties. I felt a little uncomfortable at first, but I came to enjoy it and eventually made friends with some of the girls.

I didn't like walking home at night after the class was over. One night, one of the students—a man—stopped to talk to me as we were leaving. I got nervous, so I packed up my books as fast as I could and left. I had never spoken to a man who wasn't a member of my family or a family friend. He followed me out of the classroom and the building. I didn't dare look back. I walked home as fast as I could.

I was so scared that I decided not to return to class. But I kept the textbook and studied by myself at night. I also practiced my sewing. Later, the next year, I took a cooking class where there were no men.

I liked living in Seoul. Sometimes I got bored with my chores during the day, but I could wear my hair down there and not in a bun like I did in the country. When I returned to Kongju to live, I had to put my hair up again.

I pictured Halmoni studying by herself at night, for it's a practice she has maintained throughout her life. I remember a small spiral notebook with green-lined pages that sat under her Bible on her nightstand in Houston. In shaky but legible script she dutifully copied passages from the English side of her bilingual King James Bible, over and over again, until the lines rang clear and she could recite the verse from memory. I know that while we speak, a similar notebook lies underneath her Bible on the bureau in her current bedroom.

My sister was already living in Seoul when I moved there, when your grandpa was in prison. She first went there with my grandmother when she was nine or ten to visit some distant relatives. I think some second cousin of my father's had been released from pris-

on. I don't remember why he was in prison. His family, the family who owned the pharmacies, suggested my sister stay with them so she could go to school in Seoul. She got to stay. I was so jealous, but I didn't say anything. I wanted an education, too, but I was too old. My father was already planning to marry me off.

My sister was tall, taller than me, so tall that she had to sleep on a futon at a diagonal so her feet wouldn't hang off the end. She ended up going to Ewha High School, which was the first high school for girls in Korea. It was started by Methodist missionaries from the U.S. It was next door to Bae Jae High School, the first school your grandfather went to after he left Kongju.

I didn't see my sister much in Seoul, since she was busy with school. She didn't really want to spend time with me anyway. She was only concerned with herself.

After my sister graduated from high school, she got married to a student at the agricultural college who was from our home province. He became an official in the colonial government, as the district chief of forest management for a province up north. They had a big wedding planned in our hometown at the Presbyterian church, but someone told the preacher at the last minute that the groom had been married to a local girl when he was a teenager, before he moved to Seoul to go to college. The Presbyterian minister refused to marry them, so the wedding was canceled. They had to find another minister who would perform the wedding ceremony. A couple of weeks later they found one at a much smaller Methodist church.

My sister and her husband had one son, your father's cousin Hee Sung. He's a doctor. He was born right after the end of the war the Japanese lost, in 1945 or early '46. My sister and her husband both died of diphtheria soon after his birth, within a week or two of each other. Their baby was brought back to Chongju to live.

I recognize Hee Sung's name from one of my father's notes on history. He was the one who noted the resemblance between my grandfather and Ed after being shown my grandfather's prison photograph. Later, I asked my father about his aunt Kum Bong—Hee Sung's mother and Halmoni's sister—about what he remembered of her. He didn't recall much, since she and her family rarely came to visit, but he did remember Halmoni's reaction after news of her and her husband's deaths reached the family.

"Because of the end of the war, the news of her death took a couple of weeks to reach us in Kongju. It was the first time I saw my mother cry. By that time, her grandmother and father had both died. Her sister was the only one left. Halmoni cried for a long time bent over her sewing that evening."

Your grandfather was in prison for over four years. I remember my last visit with him very well. My father came with me and brought a gray wool blanket, a really thick one that had two layers. He knew your grandfather's cell was unheated and the prison was located in an especially cold spot, at the foot of a mountain range. He also knew how to bribe the guards so his gifts could be smuggled in. On earlier visits we brought food. And clothing. I sewed money my father gave me into the hems and the collars. "He'll need the money," my father told me. I didn't ask for what.

Your grandfather brought the blanket home after he was released. It was still in good shape. It was so warm and well-made. When your father was a baby, I cut the blanket in half and used it to carry him on my back.

I could tell he lost weight while he was in prison—you could see it in his face, but he still seemed healthy at that point. He still seemed like the same person—thinking, always thinking.

During my last visit to the prison, your grandfather told me he planned to go home after he was released. He would go home for a visit, but afterward he would return to Seoul. He wanted to reunite with his comrades in Seoul, which meant I would have to return to Kongju to live with his family by myself.

When your grandfather was released from prison, I was still living in Seoul. After that much time, his father wasn't mad at him anymore and wanted him home to take on his duties as the first son. He didn't know that his son planned to go back to Seoul right away.

I didn't want to be in Kongju for the homecoming. I always felt awkward at big family events. I went home a month later. By that

time, your grandfather had already returned to Seoul to be with
his comrades. But he overdid it and got really sick. So sick he was
hospitalized.

The doctor diagnosed him with diphtheria and pleurisy, a lung
disease. It took him several months to recover in Seoul. When he fi-
nally returned home to Kongju, he was so pale. His skin looked like
rice paper. You could almost see through it. And he was so skinny,
just bones. He seemed healthier when he was in prison.

I remember men coming to visit him in Kongju. They would
come after his father had left for the day. Or in the middle of the
night. Some of them were from Seoul. I think they were his old
comrades.

He never talked about his time in prison to me. And I never asked
him. When he first returned home, his mother told me that she no-
ticed that the nails of both his pinky fingers were mangled and half
grown in.

She told me that the Japanese were responsible. They pushed
bamboo sticks underneath his fingernails to make him talk.

My mother lets out a tiny yelp. Startled, I ask her what Halmoni said.
The force of Halmoni's words are blunted in translation, but I still flinch
at the thought of what the Japanese did to my grandfather. Halmoni's face
belies no emotion. Neither does her voice. She recited her mother-in-law's
words in a steady drone.

Halmoni's hooded eyelids droop more than usual. I know she is tired. I
ask if we can continue after our trip to see Grandpa's grave at the National
Cemetery. A trip on which Halmoni has been invited. But she hasn't yet
made up her mind whether or not to go.

"Neh . . . yes," she says and walks into her bedroom to rest.

DISLOCATION

I arrive in Korea in September 2000 to what is supposed to be fall, but it is still Houston humid. The customs area at Kimpo is not air-conditioned. My jeans stick to my legs as I drag my half-empty, expandable imin gabang to the agent. The "immigration bag" is a loaner from my parents. They stuffed it with presents for the relatives on their frequent trips to Korea—Clinique cosmetics, peanut butter, See's Candies, Texas pecans, bulk vitamins—and piled in foodstuffs from the motherland on their way back home—seaweed, ginseng, barley tea, ground hot peppers, dried shrimp.

My father's cousin—who my father instructed me to call Ajeossi—picks me up at the terminal with his daughter Hansem, my second cousin. She is supposed to practice her English with me, but all she can manage is hello and red-apple cheeks of embarrassment. I try to mete out some Korean, the language I first learned from Halmoni as a toddler and promptly forgot after she left for Korea when I was in kindergarten. My mouth is thick with exhaustion.

I sit in silence on the long drive past dozens of near-identical apartment buildings. At the Coca-Cola plant, whose curlicue neon sign pulses through the thick air, we start to snake up steep hills. I am in the back, in the seat of honor behind the front passenger seat where Hansem has nodded off. Carsick, my stomach starts to jump and buckle.

Ajeossi parks. He unloads, and Hansem has the presence of mind to grab the top handle of my imin gabang before it rolls down the sharp incline. Ajeossi lives in a house, an actual house, a rarity in Seoul, where the rest of my relatives reside in high-rise apartment buildings.

I am deposited in the room of In Kyun, Hansem's brother, who was recently discharged from obligatory military duty. He is spending his semester abroad in the outer reaches of suburban Houston, living with my parents in my childhood home while he takes ESL classes at Rice University to prepare for university entrance exams.

Then there's me, a journalist in her midthirties formerly employed by *The Nation* magazine, fresh from a yearlong fellowship at Radcliffe, on a research fellowship sponsored by the government of Korea.

My relatives have decorated In Kyun's room for a person twenty years younger than me. Matching pale-green twin comforter, sham, and valance stamped with some poor cousin of Holly Hobbie dreamed up in a South Asian sweatshop. Brand-spanking new, still creased from the packaging, emanating vapors of cheap dye. My single bed for the months to come.

They think of me as a child, I know, someone just a couple of years beyond Hansem, who is freshly graduated with a French degree from a university on the city's edge. I occupy the netherworld between daughter and wife, a time much extended for some reason not understood by them.

She's in her thirties and unmarried?

What's wrong with her?

She doesn't even speak Korean that well.

Why would she want to be alone?

Maybe that's what they do in the U.S.?

On my half a dozen or so visits to Korea, I am the grandchild, the daughter, the niece, the cousin, the sister, and perhaps the potential mate of some Mr. Kim, Lee, or Park with an advanced degree and promising career in medicine or business or law. I'm not a real adult in the eyes of my relatives unless I am married and have children. I know this coming in, so why am I shocked?

I STUMBLE THROUGH THE FIRST week—I can barely keep my eyes open for Ajuma's spicy, gochujang-slathered seafood dinners. I awaken at 3:00 a.m., an hour after my night-owl relatives go to bed—Ajeossi up late with his stamp collection, Ajuma and Hansem with their dramas. I trip the alarm system trying to let out the steam through the bathroom window at 5:00 a.m. and scare the crap out of Ajeossi, who comes running up the stairs expecting an intruder.

Ajuma invites me to church on Sunday. I politely decline. I don't mention my agnosticism or the fact that the only time I step foot into a church is for a friend's wedding or an occasional, heartbreaking funeral—of a high school pal's father who died unexpectedly the week before graduation, a former housemate who was murdered by an intruder. Instead, I tell her I had already planned to sightsee.

I happen across a gay rights rally in front of the contemporary art museum in central Seoul. I sit and watch the chanting young people, some sporting multicolored faux-hawks, some holding hand-printed placards. I recognize these people, the disenfranchised. They are me, even though I'm not gay. I'm just the Korean gal who grew up with only white people around in one of the most conservative counties in the nation. The one who was always meant to feel foreign, even though I was born in the U.S.

Where are you from?

Houston.

No, where are you really from?

Houston. I'm from Houston. I grew up there.

No, really. Tell me where you're from.

I sigh and think of my cadre of gay male friends from Texas. The ones who made my high school years bearable and college years fun. The people I feel the most at home with.

I miss them.

BEFORE I ARRIVED IN SEOUL, when I thought I would be staying in the extra bedroom in Halmoni's apartment, I envisioned spending my mornings in various libraries, archives, or museums, culling through old documents in search of information on my grandfather. The afternoons I would devote to the organization of notes and writing. It would be a quiet, contemplative four months, an extension of my year at Radcliffe, where I audited Korean history courses and read everything I could find on the colonial era.

My reality is different. Each day in Seoul is filled with appointments. Meetings with my sponsor, Dr. Chung, a sociologist colleague of my father's whose research involves collecting oral histories of comfort women. The Korea Foundation introductory plenary with all the research fellows for the year, where a frantic Argentinian woman complains that her host family will not let her venture out of the apartment alone. A visit with a family friend from Houston, Dr. Lew, a historian who heads a research center that resembles a white-pillared palace. He offers his graduate student Jungmin to me as a research assistant and translator, since he knows I don't speak Korean fluently. He thinks we will get along well, and he is right.

There's no time for contemplation. Ppali ppali—hurry hurry—like life in New York, the life I supposedly escaped after I moved to Boston. That year in Boston already feels like a dream, an interlude to my supposed real life. I slept ten hours a night there with no car alarms or combative neighbors or an unraveling boyfriend to keep me up at night. I was cocooned in a community of supportive women. Nineteen ninety-nine was the last year the Bunting fellows would be all female.

I SETTLE INTO A ROUTINE of sorts. Get washed and dressed. Tiptoe downstairs so as not to wake anyone, including the two yappy lap dogs who poop all over the house. Coffee and toast by myself at the round kitchen table as I try to avert my eyes from the looming wooden relief sculpture of the Last Supper on the wall. Tiptoe back upstairs for a quick check of email to see if any appointments for the day are canceled or if someone wants to meet up at the last minute. Back downstairs, I zip up my ankle boots, which stand in a row by the front door with Ajeossi's battered loafers, Ajuma's black pumps, and Hansem's tennis shoes with the backs flattened down.

I'm off, down the street to the waiting bus below. Mine is the last stop in Shihung, the fancy neighborhood south of the Han River and west over the mountains from Seoul National University. Mine is the stop where the buses turn around and the drivers take smoke breaks.

I grab a cold canned latte from the corner store and nod at the proprietor. He knows not to engage me in conversation, since it will only result in a painful exchange of mangled syllables on my part and flushed cheeks on his, in sympathetic embarrassment for my less-than-adept grasp of my forebearers' tongue.

I board the bus and pull the 800 Won fare from my pants pocket. I take a seat by the window, two-thirds of the way back, where the rows are placed on risers for a better view. The morning rush-hour crowd has gone. In its wake, high school students with their dyed red and purple hair and hand phones text away. Empty-nested middle-aged mothers with their tightly curled perms are all dressed up for a day of shopping. Elderly folk, some in the loose hemp garments of preindustrial times, sit up front on their way to visit relatives on the other side of the city.

I am the only single woman in her thirties on the bus. I am sure of this.

My bus arrives at the Shihung subway station. A line of people has already formed to take the bus back to Ajeossi's neighborhood. Behind the explanatory placard, stick figures and arrows instruct the public how to stand in line. I witnessed a mob scene six years ago in front of the ticket counter at Kimpo Airport—complete with ticket waving from the polite passengers, and pushing and shoving from the more aggressive ones. There was no way I could force myself through that crowd and make my flight to Hong Kong to visit my then-boyfriend, two boyfriends before Ciaran. I experienced firsthand the fact that Koreans do not know how to stand in line. It's just something we Westerners take for granted.

I hurry down the steps to the subway station since I am in ppali ppali transit mode. On the platform I buy a copy of *The Korea Herald*, the English-language newspaper, fold it in half, and stuff it under my arm. A familiar underground rumble and fierce intake of air that plasters my hair to my face announce the train's arrival. Lots of empty seats at 10:00 a.m. I scan the headlines—the glow of President Kim Dae Jung's Nobel Peace Prize win last month has already dimmed; why can't he fix the economy? one editorial asks. The South Korean news cycle is even shorter than it is back home. What I'm really after is the crossword puzzle anyway. It's not *The New York Times*, but it will do.

THE GENTLE SWAY OF THE train car soon lulls me into a half sleep. In my dozy, almost dream, I replay the sounds that woke me up that morning. Metal chopsticks clink on a ceramic bowl. A newscaster drones on about the weather. A refrigerator door sucks in and out—to the rhythm of a family who lives in an apartment somewhere down the hill from Ajeossi's house. How can I hear the soundtrack of a family's life so clearly from my single bed? Sound waves ricochet in mysterious ways.

I receive the noises like they told me in the hundreds of yoga classes I have taken over the years. Acknowledge the sound, the accompanying image and thought—and let them pass by like clouds in the sky, like steam dissipating into nothingness.

A baby cries, and I am bolted awake from my hovering state. Eyes wide. A sharp intake of breath. Some latent instinct has taken over, and I almost announce to my fellow subway passengers: "Is the baby okay? Who's taking care of the baby?"

"Where's the baby?"

MY BABY LUST BEGAN IN my midtwenties, after I moved to San Francisco. The desire, the need, deep inside the gut somewhere between my belly button and pubic bone. The feeling that caused me to try to catch the eye of any baby who would have me.

Smile. Coo. Make fishy face.

I didn't care that my friends were embarrassed by my behavior or that the baby's mother or nanny looked at me with alarm. I wanted to pinch a juicy cheek, squeeze a chubby foot, poke a belly until a laugh burst through.

When I was little, I wanted so much to have a being to hold and love—like a kitten or a puppy. Neither were appealing to my parents, who thought dogs belonged on farms (Dad) and cats were dirty (Mom). When my brother Ed was born, my six-year-old self latched on to him and claimed him as my own. I picked him up when my mother couldn't, her giant stitches making railroad tracks down her belly. I gave him his bottle, slept with my naemse blanket on the rug beside his crib in case he cried. I dressed him in the outfits my aunties sent from Korea. Striped sailor suit with matching white cap. Navy coveralls with a pom-pommed beanie. I liked the yellow terrycloth onesie with a bonnet shaped like a duck head the most.

In Boston, I find a best friend who enveloped me into her young family. I spend weekends at Sabina's rented beach house in Newburyport. She and her husband, toddler son, dog, smelly cat, home-cooked adobo stew, red wine, and me, while the wind off the Atlantic blows sand and snow in swirls around the barely winterized clapboard house.

Is it her life that I really want? Could I manage a writing career, husband, and child? I have a handle on the career part; as for the rest, I'm kind of at a loss. I haven't lived in the same place for more than a couple of years at a time. When I am single, I want to be in a relationship. When I'm in relationship, I long for my single life after the headlong rush of the first couple of months have passed. And with my less-than-stellar track record, I realize that I have no idea how to find a suitable mate. I don't want to be married to any of my ex-boyfriends, even though at some point, I considered the prospect.

It has taken two years to fully untangle myself from Ciaran. The year in Boston, when I began research for my book, was but an interlude. The move to Korea, the door slammed shut. He can't call me here since I didn't give him Ajeossi's home phone number. And I can choose to ignore his emails, which I know will be sporadic. He's a talker, not a writer.

DR. SHIN

On this day in Seoul, I am on my way to visit Dr. Shin, who I first met with my parents the day before my grandfather's reburial ceremony in 1995. If anyone knows where my grandfather's records are housed, it is my father's former classmate, who is now one of the foremost experts on Korea's colonial era and a government advisor.

The Seoul National University subway stop isn't at the university like I expect it to be. I can see the buildings of the most prestigious school in Korea in the distance, miles up a steep hill. I call my research assistant Jungmin on my borrowed hand phone.

"Take a taxi up," she says in her perfect English, honed by four years at UC Irvine. "That's what I did. It's a long walk up the hill."

Without Jungmin I would be lost, that I know. I meet her in front of the history building and give her a list of questions I have prepared for Dr. Shin.

We walk up the dirt-streaked concrete stairway to the second floor. Why are all floors in Korean public buildings filthy? I wonder to myself. Jungmin firmly taps the knocker on the appointed door.

Dr. Shin greets us in his black socks and khakis with a hearty baritone. We take our shoes off at the door, and he leads us past half a dozen rows of packed bookcases to the buffed wooden desk at the back. He surprises us and booms in English.

"Your gr-r-randfather, he was a gr-r-r-eat man!"

Tony the Tiger flashes in my head. Jungmin's palm flies up to her mouth to stifle an onslaught of giggles.

"He was a gr-r-reat leader. A gr-r-reat thinker. An idealist."

Dr. Shin pauses to take a deep breath.

"If he hadn't died so young, he could have been an official in the North Korean government. Maybe even second to Kim Il Sung!"

Jungmin stops giggling long enough to lean into me and whisper, "Or he could have been purged."

I know that Dr. Shin is spouting hyperbole, but I smile and go with it. My grandfather might have been a member of the Communist Party, but he was no guerilla fighter. Although Kim Il Sung, the Great Leader, North Korea's first demagogue, might not have been either, even though his "official" hagiography claims he was.

Dr. Shin is enjoying the moment. His arms wave, his chest swells. He is performing admirably for his audience of two single women. He trots over to the far bookcase and removes a well-read hardback, the same book he showed my father while he was on sabbatical almost fifteen years ago.

"See, look here. Here's your grandfather's name—Lee Chul Ha."

I recognize the Korean characters of my grandfather's name but little else.

"He staged demonstrations against the Japanese colonial government at his high school in Kongju. He was a student leader of the nationalist movement."

WHEN I FIRST MET DR. Shin with my parents, I was twenty-eight, the same age as Jungmin. I was living in San Francisco then, the place where dissatisfaction reigned—with my art museum career, with my choice in men—but at the time I wasn't ready to do anything about it. I only knew I was unhappy.

During that whirlwind long weekend in 1995, I knocked at the same office door. A jolly man with silvering waves and a belly befitting a Samoan warlord greeted us. In fact, Dr. Shin looked Samoan or Hawaiian or Guamanian.

"Are you sure he's Korean?" I asked my parents.

"He's from Jeju Island, the honeymoon island off the southern coast," my mother said. "They look different there."

Framed photographs of Dr. Shin's various television appearances decorated the wall. "He's an advisor to the government on matters pertaining to the colonial era, when Japan ruled Korea," my father explained. Dr. Shin helped oversee the archiving of documents from the Seodaemun Hyeongmuso, where my grandfather was imprisoned with other political prisoners during the Japanese occupation. He consulted with the South Korean government in their decision to destroy the neoclassical National Museum building in 1995, since it was built by the Japanese to house its colonial government and was long a symbol of their imperial rule. He also helped usher the posthumous award of Patriot medals to students involved in the independence movement, students like my grandfather.

Years earlier, in college, Dr. Shin asked my father to translate an article he had written into English so he could submit it to an American journal. He never forgot the favor. Almost thirty years later, when my professor father was on sabbatical in Korea, he asked Dr. Shin for guidance in finding information on my grandfather. Dr. Shin was more than happy to help. To my father's surprise, Dr. Shin immediately recognized my grandfather's name.

"He's famous!" he exclaimed and pulled out the same book he later shows me on the nationalist student movement in Kongju, my father's hometown. Dr. Shin was the one whose graduate student located my grandfather's prison photograph from the Seodaemun Hyeongmuso archive and urged my father to apply for a Patriot's medal in my grandfather's honor.

MY MOTHER TOLD ME THAT the shame of my grandfather's imprisonment weighed heavily on my father throughout his life. I heard the story of their courtship from her dozens of times during my childhood, how my mother met my father in 1960 at the Christian Children's Fund office in Seoul, where they both worked translating letters between Korean orphans and their American sponsors. She noticed him, the handsome quiet guy from the countryside who was so different from the bragging, boisterous,

My father working at the Christian
Children's Fund office, 1960

My mother working at the Christian
Children Fund's office, 1960

stereotypical Korean male. They didn't speak until they ran into each other at the Korean Ministry of Education office to check their scores on the qualifying exam to study abroad. They both passed, and he asked her out to dinner to celebrate.

During their first date at a Chinese restaurant, he blurted out that he was the son of a criminal who had been imprisoned. She thought he was attempting to make a joke out of nerves, so she chose not to react, steering the conversation toward their plans of studying abroad for graduate school.

What she didn't understand then was that shame lay underneath all of his decisions—the shame surrounding his father's prison stay and his fatherless state. This is what spurred him to move an ocean away.

"Daddy was so quiet because he was ashamed of his father being in prison. He never smiled much or laughed while you were growing up. But now, he talks all the time. He won't shut up. From morning to night. I never imagined he could be so talkative. It's like his true self came out after he discovered who his father was."

THE GRANDSTANDING PORTION OF THE meeting over, Dr. Shin returns to his desk and switches back to speaking Korean. I ask him in English if he knows where I can find my grandfather's prison and interrogation records, the ones my father remembered seeing as a child, as well as my grandfather's transcripts from Bae Jae High School, the private school in Seoul he transferred to after being kicked out of Kongju High School. Jungmin translates.

Dr. Shin is all business now. Try the Governmental Records Office for the prison records. Contact the head curator at the Independence Museum, he's a former student of mine. Call various professors around Seoul—all experts on the colonial era. Head down, Jungmin scribbles down the names and places as fast as she can. I nod and silently give thanks for her efforts.

Dr. Shin begins a soliloquy about how difficult it can be to find records from the colonial era. I catch something about how most records from the colonial era were destroyed during the bombing of Seoul during the Korean War and other issues related to blind spots regarding modern Korean history, most of which relate to nationalism. I know from my Korean history classes and research that many established historians discount the links between colonial and postcolonial Korea, and how a leftist camp of scholars chooses to focus more on how Japanese colonialism instituted a state-centered, capitalist structure that replaced that of a landed aristocracy. Some argue that the economic system that produced the South Korean chaebols, the giant conglomerates like Samsung, Hyundai, and Daewoo, originated in the colonial era.

The scarcity of archival documents from the colonial era comes as no surprise in this type of politicized atmosphere. No one wanted to deal with them. It is as if their contents have been stamped in big red letters: DANGEROUS. In other words, these documents might reveal a past with which the present is not comfortable. The colonial era was a time when the ancestors of many prominent South Korean families collaborated with the Japanese; when student "nationalists" protested Japanese rule but were also members of the Communist Party; when Korean teachers beat and kicked their elementary school students, like my father, for misbehaving in front of the Japanese principal.

Dr. Shin wishes me luck with my search and tells me to call his secretary if I need anything else. He stands up, our signal to leave. Jungmin closes her notebook. I stand and immediately thrust out my hand, then realize that a bow is in order.

He walks us to the door and pats me on the back.

"You are a good granddaughter," he says in Korean. "Your grandfather would have been proud."

This I understand.

I smile and bow.

LOST IRONY

Two months have passed, and I am on the subway again. I transfer north over the Han River to old Seoul, or what counts as old Seoul since the city was pretty much demolished during the war. Back to Ewha Womans University, where I stayed the summer before my first stint in graduate school, living in the traditional Korean house at the top of the hill. The house was rebuilt with the finest materials—the thickest mulberry paper for the screen doors, the smoothest sanded ash timbers, which hold the paper in place, the whitest stucco anchoring the half-moon gray roof tiles at even intervals.

A group of six females, the eldest and supposedly most mature students in the summer language program, lived in the house reserved for ancient tea ceremonies and traditional wedding receptions, where graduates in the ladylike arts displayed their wares at the end of each academic year.

My aunt Chong Pil had been one of those graduates over fifty years before. Immediately after graduation she married a government official—in a hurry, I overhear my mother say, because their father got wind that the Japanese were recruiting Korean women her age to "serve" their soldiers during World War II, so he married off his third daughter as fast as he could.

Chong Pil had four children, whom she raised in the mansion my family stayed in during my first visit to Korea in 1976. She majored in embroidery at Ewha and has maintained her stitching skills since. Today, hundreds of tiny cotton hexagons are neatly stacked in her sewing basket. "I'm making a quilt," she tells me on my last visit to her one-bedroom in Gangnam. To display at the annual Ewha alumni craft exhibition.

"I'll make you one, too," she says with a smile. "When you get married."
I smile back and nod my head. I guess everything comes at a price.

EWHA UNIVERSITY IS THE SITE of tonight's English language club meeting, the one my uncle moderates, the one made up of young professionals, all with the dream of one day working in the United States for a year or two, or maybe forever. My uncle Chong Sae, Octopus Oesamchun, tells me on the phone that he has arranged for one of his best students to meet me at the gate so I won't get lost. I explain that I can find my way, I remember the campus from when I lived there a dozen years ago, but he insists. One of his favorite students is single and in his thirties—just like me—and will accompany his niece to the meeting.

Beom Seok is short, with bushy black eyebrows. Black blazer, slightly too big. He picks me out right away. Beom Seok talks at me the entire fifteen minutes it takes to walk to the meeting hall in the student union—he respects my uncle so much, my uncle speaks English like a native. He also tells me he works for an import/export business that ships computer chips to Silicon Valley but doesn't transport much of anything back since the tariffs are so high on American goods. He is thirty-three years old and unmarried. He asks me questions but doesn't give me time to answer. He is sweating.

I can bear it, though. For Oesamchun has given me a gift, a wondrous gift of two hours of freedom a week. Two hours when I can speak in my native tongue. Two hours when I don't have to access the deep fissures of my brain for words in Korean that Halmoni taught me when I was a child.

For that was the last time I was fluent, when Halmoni lived with us in Alief, right before Ed was born. When my mother was bedridden and my father tried and failed to braid my hair. A rat's nest, bigger than my fist, tucked at the nape of my neck. An entire bottle of Johnson's No More Tears detangler couldn't make it unfurl.

For two whole hours I am myself again—not the strange unmarried, foreign journalist from the U.S., the woman without a home or partner or any ties except to a long-dead grandfather who was imprisoned by the Japanese.

I am the person who obviously doesn't belong here.

But if I think about it, isn't that who I am back home? The person who doesn't belong? Growing up in Texas in the 1970s and '80s, I was viewed as a foreigner even after I opened my mouth and spoke English. My freshman world literature professor at UT assumed I was a Vietnamese refugee because I was shy and didn't say much in class. And why was that class even called world literature when it didn't include any works from outside Western civilization? And why didn't UT Austin offer Asian American studies classes until the 1990s, after I left the university? In Minneapolis, a museum guard where I worked asked if I was adopted, since the only Asians he knew there had white parents. In California, no one believed I was from Texas. And in the East Village, the homeless guys in the park called me geisha girl on my way to work every morning.

I'M NOT SURE WHO CHOOSES the locations for the meetings—a nouvelle Chinese restaurant in Gangnam, a subterranean pool hall near the Royal Palace, a pseudo-Italian joint that serves spaghetti with gochujang al fresco on the patio, where we all drink Chianti and my uncle serenades the group with "O Sole Mio" and a Verdi aria.

At my first meeting at the nouvelle Chinese place, I inform the group of my search for my grandfather's records, and one young man at the other end of the extremely long table, the one with the wide face and squared-off forehead, grabs the gelled hair at his temples. His voice rises over mine.

"Oh my God, I know him!"

"You know my grandfather? He's been dead a long time."

"No, I've heard this story before. Your grandfather is my great-uncle."

And so he is. In a city of eight million people, I meet my second cousin, the son of my father's schoolteacher cousin in Kongju, at an English-language club meeting. How random is that?

Joon Sung is big, like all the men on my father's side. Almost six feet, twenty-seven, a middle manager for Samsung's cell phone division. After the meeting he drives me back to Ajeossi's house in a tiny blue Kia. He knows the way, for he has been there before. Ajeossi is his uncle.

YOUNG MIN IS MY FAVORITE club member, though. He wears super pointy black loafers, which remind me of the lace-up witch boots I favored during my New Wave, club kid days in college. He has swoopy hair, almost a ducktail, and loves, absolutely loves, Janet Jackson, who is in her cyberpunk, Harajuku girl, silver lamé-wearing phase.

"Doesn't she seem like such a nice person?" Young Min coos, his eyes dreamy. "I would like to be her friend."

"I'm sure you would," I say with a laugh. Then I stop.

I forgot. Sarcasm is lost on Koreans.

Young Min always wants to talk about some American pop icon and shares seaweed-wrapped rice crackers with me. He buys me a Hite or an OB beer. He's a gentleman.

"I do not like Madonna. She looks hard."

He only has eyes for Janet.

He does, one evening in the subterranean pool hall, have a serious question for me. He cannot fathom, cannot imagine, how difficult it must be living in the United States with all those white people.

"How do you tell them apart?" he asks, dripping with sincerity.

"The white people?"

"Yes, them. They all look the same. And there's so many of them."

I start to laugh, so much so I struggle to keep the beer in my mouth from spewing forth. Young Min looks hurt.

Oh God, he's serious.

I start to tell him that usually it's the white people who ask me how to tell Asians apart, then think better of it.

"Well, some of them have blue eyes and some of them have brown. And sometimes their hair color is different."

Young Min nods. He is trying to understand.

LEADS

A week after our visit with Dr. Shin, Jungmin sets up an appointment with the first professor on the list of colonial Korean history experts he mentioned. She is unable to accompany me, so I head out to Korea University on my own. I assume the professor will speak to me in English, since he did his graduate work in the U.S. I am wrong. He only speaks to me in his native tongue. As I stammer my questions in my elementary school–level Korean, he looks me over.

Why is this hangukkye migugin wasting my time? is how I interpret his squint of dismissal. *She must be right out of college.*

"I don't know where your grandfather's records are" is how he responds, in Korean. Then he shows me the door.

I call Jungmin after the meeting and come up with a plan for future visits. I need to present myself to Korean history scholars (who are all male) as an American journalist with Harvard credentials who requires the need of a translator (either Jungmin or my mother). Then they will take me seriously.

MY FATHER HAD WARNED ME about Dr. Lew's conservative politics before I left for Korea. Dr. Lew, Jungmin's employer, heads the Syngman Rhee Center, which is funded by a group of anti-Communists who still hold the view that Rhee was a great hero of Korea, even though he's been since exposed as ordering the massacre of thousands of civilians during his tenure as the first president of South Korea from 1948 to 1960.

"Will he want to talk to me? Let alone help me?" I asked. "Did you tell him I worked at *The Nation*?"

"It's okay. He's an old family friend. He knows our politics aren't the same. He's even offered you one of his research assistants."

I meet Dr. Lew at his center with Mom, the day after she arrives for her solo visit. She is visiting Korea without Dad for the first time, since he has a new semester to teach at school. To visit me and then go on a painting trip to Jeju Island with Chung Wha, her best friend from childhood. It's been four years since Dad's lung surgery, and even she has to admit that he has fully recovered.

Dr. Lew's center is a chalk-white building on the top of a hill located in the southern part of Seoul, a building that makes me think of the Parthenon. A stately bespectacled man, he greets us with the edges of his mouth turned upward into a tiny, forced smile.

"Ah, Juhae," he murmurs. "I haven't seen you since you were a little girl."

He walks us into a vast library as if he were floating on a cloud. Jungmin waves from the far end of one of the longest tables I have ever seen.

Academics are sure treated well in Korea, I think to myself.

We sit in a grouping of high wingback chairs, and Dr. Lew's secretary brings us tea in a celadon pot. I give him my spiel, which flows easily now, about my search, my goals for the trip, research conducted thus far. He listens and nods. He tells Jungmin to find Professor Chi's contact information at Kongju University—"he was a student of mine at Yonsei University"—and gives me the name of another former graduate student, a Korean American now studying with Bruce Cumings at the University of Chicago.

"I'm sure you know Cumings's work. He's a revisionist," Dr. Lew says.

"Yes, I know. He's written for *The Nation* several times, and I've read his books." I didn't tell him that Cumings's *Korea's Place in the Sun* is a frequent subject of my conversations with my father since it challenged conventional thinking about the country's history, especially in terms of U.S. involvement in the war and the country's brutal dictatorships, including Rhee's.

Business over, Mom inquires about Dr. Lew's wife and asks if she can see her.

"I will let her know," he answers. "But she is not well and isn't taking visitors at this time."

He looks down, fingers the arms of his chair, and turns to me.

"Do you remember my sons?" he asks, his voice watery. "I remember you coming to our house and playing with them. In Houston."

HOURLONG DRIVES ACROSS THE CITY of a thousand billboards, where the only hills were the freeway overpasses. To Sugarland or Pearland or, if we were lucky, Sharpstown, which was only forty-five minutes from our house in northwest Houston where the city dissolved into Brahma bull pastureland. Dad driving in his suit and tie, Mom emanating Youth Dew and mothballs wearing her stiff hanbok. Ed and I grousing in the back seat, not wanting to go, never wanting to go.

I was the oldest kid and often the only girl at those meetings in the late 1970s. I hoped and prayed that the extra bedroom contained a TV so I wouldn't die of boredom. I learned to bring a book, just in case, something I loved and could escape into, like one in the *Little House on the Prairie* series or later one by Judy Blume. I remember Dr. Lew's two boys, the elder with a line of concern down the center of his forehead, the younger hyperactive and jumping around.

As he grew older, the elder became bitter and suspicious and told his brother at one of the gatherings: "You can't trust white people, so you shouldn't make friends with them. Only be friends with Koreans."

I told Mom about his warning later in the car, and she explained that he must have had a bad experience. Maybe some kids at school made fun of him for being different, for being Asian. She explained that some Koreans choose to isolate themselves from non-Koreans. They only socialize with Koreans, attend a Korean church, eat out only at Korean restaurants.

That's dumb, I answered. There are so few Koreans in Houston. There's only one Korean grocery store in the whole city. Who would the younger brother be friends with? Only his brother?

"If I followed his advice, Mom, I'd have zero friends."

A COUPLE OF DAYS AFTER meeting with Dr. Lew, Mom and I set off
to Kongju University to visit the foremost expert on the nationalist movement in my grandfather's hometown. Professor Chi greets us in his sparse
office with a view of the mountains. He flashes a sheepish look toward me
underneath his heavy bangs. He apologizes over and over, laments, almost,
at not being able to speak my language. I feel sorry for this young professor dressed all in black, stuck in the most conservative part of the country,
away from Seoul and the intellectual hub. He wants to address me directly,
I can tell, without the intervention of my mother, my translator for the day.

I tried numerous times to learn Korean. During my last-ditch effort
in New York through classes at the Korea Society, I master the reading of
the Korean alphabet. I can sound out words, but I don't necessarily know
what they mean.

I love the singsong syllables, though. The way they lilt up and down
the scale like in a nursery rhyme or a pop tune. They are the sounds of
a mother's soothing, of a childhood verse about a baby cow—song-ah-a
gee, song-ah-a gee—of comfort food. My musical ear can catch inflection,
emotion, emphasis, but my brain has difficulty with the meaning part.

Foreign languages have never quite been my thing. Eight years of
German have barely permeated the outer layer of my brain—eins, zwei,
drei, g'suffa? Squarely into my thirties, I am resigned to not fully understanding the language of my forbearers. I can get the gist. I can observe
Professor Chi and drift off when he gets into the nitty-gritty of historical
facts that I can look up later.

Professor Chi's discomfort melts away as he switches into lecture mode
and imparts his knowledge of the nationalist student movement in Kongju.
The young assistant professor with the Prince Valiant haircut exudes pas-
sion about his subject matter. I can easily imagine him with a megaphone

in hand and slogan emblazoned on a sash across his chest, shouting orders to the mass of student protestors at Yonsei University, his alma mater, where he studied under Dr. Lew.

PROTEST HAS BECOME A RITE of passage for students in Korea. Protesting is what you do in college, after surviving years of all-nighters in high school preparing for the college entrance exams. College is the prize for all that hard work. Students can take the time to participate in noisy protests against some wrong the South Korean government has committed. The well-choreographed clashes involve maybe some rock throwing and fists punched into the air in time to an old Korean peasant song, as well as riot gear–clad policemen as young as the students themselves.

Some say the student protest movement in Korea began on March 1, 1919, when dozens of religious and political leaders gathered to declare Korea's independence from Japan and spurred a nationwide campaign across the country. The Japanese responded with a brutal crackdown resulting in tens of thousands of arrests and thousands of deaths. March 1 is now a national holiday in South Korea and commemorated by the reading of the 1919 Declaration of Independence in Seoul's Tapgol Park, the original site of the demonstration.

In the summer of 1988, the last time I spent more than two weeks in Korea, the television was full of images of clashes between students and police. I even came across one or two gatherings on my treks through the city streets. I don't remember what they were protesting—maybe the strong-arm tactics of the recently departed president Chun Doo Hwan— but the world was watching Seoul, since the Summer Olympics were to be held there that September.

As a college graduation present, my parents had offered me a summer in Seoul. At Ewha Womans University, the offshoot of the private high school my mother—and Halmoni's sister—attended. "You should spend some time in Korea. You can take language classes in the morning and have fun in the afternoons," Mom said on the phone. My parents knew to target my guilt at not knowing their native tongue.

I had envisioned a lazy, margarita-laden three months in Austin sleeping in after late nights checking out the new bands in town. A last summer off before starting an art history graduate program in the fall.

"Uh, how about you give me a computer instead?"

"Well," Dad piped in, "it's already paid for. So you have to go to Korea."

I GIVE PROFESSOR CHI A quick summary of what I know about my grandfather and the particulars of the search for documents concerning him—the various leads Dr. Shin Yong Ha had suggested at the Independence Museum and various libraries and the dead end at the Governmental Records Office.

He nods his head.

"I know your grandfather's name. He was one of the leaders of the student nationalist movement in Kongju," he tells me, then picks out a book from the shelf behind his desk. It's the same one Dr. Shin pulled from his shelf at our meeting the month before. In one chapter, my grandfather's protest at the high school is described and analyzed. (Professor Chi will publish an article about my grandfather later that year.)

I mention the name of the student group my grandfather joined in Seoul, the Chosun Haksaeng Kwahak Yonguhoe. I ask Professor Chi if he knows of any primary sources concerning the group or any others from the same time.

He informs me that the students at that time transmitted information orally so they wouldn't leave a paper trail for the Japanese. Or if they did receive documents, they burned them immediately after they read them.

"The only way to know what your grandfather was thinking at the time is to interview people who knew him, like your relatives. I do not know if the libraries will have anything, either. Records from the colonial era are difficult to find, especially with the bombing of Seoul during the Korean War. Not much survived."

Professor Chi asks what I will do if I cannot find the documents. I tell him that I had met with Dr. Lew and he gave me a list of names of colonial era scholars to contact. Professor Chi bristles at the mention of his former advisor.

"His politics are much different than mine. He's become very conservative since I was in school."

I explain that Dr. Lew is an old family friend from Houston. He and my father were both young professors from Korea who found themselves working in the humid sprawling city—he at the University of Houston, my father at the University of Texas School of Public Health. They were members of a small group of Korean academics who stuck together, no matter the political affiliation. They were also part of the same Korean fellowship group that met at monthly meetings in the far reaches of the city, wherever a Korean might live.

DR. CHI SAVES THE BEST for last.

"I found an article that might help you," he says. It's about Lee Hyun Sang, the Communist ppalchisan revolutionary, about his 1928 arrest. "The professor who wrote it found his police interrogation records and quotes them at length. Your grandfather's name is mentioned at the end, as one of Lee Hyun Sang's comrades. There's even an abstract written in English."

My heart jumps. My mother and I lock eyes. She nods. This could be the lead I was searching for.

He hands me the article. I quickly scan the abstract for information on Lee Hyun Sang, who Jungmin told me about in Dr. Lew's office. The one who has been celebrated as a folk hero in a bestselling novel and a subsequent film.

Professor Chi advises me to contact the professor who wrote the article and ask him where he found the records. Since Lee Hyun Sang was involved with the same student group as my grandfather and was arrested in the same year, my grandfather's records should be located in the same place as his.

CHESTNUTS

Ajeossi agrees to drive my mother and me to Kongju so I can interview my father's great-uncles, who are both octogenarians. I wake at 4:00 a.m. for a departure at 4:30. Still jet-lagged, Mom is already dressed and ready to go when the alarm buzzes. Ajuma has somehow gotten herself up as well, six hours before her usual wake-up time, and sets out rice and soup for us before our journey. Ajeossi looks exhausted, with dark half-moons under his eyes. His wife hands him a thermos full of instant coffee. I glance longingly at the bag of Starbucks ground I had brought from the States as a gift, which sits by the empty Braun coffeemaker, unopened.

We pile into the Hyundai 4x4 and set off down the steep hill and to the main thoroughfare, where the Coca-Cola plant lies dormant in the dark. I have never seen the streets of Seoul so deserted. We quickly hit the highway south as the sun peeks over the horizon. Its rays already diffused by the ever-present pollution haze.

Ajeossi and Mom are deep in conversation. I can barely make out what they are saying over the roar of the diesel engine from the back seat. It's too early to focus my synapses on comprehending Korean so I just let the particulars of their conversation fade into the background. I have more important things to concentrate on. Like grabbing the handle above the window so I don't careen over the slippery leather and into the opposite door. The Hyundai Jeep is in need of a new suspension.

The more Ajeossi speaks, the slower he drives—I watch the speedometer dip from one hundred kilometers per hour to sixty. Cars and buses zoom past, the faces of their drivers turned to us in disdain. Ajeossi is in the fast lane.

My mother tells me later that he was recounting stories from his child-hood in Kongju. Memories of my father, who is ten years older than him, and Halmoni, the matriarch of the family. When Mom speaks, a light goes on in Ajeossi's head. He pushes the accelerator pedal to keep up with everyone else on the highway out of Seoul.

We stop at a rest area at the outer edge of the sprawling suburbs, where white concrete apartment buildings give way to stepped rice fields. In the parking lot, buses spew forth swarms of retirees wearing identical wind-breakers. They are on their way to some sightseeing excursion down south. Ajeossi picks up another cup of instant coffee. He's already gone through the thermos. Mom and I grab a couple of soft drinks—green apple flavor, my favorite—and a bag of pink shrimp chips.

Back in the car, the terrain surges up and down as we near Kongju. Vendors appear on the side of the road with giant clear plastic bags of shiny brown nuts. Ajeossi explains that the onset of fall means chestnut season, especially here in the Chungcheong province, where the country's chestnut trees are centered. Without warning, Ajeossi veers onto the shoulder and stops to buy a bag. The week before I told him chestnuts were my favorite and explained that Americans used them to stuff their turkeys for Thanksgiving. He had smiled, proud his cousin's American daughter loved Korean things.

"You are really Korean, not American," he joked. "You even use chop-sticks better than my son."

In the valley between the two largest mountains lies Kongju. We drive through the town's center—past the dusty shop fronts on a street full of potholes. Kongju looks like a slab of a poor neighborhood in Seoul. No giant apartment buildings or glass-encrusted office buildings. The horizon line of the buildings here hovers low so as to not compete with the spectac-ular peaks that surround the city. The mountains were the reason Kongju was the capital of the Paekche dynasty over 1,500 years before. There's gold in those hills, which supplied the royal family with filigreed crowns, thick-hooped earrings with dangly yin-yang shaped amulets, and treasure to trade with the Chinese. I spy the giant groves of chestnut trees, which still protect the palace remains, high up on the hill overlooking the city.

We turn off the main thoroughfare out of town and onto a dirt road. Ajeossi says he still remembers the way from his childhood trips to his uncle's house. "We always came here at this time of year," he says. "To get chestnuts."

Great-uncle Choong's house stands on the edge of a chestnut grove north of town. It's harvest time, and my eighty-something uncle still gathers the nuts himself with the help of his sturdy wife. They had no children to help them.

Choong waves at us from the embankment. He's stooped, with a bulging hemp bag of nuts on his back. His smiling wife greets us at the top of the road by their ramshackle home, her squat form framed by a tangle of kiwi vines that wind through a trellis arch. Tanned and robust, you can tell she has grown up among the orchards surrounding Kongju. Her husband's Lee-family high forehead and white, pointy beard give him a more intellectual air, like that of a yangban scholar, of his landowning ancestors.

CHOONG'S WIFE BECKONS US INTO the house and has a steaming plate of nuts waiting on a low table. Gnats drift in the October air, but they will soon be gone with the onset of the cold. Sunlight illuminates a small rosewood dresser in the corner of the otherwise dank room, which functions as both the living room and bedroom. Above the dresser hangs an old map of Korea, darkened with age and sans the jagged dashes of a country divided into two.

I remove my patent leather sandals and tiptoe barefoot across the sticky linoleum to a pillow by the table. I silently berate myself for wearing the wrong thing, yet again, as I attempt to maneuver my legs underneath my slightly too short polka-dot skirt so as not to expose my nether regions to elderly relatives. Life on the floor is difficult for my American limbs, even with the benefit of years of yoga classes. I know my sit and ankle bones will throb by the time we leave.

When I crack chestnuts, the hard shells disintegrate into shards. In Choong's wife's expert hands, the shells come off in one piece. The fruits of the nuts lie steaming on the plate, like tiny brains marked with furrows of experience. She hands me the plate, and I pop one in my mouth. Chalky and dense, slightly sweet. In my mouth it feels like something in between fruit and flesh.

We exchange niceties and sip our coffee. Mom extends good wishes from my father in Houston. I smile my *I can kind of understand what you are saying but I can only answer you in English* smile and tell Choong that I am here not only to eat his chestnuts but to ask him questions about my grandfather. He is one of only two relatives alive today who knew him. Choong tilts his only working ear toward me and nods.

"Okay," he answers. "I will tell you what I remember."

I LAST SAW CHOONG AND his wife the summer before at Halmoni's wake. They sat quietly across the table from my father, more interested in the food before them than in conversation. My soft-spoken father raised his voice to ask his favorite uncle what he thought about the reunions of family members separated by the Korean War that summer. The reunions that accompanied the first talks between the leaders of North and South Korea, between Kim Jong Il and Kim Dae Jung. The Korean Broadcasting Service had blasted round-the-clock video of weeping and wailing halmonis and harabojis, hugging loved ones they thought they would not live to see again.

A cousin had shushed my father before he could ask Choong if he planned to apply to the government for permission to see his long-lost family, whom he had left behind on an ill-timed trip home in June 1950 at the beginning of the war. The cousin pointed at Choong's wife from underneath the table to remind my father that she didn't want to hear about her husband's former family and changed the subject to something more benign, like the early onset of monsoon season. Choong's wife stared straight ahead and pretended not to hear my father. Instead, she loudly slurped the last of her warm boricha tea. Even after almost half a century of marriage, she still felt threatened by the wife and children her husband inadvertently abandoned at the beginning of the Korean War. She wanted to forget that that part of her husband's life ever happened.

"WHAT DO YOU REMEMBER OF my grandfather?" I ask my great-uncle.

Choong answers slowly, thoughtfully, in his Kongju drawl. He sits ram-rod straight, his skinny legs entwined with the ease of a yogi master. He answers in a cadence I recognize from my father—rolling phrases undulating like the rounded mountains of their native landscape, phrases interposed by deep breaths. The valleys in between.

> *Your grandfather was my cousin. I was six years younger, so we weren't that close, but our families were. We lived near each other in the outskirts of Kongju.*
>
> *When he left for high school in Seoul—I think it was in 1927—I was twelve years old. He returned to Kongju a year later. I remember him coming over to our house wearing his Joongdong High School uniform and cap. He was carrying a big box of books. He told my father he was on the run from the police. He came to our house first because he didn't want his father to see the books. He asked my father to burn them as soon as he could. He didn't want the police to find them. After he left, I asked my father to save them since they looked interesting. They were like no books I had seen before.*

Choong pauses, allowing my mother to fill in the gaps for me. I can only understand the gist of what he says in Korean, but with Mom there I can focus on his expressions, mannerisms, and body language. While he slowly chews the tender nuggets of the morning's harvest, I am struck by the familiarity of the faraway look he assumes. Thinking, always thinking. It's my father's face as he folds origami animals after dinner in his recliner chair. The hobby Mom suggested for him in the hospital to help him recover from lung surgery, to make his fingers nimble again.

> *After my parents died of cholera three years later, my sister and I moved into my uncle's house, not your great-grandfather's but his brother's. I took the books with me. I left Kongju a year later, when I was seven-*

teen, to become a sailor on a merchant ship in Japan. I worked abroad
for a little over ten years and went to night school between voyages. In
1944, the year before liberation, I returned home for a visit. When I
arrived at my uncle's house, I found the walls papered with the pages
of your grandfather's books. Paper was scarce at the time and it had
been a cold winter, so my uncle used the pages as insulation.

My uncle told me the Japanese police had been there earlier, on
one of their routine checks of homes in the area. They saw the pages
on his walls and threatened to arrest him. Apparently, the book pag-
es defied their rule somehow. My uncle told the police he had no idea
what those pages said since he could not read classical Japanese. After
a long argument, the police realized my uncle was telling the truth.
They searched the house for the remaining books and confiscated them.

"DO YOU REMEMBER ANY OF the titles of the books or what they were about?" I ask.

Choong pauses, and the furrows of his wide forehead deepen. He glances over at his wife and says, "I only remember that some of them had 'ism' in the title."

I push him, asking if any of my grandfather's books concerned politics, history, philosophy, even literature. I mention Marx, Lenin, Trotsky. Kant, Hegel, Goethe. Tolstoy. None seem to ring a bell.

"I'm not sure," he says, wringing his weathered hands. "It was too long ago."

I sense Choong is hiding something. Or he doesn't feel comfortable speaking about what he remembers in front of his wife, who isn't interested in knowing anything more about his life before the war, before she met him. He is a just a chestnut farmer to her. She is fine with that characterization.

She emits a glare of warning at her husband of almost fifty years. I am meant to see it. Out of deference to him I relent.

I TRY TO IMAGINE THE book pages decorating the walls of Choong's uncle's house in the countryside—columns and columns of Japanese script, indecipherable to the household's inhabitants, expressing ideas unaccept-able to the Japanese colonial police. I know that since Choong had lived and studied in Japan, he was probably the only family member who could have read the errant wallpaper.

I picture my teenage grandfather—whom my brother Ed resembles so closely—trudging with a heavy box of books all the way home from Seoul. He dared not bring evidence of his transgressions home. Their possible discovery by his father, the head of the clan, would only result in further restrictions on his behavior, since his father did not approve of his political views or activities.

I change the subject and ask Choong about his own life. "What did you do after you were a sailor in Japan?"

> *In 1944, I came home to look for a job. There weren't any in Kongju, so I traveled up north to Wonsan where a relative was living. I worked at a small ironworks shop. One of the managers heard I had worked as a sailor and had drafting experience, so he gave me some drafting work. Later, I worked at the Wonsan shipyard. At first, I drew small parts of engines, but soon I was drawing entire ships.*

I ask Choong if he had been involved in politics or if he had talked to my grandfather about his involvement in the nationalist movement.

Choong tugs the end of his pointed white beard.

"No, we never talked about any of that."

He would only say he learned about the nationalist movement from a fellow sailor who had somehow been affiliated with the provisional Korean government in Shanghai in the early 1940s. The government-in-exile that had been established in 1919 in China during the Japanese occupation. He couldn't recall the details.

I ask when he last saw my grandfather.

> *I think your grandfather might have still been involved in the nationalist movement after he was released from prison and used the hatchery as a front. I don't know for sure, but it makes sense with his involvement with the JoongAng Ilbo. I visited the chicken hatchery in Chongju, around 1934 or 1935, when your father was a baby. I was on leave from one of my tours at sea. My sister lived in Chongju*

then, so I stopped by to see your grandfather on the way to her house. Halmoni and my sister are the same age. Halmoni was the one who introduced my sister to her husband, a neighbor Chongju boy.

Your grandfather gave me a tour of the facility. I was impressed by how large it was. He must have had many people working for him. He also talked a bit about his work at the newspaper. He was in charge of the provincial branch of the JoongAng Ilbo newspaper, which was headed by Lyuh Woon Hyung. Lyuh Woon Hyung was famous for doctoring a photograph of the Korean marathoner who won the gold medal for Japan at the Berlin Olympics in 1936. He superimposed the Korean flag over the Japanese imperial flag that flew at the medal ceremony. The Japanese closed down the newspaper after that and put Lyuh in jail.

I ASK MY GREAT-UNCLE TO elaborate. Choong refuses to meet my gaze. I ask him to speculate further on my grandfather's involvement in the movement. His eyes still askance.

My mother takes over.

"Do you think Juhae's grandpa was in direct contact with Lyuh Woon Hyung?"

Silence. Still no eye contact. And then a mumbling of "I don't know."

I look at Mom and shrug my shoulders.

Then Choong becomes forthcoming for the first time and relates a childhood story.

When I was a child, your grandfather's family and my family lived next door to each other in a mountain village outside of Kongju. Your grandfather was much older, so I didn't interact with him very much. Plus, his nose was always in a book. But he was always kind to me. I didn't play with his brothers either, since the middle one was sick all the time. The youngest, Kwan, was only a year older—he didn't want to have anything to do with me. So I played with the peasant children outside the walls of the family compound, the tenant farmers' children. I liked to fly kites with them above the tree line where the wind was strong.

The adults in the family discouraged me from playing with the workers' children, but I kept sneaking away to play with them. I was lonely. I was too young to understand the difference between my cousins and the boys in the village, except the village boys wanted to play with me.

After one long kite-flying session, I walked home through the woods, well after suppertime. I tried to sneak into the house without my father noticing, but he was waiting for me. I lied and told him I was off by myself and lost track of time. He didn't believe me. He told me that my playmates were not my friends, they were beneath me. I was only to play with other yangban children like my cousins. I wasn't allowed to leave the house for a week afterward.

Uncle Choong's bright eyes begin to cloud over. The strain of transporting himself into the past has taken a toll on him. He unfolds his legs from his cross-legged position and stands, pulling his tightly cinched pants even farther up his bony torso so there is absolutely no danger of them ever falling down. Ajeossi jumps up and takes Choong's arm. Choong's wife clears the dishes. The interview is over.

As we file out of the room, Mom leaves an envelope of money on the bureau. No one sees except for me.

We take a couple of snapshots on the porch. I feel enormous, like a beef-fed Amazon, a head taller than Choong and his wife. We all smile broadly, my pearly whites and their yellow dentures, under the arbor of kiwi vines.

After the last photo, great-uncle Choong pats me on the back.

"You are a good granddaughter," he says. "Your grandfather would have been proud."

THE NEXT DAY BACK IN Seoul, I call my father. I tell him about our visit to Choong's house, about what his uncle said about the house papered in Grandpa's contraband books, about the story of him as a boy playing with the peasant children.

My father's "I'm thinking" silence ensues for two, five, ten seconds. Finally, he speaks.

"I think the childhood story was Choong's way of telling you he identified with the peasant class, rather than his yangban ancestors. He didn't
think it was right for him to be separated from the workers' children. He
thought they should all be equal. It was his way of explaining how he became a socialist."

"What?" I practically yell. "A socialist? Are you sure? He wouldn't talk
about politics at all."

"Actually, he was a Communist. He became an officer in the North
Korean Army when he lived up North."

I am speechless. Shocked.

My father continues.

"I didn't want to tell you until after you spoke to Choong. He probably
didn't talk about it because his wife was there. I heard the story from my
other great-uncle when I was young.

"Apparently, Choong attended Pyongyang Industrial College around the
time of liberation. The college was renamed Kim Il Sung University, after
the leader of North Korea in 1946, the year after the Japanese lost the war.
He met and married his wife while he was in college. The new government
in the North recruited Worker Party members who were originally from
the South to be officers in the North Korean Army. Men like Choong. They
were recruited to manage the propaganda effort among civilians in the South.
Choong was responsible for the South Kyongsang province, where Pusan is
located. He traveled down there to organize a couple of months before the
Korean War started in 1950. After it began, he was stuck in the South.

"He found his way to his sister's house in the mountains outside of
Kongju. Many of his comrades, who were also trapped behind enemy lines,
became members of the ppalchisan, the Communist guerilla group led by
Lee Hyun Sang. Now, some people call Lee Hyun Sang the 'Che Guevara
of Korea,' since he and the last of the ppalchisan holed themselves up atop
Mount Jiri near Kyongju and never surrendered. Instead, they were all
killed in 1953, just like Che Guevara was in Bolivia.

"Choong's uncle is the father of your other great-uncle Wan in Taejon.
He's the one who told me this story years ago. He was a local politician

and went to see Choong at the house in the mountains. He found Choong wearing a tattered North Korean army uniform. They burned the uniform, and he took Choong back home to Kongju. Because of his influence in Kongju, he was able to protect Choong from prisoner-of-war camp.

"Choong turned himself in years later, well after the Korean War was over, after the prisoners-of-war were released. He wasn't punished, but he couldn't get a decent job because of his past. So he married a local peasant girl and became a farmer. He has lived in the house you visited in the chestnut groves ever since."

I TRY TO DIGEST THE new information. I knew Choong had left his wife and children behind in the North but had assumed he was just visiting family when he found himself trapped after the war started. I had no idea Choong had been a Communist like my grandfather, let alone an officer in the North Korean Army.

My thoughts snap toward my grandfather. What would he have done if he had lived to see the end of the Japanese occupation? Would he have made his way up North like Choong? Would he have taken his family with him?

Would he have joined the army or been involved in the formation of the North Korean government? He would have surely been afforded many opportunities because of his involvement in the student nationalist movement during the colonial era.

The memory of Shin Yong Ha's Tony-the-Tiger rolling Rs flashes in my head. "Your-g-r-r g-r-r-randfather could have been second in command to Kim Il Sung!"

I tell my father that Choong and my grandfather must have talked politics when Choong came to visit him at the chicken hatchery. Maybe even in depth. Or at least my grandfather was an influence on his younger cousin. And Choong must have known the titles of the books my grandfather left behind with his family. Like *Das Kapital*, *The State and Revolution*, *The Communist Manifesto*—texts I had first read in my Methods of Art History course in graduate school. He had been a Communist just like my grandfather.

My father agrees with my assessment and continues.

"Maybe Choong will write me with more information. I had your mom include a letter from me with the money she left him. I told him to contact the government office in charge of the reunions of families separated by the Korean War. Even if his first wife isn't alive, his children most likely are. The North Korean government would have treated them well, since Choong had been an officer in the army. Perhaps Choong would have even been considered a hero in the North. You never know, maybe he was declared a Patriot just like your grandfather was in the South.

"A couple of years ago, Choong wrote me a letter. He heard that a former student of mine, another Dr. Shin, the one who runs the private hospital in Seoul, was organizing a medical mission in North Korea to vaccinate children. Choong wanted to know if Dr. Shin could try to contact the family he left behind in Pyongyang while he was there. He wrote the names of his wife and three children, two sons and a daughter.

"He also wrote about his life after the end of World War II. In 1945, he worked as the technical director for a shipping company in the Wonsan shipyard. The company sent him to the executive program at Pyongyang Industrial College. He was recruited into the North Korean Army there.

"He didn't want his wife in Kongju to know he was trying to contact his family in the North. That's the reason he wrote me and didn't call. He didn't want his wife to overhear our conversation.

"I gave the information to Dr. Shin before his trip to North Korea, but he was unable to contact Choong's family. Dr. Shin wasn't allowed to contact anyone outside of the clinic. All of his interactions with North Korean citizens were supervised, either by a clinic staff member or a soldier.

"I hope Choong applies to the South Korean government for a reunion with his family in the North. I don't know if he will, though, since his wife doesn't want him to. Or maybe he's given up hope. It's been fifty years since he last saw his family. That's a long time. A lifetime.

"When you're his age, maybe it's just easier to forget."

COLLABORATOR

Kwan was my father Eun Sul's uncle, the younger and more impulsive of my grandfather's two brothers. The one always in motion, the one the neighbors described as "enterprising." Flailing arms and fast chatter—that's how my father remembered his uncle. He made a good living as the chief mechanic for the U.S. Army unit stationed near Kongju, the unit that arrived after the Japanese lost World War II in 1945 and Korea was split in two. The Americans inherited the southern end of the peninsula, everything south of the 38th parallel, their spoil of war. Everything above the 38th parallel was under control of the Soviets, who occupied the North.

Kwan got the job with the Americans because he was the only mechanic in town who spoke a little English. He had learned English from the Methodist missionaries who ran his school. He wasn't allowed to attend Kongju High School like his eldest brother because Chul Ha had been expelled for staging protests against the Japanese principal in 1928.

After high school, Kwan became an apprentice at the local bus company and learned to be a mechanic. He worked as a driver for the ruling Japanese magistrate in the area and became his confidant. He was the recipient of the magistrate's beloved bonsai collection after the magistrate and his family were forced to leave Korea in disgrace after the Japanese emperor surrendered. Then the Americans came, and Kwan got a job with them.

My father remembered that the American soldiers regularly gave his uncle cans of Spam—the pink spongy meat his wife fried and put on top of Kwan's rice as a special treat for breakfast.

Kwan and his family prospered. Their new house was located in the nice part of the town, where all the city officials lived. But after June 25, 1950, the day the North Korean army crossed the 38th parallel and invaded the South, everything changed.

HALMONI WAS IN SEOUL ON the day the war began—to explore the possibility of her family moving there. She left the capital two days later, with thousands of others trying to escape. On her walk to the train station, Halmoni saw hundreds of wounded soldiers carried in a convoy of trucks driving toward Seoul National University Hospital. Her train was one of the last to leave Seoul before the Han River Bridge was blown up without warning by the South Korean Army on June 28 to deter the North Koreans' advance.

The typically two-hour train ride south to home took over twenty. The train stopped every couple of minutes, it seemed, to yield the track to military transports. At the stop before Kongju, the train was detained overnight. Halmoni decided to get off and hitchhike home. No one offered her a ride, so she walked the forty kilometers to town. On her long walk, she made the decision to prepare her family to leave Kongju as soon as possible, even though the radio announcements assured people that the South Korean forces would expel the invaders soon.

KWAN CAME TO VISIT HALMONI a couple of days later. It was early in the morning, still dark when he pounded on the door, waking Eun Sul and his brother. Eun Sul told his uncle that Halmoni was at her dawn prayer meeting and would return soon. Kwan paced a path through the long grass in front of the house while he waited. When she arrived, he led her to the backyard to discuss something in private away from his nephews.

He didn't know that Eun Sul listened to their conversation from inside the house. The windows were open to let in the summer breeze.

I know you saved them, Kwan said to Halmoni. *Those papers, those papers of my brother's can finally be of value to the family, now that the North Koreans are taking over.*

Uncle Kwan went on and on, as was his habit. Halmoni stood expressionless throughout his tirade until he said something that piqued her interest.

The North Korean government would surely reward your sons for their father's efforts with free education. He was a Communist, after all, and protested Japanese rule. Plus, if I present the papers to the North Korean authorities, I will be given an honorable position.

HALMONI RAISED HER EYEBROWS. SHE knew Kwan was an opportunist, that didn't surprise her. He had intercepted crops from the family's tenant farmers to keep for himself more than once. The possibility of free education was what aroused her interest. She wanted to move the family to Seoul so her sons could attend the best schools in the country. Education was the most important thing—that's what her late husband told her on her visits to the prison in Seoul. Education was what she had yearned for most after her mother died when she was a child. She allowed her mind to wander for a second with the hope that perhaps her husband's disgrace could somehow be transformed into something to benefit her sons. God knows there hadn't been any previous benefits.

With a quick shake of her head, she thought better of it.

No. No, I will not give you anything.

Kwan protested, then tried a different angle to his argument.

Those papers could benefit you as well, since you are the widow of a Communist revolutionary.

Kwan pushed too hard, as usual. Halmoni silenced him with a flick of her palm.

He knew her mind was made up. It wasn't worth his time to try to change her opinion.

BEFORE DAYBREAK ON JULY 13, a loud explosion shook Eun Sul's house—the American troops had blown up the bridge over the Kum River as the North Koreans made their way south toward Kongju. The explosion was their signal to leave. They abandoned their home and walked over an hour and a half to the safety of the hut of the family's cemetery caretaker at the base of the Sobaek Mountains. Halmoni had made sure no evidence of her late husband was left behind for her brother-in-law Kwan or the North Korean soldiers to find. The night before she had burned all of it—the prison documents, letters, writings on political theory, newspaper articles, even her husband's books.

LATER, AFTER THEIR ESCAPE, EUN Sul asked his mother why she did not hand over his father's papers to Kwan. Why she destroyed the paper remains of his father's life in the kitchen hearth.

Halmoni told him that deep in a prayer session at home the morning before Kwan came to visit, she stared at the two spears that hung on the far wall of the main room. These family heirlooms, the weapons the Tonghak peasant army had left behind after they took over the old Lee family compound at the end of the nineteenth century. Crudely forged in black iron, one spear hung lower than the other, the end of its shaft broken off during what would be the peasants' last battle in the outskirts of Kongju.

The first Tonghak insurgence began as a revolt against yangban landowners, like Eun Sul's ancestors, as well as increasing foreign interests. The frightened Korean government asked China's Qing dynasty to deliver troops to quell the peasants. The Japanese countered with forces of their own, citing the breaking of the Tientsin Convention agreement, which established Korea as a co-protectorate of both China and Japan in 1885.

What had begun as an indigenous social movement exploded into a battle between the ruling powers of Asia for the control of Korea in the form of the Sino-Japanese War in 1894. In less than a year, the Japanese prevailed and gained their footing with the diminished Korean monarchy.

During this time, a second peasant uprising swelled up in opposition to the newly formed pro-Japanese government in Seoul. The Japanese-backed government army—outnumbered by thousands of Tonghak fighters but armed with modern weaponry—set a trap for the peasants in Kongju's center. They shot cannonballs and artillery into wave after wave of Tonghak forces who were carrying only spears and bows and arrows. The poorly armed peasants put up a good fight but were soon defeated.

THE TWO SPEARS REPRESENT TWO rounds of war, Halmoni explained to Eun Sul.

Look at what happened to the Tonghak in their two rebellions. They didn't know their uprising would lead to a war between China and Japan.

You never know what will happen. History is the proof. Kwan thinks that the North Korean invasion will surely result in their rule. I don't know if that will happen.

You can't divine the future. Nothing is ever certain, especially in war.

THE NORTH KOREAN ARMY SLICED their arc of influence deep into the southern part of the peninsula—through Kongju and beyond. By the end of the summer, they reached Pusan, the southernmost port. It looked like the peninsula would be theirs.

Kwan remained in Kongju after Halmoni and her sons fled to the mountains. He sidled up to the North Koreans after they arrived, just like he did with the Americans after the Japanese left in 1945. He joined the local Workers' Union and became the chairman. A month later, in mid-September, U.S. General Douglas MacArthur staged a surprise invasion at the port of Incheon and eventually pushed the North Koreans all the way back over the 38th parallel.

The North Koreans left Kongju as quickly as they arrived. Halmoni and her family returned to town. Kwan found himself branded as a collaborator of the enemy and feared persecution or worse. He hid in Halmoni's house for more than a month while his wife and children stayed in their home and pretended that he left with his Communist comrades from the union. Kwan's wife asked Halmoni to give her rice gathered by the family's tenant farmers so she could bribe the local police detective to consider a lesser punishment for her husband. Halmoni reluctantly agreed, even though the family's only source of annual income would be depleted to almost nothing.

Kwan turned himself in after the final bribe of rice was given. Instead of a jail term, he was permitted to join the civilian driver corps of the South Korean Army and serve his country that way.

The Korean Armistice Agreement was signed on July 27, 1953, and ensured "a complete cessation of hostilities and of all acts of armed force in Korea until a final peaceful settlement is achieved." After the war, Kwan couldn't find anyone to hire him as a mechanic. He was a North Korean sympathizer. He was affiliated with the enemy. Everyone in Kongju knew— they didn't care that he was motivated by self-interest instead of conviction.

Kwan lost his house. He lost his livelihood.

He ended up driving a taxi instead.

SOLITARY
CONFINEMENT

I settle into life with my father's cousin's family in their big house on the hill. Ajeossi is semiretired, it seems. He wakes close to noon after late nights with his stamp collection or developing color photographs in the darkroom upstairs. I'm not sure what he does during the day.

"I think he manages office buildings," my mother tells me. I know that one of his tenants is Pizza Hut since he brought home a couple of greasy pies the week before. They looked like pizzas, but the cheese didn't quite melt. Instead, it floated on top of the pepperoni slices. A weird unearthly orange color, the consistency of slightly molten plastic.

When I peer into the open door of his office, Ajeossi is holding tweezers in one hand. The tweezers grab hold of one of his precious stamps, which he places gingerly on a page of acid-free paper in an oversize album.

He glances up and beckons. "Juhae, come in."

I walk into his sanctum, which is located adjacent to the family room, where he works with the door open to keep watch over his wife and daughter while they sit on the floor and watch their favorite soap operas on the enormous backlit television. It's the first time I've ventured into his office. My curator's eye takes stock of the blue-and-white Chinese vases (Ming dynasty) and antique wooden Korean rice chests (most likely nineteenth century). Ajeossi has good taste, I think to myself, unlike his wife, who decorates the house with Austrian crystal animal miniatures and the wooden Last Supper sculpture over the kitchen table.

Seodaemun Prison History Hall, Seoul, Korea

I sit carefully on the edge of the armchair facing Ajeossi's vast desk so as not to disturb the stacks of papers, catalogues, and photographs that cover most of the floor. He tells me in his broken English that he has collected every stamp Korea has issued. That's why he spends so much time in his office, to keep up with the regular shipments of stamps from the South Korean postal service that arrive for him every week in brown cardboard boxes.

He shows me Korean Stamp #1 from November 1884, which was printed in Japan. I learn later that this stamp saw little use, since the country's post office was burned down in an attempted coup one month after it was released. Ajeossi points at the dozens of leather-bound stamp albums lining the wall, organized in chronological order. He tells me he is branching out into different media for his collections. Like postcards. He reaches over to a pile from the upper right quadrant of his cluttered desk and hands me the one at the top.

A man, stripped to his waist, lies splayed out on a rough-hewn wooden plank. What looks like a rice sack has been placed over his head. His voluminous peasant pants identify him as Korean. I have seen old harabojis on the subway wearing versions of those white hemp pants, with their white padded socks stuffed into Nike tennis shoes. Standing over the humiliated Korean is a man in uniform, laughing, with a greasy moustache, pegged pants, and a smart cap with a tiny brim, obviously enjoying the other man's subjugation.

One glance and I know what's happening.

A COUPLE OF WEEKS LATER, I visit the Seodaemun Hyeongmuso, the prison museum. The red-brick complex, built by the Japanese during the early years of their occupation, is located in what used to be the outskirts of Seoul. Now it's smack dab in the middle of the city, just northwest of the grand avenue where all the embassies are located on the same thoroughfare as the Olympic Stadium, which was built for the 1988 games.

The Japanese housed all the political prisoners at Seodaemun, or what was then known as the North Gate Prison. It housed the anti-Japanese protestors, the Korean nationalist intellectuals, the avowed Communists with contraband screeds from Russia and China—all of them, including my grandfather. The structure somehow survived the end of World War II and the relentless bombing of Seoul during the Korean War. During the 1980s, the South Korean government decided to turn the prison's decrepit buildings into a museum.

I email Jungmin and ask her to meet me there at 10:00 a.m., when the museum opens. I'm early, but not as early as the swarms of schoolchildren yelling and running around the entrance. Each class is color-coded with uniforms of yellow, red, or blue—and matching backpacks, of course, on which the name of each school is emblazoned in large block characters.

It's a beautiful, crisp fall day, still quite warm in the sun. Clad in appropriate layers, I remove my cardigan and absorb the rays into my sun-deprived arms. Jungmin arrives out of breath. Her commute from the apartment she shares with her mother in Ajou has taken an hour and a half that day. She tells me she has a couple of hours before she heads off for Dr. Lew's office at the Syngman Rhee Center nearby.

We enter the main gate of the prison behind all the kids with black, velvet-haired bowl cuts. They are rambunctious in the way Korean kids have become, with their permissive, Westernized parents who let them run wild. Their minders guide them into the front door away from the brilliant fertilized green of the lawn, which twinkles with dew in the sun.

Prison interrogation rooms have been transformed into a gallery of sorts. Jaunty woodcuts of what look to be frolicking peasants decorate the walls. At closer view, though, the peasants are posed in various scenes of capture, arrest, and even warfare. They are the Tonghak peasants from the rebellion a century before, the ones who occupied my father's family compound outside of Kongju.

Two sides of a giant rice basket, large enough to hold an adult, are displayed on a white riser in the middle of the room. With my poor grasp of written Korean, I can't understand the explanatory label, so I ask Jungmin to translate.

"It's an imprisonment device. The Japanese would wrap a prisoner up and place him in the rice basket. They would hold him there until he talked."

Other torture devices are laid out for display as if they were artworks. Shackles, crude wooden handcuffs, disintegrating leather whips, and a rough wooden plank, just like the one on Ajeossi's postcard. This one is inhabited by a chubby boy of eight or nine with his arms splayed wide, Christ-style. A cluster of schoolmates gathers around. Two boys whip him with imaginary bamboo sticks as the prisoner giggles and writhes in mock pain.

We step outside to get some air and escape the chaos of the school-children. A photographer has set up a tripod on an expanse of lawn in a protected alcove. The look is decidedly retro, Old World even in a Western way, since there are no other surviving red-bricked buildings in Seoul. A young bride and groom stand in front of the photographer and anxiously wait for direction.

Jungmin and I watch as the photographer and his assistant arrange the ten-foot white satin train just so over the emerald blades. The bride's surgically enhanced eyelids blink in the sunlight while her trusty tuxedoed groom grabs her elbow to keep her from tottering over.

"Ugh, can you believe they are taking wedding photos at a prison?" Jungmin whispers to me. "It's bad luck." Jungmin pauses. "I think they will get a divorce."

We watch for a moment longer, then make our way down the steps to a back gallery with a warning sign out front: MAY NOT BE SUITABLE FOR CHILDREN.

"Great," I say. "No kids here."

A full minute passes before my eyes can adjust to the dank galleries that smell vaguely of mold. Once my eyes come into focus, I am surprised to be surrounded by life-sized, dust-covered mannequins, like those from a 1970s-era history museum back home—pioneers building fires on the plain, Native Americans huddling in their teepees—except these human facsimiles are reenacting scenes from the prison.

A dastardly Japanese soldier flicks cigarette ashes onto a poor Korean man who lies on the ground, his hands and feet bound. Western-clothed interrogators in their white shirtsleeves laugh while one pulls the fingernail out of a screaming woman's hand. A young man is somehow stuffed into a wooden box that would comfortably fit only a three-year-old child. Gruesome torture scene after torture scene, complete with fake blood and high-cheekboned Korean faces contorting in pain. Their moral impact blunted by the chips of paint that fall off the poorly modeled latex forms and the heavy-handed message of the supposed true-to-life representations—Japanese Bad! Korean Good!

Shocked at first, my postmodern sensibilities take over and I swallow my horror at what the Japanese staff inflicted upon its prisoners. I have become skilled at ignoring my initial, authentic emotion and intellectualizing it. Isn't that what graduate school theory classes teach you? Or to go back further, isn't that how I learned from my father to deal with uncomfortable emotions?

I begin to laugh at the fauxness of it all. I'm incredulous such a display could exist, let alone be taken seriously.

"Can you believe this place?" I say to Jungmin.

She shakes her head, mouth downturned. We can't get out of there fast enough.

As we are leaving, I see a mother, younger than me, who has elected not to heed the warning at the door. She is speaking softly to her baseball-capped son, who is barely out of toddlerhood. She points at the figures in one of the dioramas. His eyes stretched wide, the boy nods and grabs his mother's hand for comfort. He gets the message—the real message that I chose to ignore.

I pause. That hovering feeling of being caught in between reverberates. I long to be comforted by a warm touch—of my mother, of a loved one—while at the same time, I want to be the one who can comfort someone who might need it.

JUNGMIN AND I ENTER THE main building—pitched ceiling double-height with wooden plank walkways on the second floor. The interior freshly painted in institutional green and off-white, which feels not quite inviting but at least aesthetically pleasing in a stark, barren way. Donald Judd's minimalist boxes come to mind. The ones I saw in Marfa, in his converted military base, before moving to New York City.

We climb upstairs and I enter one of the cells, a tiny one, in front of which a small placard informs the public it was originally reserved for solitary confinement. I shiver in the small space. The damp cold of night has been captured in that tiny cell. The chill of the night before and those of the previous winter. And back through time, back seven decades, all the way to 1929, when my grandfather was held in solitary confinement.

That's the reason he needed Halmoni to deliver him the finest wool blanket she could find. The frigid air was caught in his young lungs, never to leave. Not even after he was released. Two years later, he died of a lung ailment. Halmoni told me he succumbed to neungmagyeom, or pleurisy, a precursor to tuberculosis.

That's what hits me.

A chill straight to the bone.

RECORDS

The first snow dusts Seoul in powdered sugar. My boots make neat little exclamation points on the flagstones over the koi pond as I leave the house. *Slam* goes the black metal gate to the steep street below. A schoolboy decides to use his backpack as a sled and careens past me down the icy incline. Giggling girls in pigtails and navy-blue pleated skirts hold on to each other as they half slide to the bus stop. I am glad I bought the cheaper rubber-soled boots instead of the leather-soled ones at the basement fire sale at the Lotte department store, but I am still forced to grab a couple of car door handles on the descent into civilization.

It's mid-December 2000, and I have only two weeks left in Korea. After visits to all the repositories of governmental records and most of the major universities, I am left with one lead. A certain publisher/keeper of official records in the northern reaches of Seoul. Professor Yun in his pink oxford shirt at Hansung University hinted that he procured his materials from this mysterious figure for his article on Lee Hyun Sang, the Communist guerilla fighter, the article that mentioned my grandfather by name.

"You might need to pay him," he warned.

Jungmin suggests a meeting point at the mouth of the northernmost subway station at 10:00 a.m. I give myself two hours to get there. A bus ride to the subway station and two transfers—I'm not sure exactly how long it will take. Jungmin's commute is even longer.

I get there early, as is my habit. The cold seeps up from the sidewalk to my toes. I can feel the rubber stiffening underneath. The snow here has already turned into slush, and a brisk wind picks up tiny granules of ice, which hit my face. It's starting to get painful.

Steamed-up floor-to-ceiling glass windows face the street. I can wait in there for Jungmin, I decide, on one of those lipstick-red swivel seats. I open the door to the establishment, and I'm greeted by the familiar smell of toasted white bread and warm processed meat. Arby's has made it to Seoul. The odor of fast food feels comforting, even though I would be repelled by it at home.

I wipe a circle in the condensation on the window and enjoy a small Styrofoam cup of coffee so hot I cannot taste it. I only feel the heat flow down my throat and into my stomach.

Jungmin emerges from below and sees me waving to her from my seat. She shivers in the swirling wind. I walk quickly to the counter before she can get there and buy her a cup of something hot. I try to treat her whenever I can. When I offered to pay for translator and research services in September when we first met, she refused. It was an honor for her to help me, she answered.

I hope Dr. Lew pays her well. I offer English-language editing or letter writing services, all my limited skill set can furnish, or at least a place to stay if she decides to visit the U.S. It's the least I can do.

Jungmin and I leave the warm confines of Arby's and walk down the street to Mr. Shim's office with our heads down into the wind. The street is devoid of humanity, save for a huddled food vendor selling hotteok, cinnamon pancakes filled with honey. Mr. Shim's publishing business is located in a second-floor walkup above an abandoned tailor's shop, where a pair of headless mannequins stand in the window, seemingly left behind. We climb the dark, rickety staircase to a landing cluttered with cardboard boxes.

Mr. Shim greets us formally with a barely perceptible bow and nod of the head. He motions us over to a well-worn chocolate-brown couch in the center of a large room lined with bookshelves. We both try to sit on the edge of the cushion but are soon as one with the sagging coils.

Jungmin succinctly explains our reason for being there, dropping all the important names—Professor Shin Yong Ha from Seoul National, Professor Yun who gave us Mr. Shim's name—and my story of an American journalist in search of information on her long-lost Korean grandfather.

An oily light shines through the dirty window behind Mr. Shim's desk, where he stands listening, seemingly unmoved. Meonji, I think to myself, conjuring up the childhood Korean word as I watch tiny dust particles dance in the cold winter sun.

Mr. Shim speaks. Jungmin translates. "I have many Korean family members from America come looking for information on relatives."

I can tell Mr. Shim doesn't take us seriously, even with the phalanx of names and credentials. We are just two girls to him. Two girls without husbands dressed in their long wool skirts and high-heeled boots.

We give Mr. Shim a brief rundown of the path of our search for my grandfather's records. Dead ends at the National Archive; at the Governmental Records Office, where the archivist said that all the documents from 1928 were destroyed in a fire; at Bae Jae High School; and at Independence Hall, where Professor Shin's assistant had originally uncovered my grandfather's prison photograph.

Mr. Shim nods. "Records are difficult to find in Korea."

I ask where he has acquired his information.

His eyes shift, and he says nothing for a couple of seconds. Then he mumbles something about a contact at the Seoul Municipal Court.

"I have what you want," he finally stammers.

He straightens his spine to appear taller. The stiff collar of his white dress shirt gapes, exposing the folds of his chicken neck. The lapels of his polyester-blend suit shimmer from too many pressings.

"It will cost you. Seven hundred thousand Won. Cash."

I quickly do the math in my head. According to the exchange rate, which I had glanced at in the pages of *The Korea Herald* on the subway earlier that morning, 700,000 Won equals approximately $600.

I am taken aback by the price. I don't know where I can come up with so much money before I leave.

"Can we take a look at the documents?" I ask in a feeble voice.

"They are right here," he answers and pats a stack of seven bound volumes on his desk. On the spines of each, the name "Lee Hyun Sang" in Korean characters is stamped in gold. Lee Hyun Sang, the subject of Professor Yun's article, the most famous of my grandfather's band of student revolutionaries.

I ask if I can purchase the volume or volumes that contain information on my grandfather, rather than buying the entire set.

Mr. Shim shakes his head. "They come as a whole."

Jungmin looks at me with her eyebrows raised above her wire rims. What should we do now? she silently asks.

"Can we thumb through the books to make sure my grandfather's records are in there?"

Again, a shake of the head no. "You need to pay me first." He pauses. "You can't read the documents anyway since they are written in classical Japanese."

He has us there.

I tell Jungmin to explain that we need to come back since I don't have that much money on me. Please make an appointment for a week from now.

We will need reinforcements.

WE RETURN WITH OESAMCHUN IN tow. If anyone can butter up the so-called "private publisher" and sniff out a ruse, it's my favorite uncle. He can pretend to be friends with anyone, after decades of honing his skills as a diplomat. He can also read classical Japanese.

My father fronts the money. "If the volumes are what Mr. Shim says they are, then the $600 will be well worth it. We can donate the books to a library later," he suggests. "They are important historical documents and should be in an archive somewhere."

I brief Oesamchun over the phone. First, I want to make sure the materials are authentic before handing over the money. There should be official Japanese government seals on each page, and the dates should correspond to my grandfather's time in prison: 1929 to 1933. There is also the question of where Mr. Shim acquired the documents. His suspicious nature makes me wonder if he has stolen them from some government depository. If these documents are what he says they are, they are an essential part of Korea's history and belong somewhere where scholars and journalists and family members can access them readily. Why is Mr. Shim selling copies of colonial-era historical documents from a dusty second-floor walkup in a remote part of Seoul?

Oesamchun and I take the subway together to the appointed stop. Jungmin, ever the loyal trooper, meets us there. After investing four months of her life to my cause, she is eager to see the harvest of our combined labor. I come prepared. I have seventy crisp 10,000 Won bills in my red leather billfold, a collapsible tote bag in which to carry the seven volumes, and a translated version of Professor Yun's article that led me to Mr. Shim's office in the first place.

"I've never been to this part of Seoul before," Oesamchun says when we emerge from below. "We're close to the North Korean border, you know."

I nod. I can feel it. Desolation seems to have seeped over the border to this deserted part of the city.

MR. SHIM TAKES A STEP back at the sight of the three of us on his doorstep, which has been cleared of boxes since the week before. Oesamchun emanates charm and command, and Mr. Shim responds with immediate courtesy and deference. A deep bow, a big smile that shows off his yellowing teeth, the allowance of a wide berth for his new visitor. A total about-face from his demeanor the week before.

Oesamchun cracks a joke. Mr. Shim cackles. Jungmin and I take our place on the couch. Mr. Shim invites my uncle up to his desk, where the seven volumes sit stacked in the exact place they were the week before. Jungmin pokes me in the arm with her index finger. I look over. She smiles.

Mr. Shim opens Volume Four for my uncle and stands over him while he reads. Oesamchun nods and tells me in English, "Your grandfather's police interrogation records are here. There's a couple of sessions."

I silently cheer.

Oesamchun proceeds to ask Mr. Shim in the nicest way possible how he came across these records. He must be a detective of some kind to be able to uncover such important documents. He is doing such good work in making sure the history of Korea is being saved.

Flattered, Mr. Shim puffs out his chest a little and tells his tale.

Mr. Shim has a friend at the Seoul Municipal Court who told him about stacks of official records in the basement. Stacks and stacks of paper no one had bothered to go through. Documents handwritten in Japanese that dated back to the colonial era. Some waterlogged from leaks during decades of summer monsoons. Some whose edges had been chewed off by generations of rodents. Mr. Shim got free reign of the basement one afternoon and took photographs of one page after another with his flash camera. As much as he could until his friend came back and told him to leave.

Mr. Shim didn't know what he had until the film was developed. A complete set of interrogation records of Lee Hyun Sang, the famous leader of the ppalchisan band of Communist guerillas who died fighting on Mount Jiri during the Korean War, and those of his comrades in the Chosun Haksaeng Kwahak Yonguhoe student group. Surely these documents would be of interest to scholars and historians. He printed all of the documents and had them bound into seven volumes.

"The seven hundred thousand Won barely covers the cost of film, developing, printing, and binding," he explains. "I'm not in it to make a big profit."

"Why were the records not archived?" I ask.

"No one wants to deal with them," Mr. Shim answers. No one wants to take responsibility for the information contained in records from the colonial era. It isn't a crime to be a Communist from that era anymore, but today, who wants to discover that a family member could be implicated as a collaborator with the colonizer, with the Japanese? It's a taint no one wants to acknowledge.

No one wants a witch hunt. Especially prominent families.

I HAND OVER THE STACK of crisp bills to Mr. Shim. He shoves them into his suit pocket, not bothering to count. Jungmin helps me pack the volumes into my duffle bag. I can barely lift them off the desk. Oesamchun takes one handle and tells me to take the other. Together, we lift the heavy tomes and bow together in unison to Mr. Shim.

Outside on the landing, we stop to put on our hats and gloves. Jungmin gives me a high five. "We did it!" she says with a wide grin. "Yes, we did," I answer. "It was a group effort."

I want to skip to the subway, but the books are too heavy. The weight of history still weighs me down.

DEFIANCE

J apanese police investigator Araki is new at the job. New to the West
Gate Police Station. New to Seoul. New to Korea. He is nervous.
Much more nervous than the prisoner he is about to question who
sits on the wooden chair in front of him. The prisoner who has been
arrested on September 19, 1928, for breaking the Law of Maintaining
Public Order, the National Security Law, and the Publication Law of
Imperial Japan. The prisoner who has no expression—his wide mouth is
closed in a horizontal line.

Luckily, Araki's superiors have given him a list of questions to ask. All
he needs to do is wait for the answers.

Araki wipes off the sweat gathering in the space between his nose and
the top of his waxed mustache, the mustache that took him almost a year
to grow. He's trying not to appear nervous in front of the prisoner and the
scribe, both Koreans, but he fears he is not succeeding.

WHAT IS YOUR NAME? HE asks.

Lee Chul Ha, the prisoner answers.

How old are you?

Nineteen.

Just three years younger than me, Araki thinks. What is your current
address?

5 Whachung-jung, Seoul.

Permanent address?

394 Shinki-ri, Juwoe-myon, Kongju-kun, Choongnam-do.

Tell me about your family and family's living standard.

My family includes my father, Kun Sung; my mother, Hahn Si; grandmother, Oh Byung Kun; wife, Min Kum Soon. Younger brothers, Jung Ha and Kwan Ha, and younger sister, Ha Soon. The family consists of eight persons including myself. We have income from farmland and my father's operation of a ceramic store. We are in the middle class.

What is your occupation?

I'm a student.

Where?

I'm a fourth year student at Joongdong High School in Seoul. Before that I was at Namdaemun Commerce School. That was the first school I attended when I moved to Seoul in April 1927.

Where did you go to school before coming to Seoul?

I completed three years at Kongju Secondary School. Before that I was at Kongju Public Elementary School.

Why did you move around schools so much? Araki is straying from his script, but he is genuinely curious, even though he's been instructed not to be.

For the first time the prisoner looks him in the eye. For the first time, the prisoner looks alive.

I was expelled from Kongju Secondary School for staging a protest after the Japanese emperor died. A group of us wore Korean mourning clothes instead of the black armband the principal told us to wear. As punishment, I was beaten in front of the entire student body since I was the instigator. Afterward, I moved to Seoul to finish high school.

Araki is surprised. This young man from the countryside is resilient. He didn't stop his activities after being publicly humiliated.

Please state your position on the charges against you.

When I first came to Seoul in 1927, I looked up Mr. Kim Pok Chin, who originally came from the same region as me. I wanted to get to know him because I agreed with his views expressed in a newspaper article in the Dong-A Ilbo regarding a theory of the arts. I first visited him at his residence. We talked about the arts, but I did not know that he was a member of the Communist Party at that time. Last April I ran into him in front of a bookstore on the way to school. He told me that the Communist Party was being organized in Seoul. He bluntly asked, as though he was ordering, for me to join. I reluctantly agreed because I respected him. He said that since I was a student that I should participate in the Chosun Haksaeng Kwahak Yonguhoe (CHKYH), and I would get directives through the executive director.

What kind of organization is the Communist Party?

It is an organization to promote Communist ideology. It denounces private ownership of property and tries to reform the present economic system to establish a community state.

Have you carried out any activities following the directives of the party through the executive officer of the CHKYH?

I was directed to organize reading clubs in every school and to distribute leaflets. I was also asked to assess the status of "scientific studies" at several schools. I understood that the activities of the group would be linked to the Communist Party's objectives. The student movement intends to protest schoolteachers' class-oriented views, as well as oppression and tyranny, through school boycotts and other means.

How did you distribute the leaflets?

In May I received thirty-five copies of the so-called "illegal" leaflets regarding a school boycott at the Seoul Girls' Commerce School, sent by the Chosun Youth Federation in Tokyo. I also received thirty-two copies of another leaflet regarding another school boycott that were sent from another group of organizations in Tokyo. I received leaflets two other times to distribute to various high schools. One time, my landlord, Min Kang, found a stack of leaflets under my desk and burned them, so I could not distribute those.

Did you know that these leaflets are prohibited to be published and distributed by law?

Of course I knew.

At this point Araki hands the suspect a leaflet marked Exhibit #1 that was confiscated from the CHKYH office.

Is this the leaflet you distributed?

Yes, that's the one.

End of questions. The suspect has confessed to distributing the offending leaflet. Araki and the prisoner wait for the scribe to finish. His penmanship is exemplary, Araki thinks to himself. Much better than his own, and the scribe isn't even Japanese.

The scribe finishes and gives the form to Araki to look over. Araki gives it a passing glance, hopefully long enough that the scribe and prisoner think he has read it. He hands it to the prisoner to sign.

Araki watches the suspect read—every sentence it seems, for he squints his eyes in concentration and it takes him a couple of minutes to finish. The prisoner is careful. Focused. An intellectual. Who understands what he did and knows the consequences of his actions.

He is unafraid.

OFFERING

I fly back home to Houston for Christmas. My father spends a week translating my grandfather's interrogation records with my mother's help, since she better remembers the Japanese they were forced to learn as children. Photocopies of photographs of handwritten pages the private publisher had painstakingly gathered into a whole. Looping classical Japanese characters originally rendered in India ink and brush by a court scribe. A Korean, not a Japanese scribe, as evidenced by the name at the end of the documents.

I sprawl on my childhood bed with the rainbow sheets and the pink slippery satin quilt Halmoni brought from Korea in the 1970s. I sleep twenty-two hours the first night and day and night, until Mom wakes me, afraid that something might be wrong. *Is she unconscious or, God forbid, did she die in her sleep?* She gently shakes my elbow.

"Juhae, Juhae, come eat."

I groan and turn over. Then she squeezes the tender skin on the underside of my upper arm. Hard.

"I made your favorite. Tteokguk soup."

THE FIRST WEEK HOME I am in zombie mode. Sleepwalking, almost, for time has turned around. Houston is thirteen hours behind Seoul, and jet lag is always worse when you go against the rotation of the earth. Going against time is unnatural.

When I was a kid in Alief, Dad led me into the darkened hallway that connected our bedrooms with a flashlight in hand. He asked me to turn our McNally globe slowly to illuminate the state of Texas.

"Look," he said. "When the sun is shining in Houston, it's dark in Korea. When we are awake here, Halmoni is asleep in Seoul."

These after-dinner lessons occurred on a nightly basis when I was a child, in the years before I hit puberty. After that I didn't care to learn much of anything from my father.

REENTRY INTO MY FORMER LIFE proves difficult. I sit in front of the television. If jet lag isn't disorientating enough, CNN attempts to dissect a botched presidential election. Chads, broken voting machines, a recount in Florida, all the way to a Supreme Court decision.

"What the hell happened while I was gone?" I half yell at the TV. Bubba's president and there's nothing we can do about it, even though Gore won the popular vote.

I drink lots of water. I ask my mother not to make Korean food. "How about spaghetti and meatballs?" I call my friends in Boston. Buy a plane ticket back. I need to start my life again.

My father scurries down the stairs from his office. He is excited. He is smiling. He's the outgoing Dad that has emerged since discovering who his father was in 1992. Not the Dad I grew up with.

Look, your grandfather devised a secret code for communicating with his comrades. It's based on assigning numbers to the letters of the Korean alphabet. Your grandfather assigned the numbers one through ten to the ten vowels of the Korean alphabet. One through nine with a superscript dot assigned to consonants. Double digits assigned to the four heavy consonants. He even gave an example to the interrogator of how his own name would be coded. Lee Chul Ha would be 4'108'9'34'9'1.

Dad shows me the chart he has made with the Korean vowels and consonants and the numbers assigned. I nod, not quite comprehending. Korean characters have reverted back to chicken scratch. Did I already forget the language I became reacquainted with for the past four months? Did the blocky characters dissolve in my brain over the Pacific Ocean?

I am in the U.S. now. Maybe that's why I can't read Korean anymore.

But the fact that my grandfather devised a secret code for the transmission of "sensitive" communication between his comrades—it's something out of a spy novel or a James Bond movie or even the Encyclopedia Brown series I loved so much as a kid. Didn't he crack cryptograms in some of the stories? Dad's explanation of the secret code adds a scene to the sweeping movie of my grandfather's life that plays in a loop in my mind.

Under low lamplight, the handsome teenage revolutionary transcribes furtive missives from the Chosun Youth Federation in Tokyo with the code he devised. His fine hand never once touches the paper, only the tip of the ink brush, which is the technique he was taught to render Chinese characters as a child from his father back in Kongju. The brush dances over the paper. Teenage Grandpa gently blows on the ink to help it dry. He folds the message carefully into even rectangles and inserts it into an envelope. He hands the envelope to his comrade for delivery to other members of the secret organization under the cover of darkness.

ACCORDING TO MY FATHER, THE seven volumes I brought back from Korea contain the chronology of investigation by the Japanese colonial police into the Kiyuk Party, a secret student organization under the auspices of the Korean Communist Party, which was founded in Seoul in 1925 and recognized by the Comintern in the Soviet Union. In one of my grandfather's transcribed interrogations, he explained that Kiyuk, which is the first character in the Korean alphabet, was used to symbolize the first secret student organization and was not used to represent the first letter of "Communism" in Korean, as the interrogator implied. My grandfather was one of eighteen high school and college students arrested after a police sweep of the organization's central office in Seoul on September 13, 1928.

In the seven volumes, Dad found the following documents that concerned my grandfather: four interrogation sessions, one assessment of the prisoner's behavior, and one observational report by the prison warden before his trial in 1930. All neatly translated by my mother and printed out in Microsoft Word. His first interrogation took place at the West Gate Police Station on

教育ノ程度並ニ本人ノ經歴	老衰者又ハ癈疾者ナルトキハ扶養者ノ氏名住居	改悛見込ノ有無	備考
金海公立普通學校ニ入リ一年位ニテ中途退學撤立高等普通學校二年編入翌ヘ年落第本年三年ニ進級シタルモノナリ	該當者ニアラズ	改悛ノ見込ヒナシ	本名ハ叔父姜光泉モ共立主義者ニシテ朝鮮共産黨員タリ本名モ之ニ倣ヒ思想悪化シ來リタルモノニテ排日思想濃厚ナルモノ 本調書ハ所轄金海及東大門両警察署及吉署ニ於テ調査シタル所ヲ綜合作製シタルモノナリ

右之通ニ候也

昭和三年十月　　日

京城西大門警察署

司法警察官事務取扱

道巡査　荒木菊雄

被疑者素行調書

様式第四十三號

資産並収入ノ状況	家庭並生活ノ状況	素行並對人ニスル世評	性質	本籍住居職業氏名年齢
本人ノ資産ナク父及祖父ノ資産トシテ（歯不動産）畑・建物約一万五千円位ヲ有スルモノ年穀ノ収入ニ三百石位アル外ナシ	父安孝駒外十五名ノ家族ニシテ職業ヲ有スルモノハ父ガ靴下製造ヲ為ス外ナシ年收穀約三百石マリニシテ以テ生活シ居ルモノニテ中流ノ生活ヲ為レ居レリ	素行普通ナルモ傲慢ニシテ世評良シカラズ	性陰險傲慢且ッ頑固ニシテ意志強固ナリ	本籍　慶尚南道金海郡下界面蟻田里二七二番地　住所　京城府崇二洞二八　職業　學生　安三遠　明治四十一年二月七日生

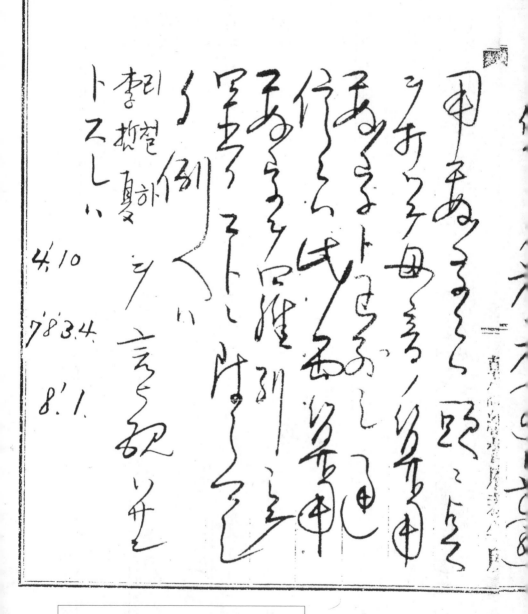

Copy of my grandfather's prison record with the
secret code he and his comrades devised, 1928

ㅏ ㅑ ㅓ ㅕ ㅗ ㅛ ㅜ ㅠ ㅡ ㅣ
1, 2, 3, 4, 5, 6, 7, 8, 9, 10.

ㄱ ㄴ ㄷ ㄹ ㅁ ㅂ ㅅ ㅈ ㅊ
1, 2, 3, 4, 5, 6, 7, 8, 9

September 18, a few days after he was arrested, by a criminal investigator named Araki. My grandfather described how he became involved in the student movement through his association with Kim Pok Chin, a pioneering Korean sculptor who studied art in Japan and worked in a representational style. Kim was also a leader in the KAPF (Korea Artista Proleta Federatio, Esperanto for Korea Federation of Proletarian Art), the cultural wing of the Korean Communist Party, and wrote art criticism and reviews for leftist publications in which he espoused a theory of "art for life" that interested my grandfather. The colonial police arrested Kim three weeks before my grandfather as part of their regular sweeps of Korean Communist Party members.

The behavior assessment report included a summary of my grandfather's character, where he was described as bright, mild-mannered, studious, and known to be well-behaved—all descriptors that befit my father. The criminal investigators interviewed his high school teachers, who spoke highly of his aptitude in the sciences, especially biology. The assessment also cited a report from the Kongju police, who noted that his father cared about him deeply and would work to "straighten out his son's bad behavior."

The documents I found deepened my father's and my understanding of who my grandfather was. He wasn't the naïve boy from the countryside who got caught up in a movement he didn't understand. He sought out one of the leaders of the movement, Kim Pok Chin, because he was interested in his theory for the arts, which he read about in a local newspaper. He joined a secret student organization, the Chosun Haksaeng Kwahak Yonguhoe, and soon became an officer in the organization. He distributed leaflets for school boycotts and organized reading clubs at various high schools around Seoul. In the interrogations, he concisely described the tenets of Communism. He received a four-year prison sentence for his involvement in the organization of a boycott of Bae Jae High School, an elite boys' high school where the Korean Communist Party recruited many of its members. A student leaked the plan for the boycott to school authorities, who in turn informed the colonial police.

The last report, written by the prison warden, lists the books my grandfather read in his cell, in solitary confinement:

- Fabre's *Social Life in the Insect World*, Volumes 1 to 4
- Introduction to philosophy, 2 books
- Japanese literature series, 3 books
- Lectures on political economy
- Understanding the views of materialistic history
- Biography of Abraham Lincoln
- Lectures on algebra
- Korean dictionary

HE WAS WELL-READ, MY GRANDFATHER. Science, philosophy, literature, economics, history, math. Thank you, Japanese prison administrators, for keeping such detailed records on what he read, for being exemplary record keepers.

The list includes some of the books my father remembers seeing hidden in Halmoni's dresser as a boy. The prison seal clearly stamped on each one's frontispiece. The court documents mailed to the family after my grandfather's release from prison. Perhaps these documents were the typed-up version of the freehand summary report contained in the seven volumes I procured—with additional information concerning sentencing. The oversized envelope with the colorful Japanese stamps, the thin onionskin paper pages the court document was printed upon. My father can still see these items in his head and hear the crinkly sound the pages made as he thumbed through them in secret as a child, when Halmoni left the house.

The material evidence of his father's existence, hidden in his mother's dresser.

IT WAS HALMONI'S INTENTION TO destroy the court documents in the kitchen fire before the North Koreans invaded their hometown in the beginning days of the Korean War. In the process she threw in all the books with words like revolution, communism, socialism, nationalism— the words that would put her family square into one camp of the two opposing camps of war. She didn't understand what these words meant, but she knew they were dangerous. Dangerous in a conflict that could go either way. When the North Koreans pushed the South Korean army all the way down to the bottom of the country, when the North Koreans looked like they won control of the peninsula, her late husband's papers and books could prove valuable—they would identify him as a Communist, as someone who might have supported the North Korean cause if he had lived long enough. After General MacArthur landed in Incheon and surprised the North Koreans, the conflict looked as though it would go the other way. Then the papers could implicate the family as that of an enemy.

That's why she destroyed the material evidence of her husband's beliefs. She was not interested in the content. She could not divine the outcome of the war. Her job was to ensure survival. Of herself. Of her children.

III

THIRD INTERVIEW

WITH HALMONI

My grandfather, Lee Chul Ha, after he
was released from prison, ca. 1933

HATCHERY

I t's March 1999, and Halmoni tells Dad that she will accompany us to the National Cemetery so she can see her husband's grave for the first time—since I am visiting, since I am writing a book about him. She means to be supportive, she really does. Dad is elated, his emotions bubbling through the barricade of accumulated facts and mathematical certainty he has built up throughout a lifetime. He's excited, smiling, like the carefree kid he never got to be. Halmoni changes her mind.

"I have too much to do at church," she says.

We are all dressed and ready to go.

Dad's face falls. Halmoni refuses to look at him.

"You go without me. I'll see you tonight when you get home." She walks into her bedroom and shuts the door.

THE NATIONAL CEMETERY IS DESERTED on a weekday afternoon. No buses of schoolchildren or families gathering for ancestor worship ceremonies. We stop at the visitor's kiosk at the entrance and buy some white daisies to place at the grave. Ajeossi drives us up the hill to the back of the cemetery, past the giant stone turtle sculpture and the socialist realist rendition of revolutionaries bursting forth into the heavens, hands raised in fists, some carrying rifles.

My grandfather occupies a prime corner location—at the intersection of the main walkway and the first tier of Patriots. He is easy to find.

Mom extracts a folded piece of tracing paper and a charcoal pencil from her tote bag. I had asked her to make a rubbing of the poem etched into the back of the base of the obelisk, the poem my father's friend wrote for the reburial ceremony. Dad stands in his customary stance—head bowed forward, hands propping up his back and pushing forth the widest part of his thickening belly. He's thinking, I know, as I soak up the view of the evenly spaced grave sites creeping up the hill, so many more than when I last visited four years ago.

I take pictures with my pocket Canon. Mom kneels in her floppy sun hat and oversized long-sleeved shirt, carefully rubbing the circles and lines of the hangul characters. Dad squats beside her, holding the edges of the paper to the base of the marker.

My smiling parents stand in front of the gravestone, Dad's arm around Mom's shoulder. They look happy, like they are on vacation. I snap a picture.

Mom asks me to pose with Dad next to the tall marker. He's sporting a wide-toothed grin. My father is proud of me, I can tell. Proud I have finally taken an interest in the past.

WE RETURN TO SEOUL, AND the next morning I sit down with Halmoni for our last interview session before I return to New York. Her initial reluctance has waned, thank God. She plants herself on her pillow, her knobby knees hidden underneath a full gray skirt. She nods in her stern way, and I turn on my tape recorder.

"Tell me about your life after Grandpa returned home from prison."

> *Your grandfather returned home to Kongju to recuperate from pleurisy, so he could try to get well. During his recovery, someone suggested he eat dogmeat to gain strength. The family prepared it for him, but he didn't like it. He was sick in bed for months, it seemed. He was never really healthy after that. Coughing all the time. At the end, he was coughing up blood.*
>
> *He was so weak and was supposed to take it easy, but he still kept busy. Too busy. His family worried about him. He reconnected with his old friends in Seoul and hid his books and papers in my dresser so his father wouldn't find them. He even burned letters from Seoul in the outhouse after he read them.*

*While we were still in Kongju, I asked your grandfather why he
never talked about his time in prison. He said, "Why would I want
to talk about such a painful thing?"*

I make a mental note of the similarity of responses—of the words
Halmoni attributed to her long-dead husband and her initial question
when I began the interview process with her.

We don't talk about painful things in our family. We swallow them
whole and let them fester for generations. It's a lesson I learned as a child
without even knowing it. Swallow the fear, the terror, the pain—and hope
that it is gone forever. Push it down until you can't feel it anymore. That's
what Halmoni did to survive, and my father.

Halmoni stops to sip her tea. It's time for a new subject.

I move on.

"Why did you and Grandpa decide to move to Chongju and set up the
chicken hatchery?"

*Your grandfather came up with the idea to start a chicken hatchery.
My father promised to finance it but only if it was located near him
in Chongju—so he could oversee the project. My father even built
the structure for the hatchery, since he was in construction. Your
grandfather did a lot of work to plan for it. He ordered thousands
of baby chicks from Japan. He bought the latest hatching machinery
and researched modern farming methods. He wanted to set up the
most modern chicken hatchery in Korea.*

*We moved to Chongju when your father was three months old.
When we got there, the living quarters weren't quite finished, so
we rented a house nearby. It was new, too. So new the ondol floors
were still wet. The chicks arrived soon after, and your grandfather
kept busy raising them and overseeing the building of our house. He
made a tin sign for the hatchery and painted it himself. It looked
like a weathervane with a hen on top. He put it on the roof.*

*Your grandfather was a good businessman. He was smart. He
developed a system to deliver fresh eggs every morning to restau-*

rants in the area. The business did very well. He brought in his brother, the sickly one, to manage the day-to-day supervision of the chicken farm once everything got running.

After that he began to spend more and more time at the newspaper. He managed the provincial branch of the JoongAng Ilbo. I think Samsung publishes it today. He also wrote articles, mostly on sports. He kept a scrapbook of all the articles he wrote. He wasn't that interested in the details of what was going on at the hatchery after he began working at the newspaper. Or spending that much time with the children, for your uncle Eun Suk had been born by then.

But he insisted on sleeping with your father at night on the porch. He didn't like sleeping on the warm ondol floor inside. He said that he felt like he was suffocating inside lying on the ondol. He would wrap your father up in the other half of the nice wool blanket, the one I delivered to him in prison, and put his arm around him to sleep. Your father was such a good baby and never cried.

While we were living in Chongju, your grandfather confessed that he hadn't been interested in getting married. His parents made him do it. He was more interested in politics, in taking part in the nationalist movement.

Halmoni excuses herself. It's time to stop.

I THINK ABOUT HOW MARRIAGE was foisted upon my grandparents as teenagers, as children. Marriage before high school for my grandfather, marriage in lieu of an education for Halmoni. Not that they had any say. And how Halmoni didn't really even get to know my grandfather until she visited him in prison. I think about my cousin's ill-fated, short-lived union, "brokered" by two sets of parents in the aftermath of the IMF crisis in 1997. I think about how I have escaped the tradition of brokered marriages, having been raised in the United States, how I always refused my mother's gentle offers to set up "meetings" with a future "very special male friend" of Korean descent.

"Mom, Korean guys won't like me. I don't clean. I barely cook. I don't know how to make kimchi. I'm stubborn. I hate being told what to do. I'd make a horrible Korean wife."

Left to my own devices, I choose educated white guys—most who need some mothering, some with alcohol issues, all who love music. None who have worked out for the long run. Like Ciaran.

But I'm free. At least I'm free. Of patriarchal Korean culture. Of my parents' expectations. Of my own bad choices.

I GIVE THE REST OF my questions and my tape recorder to Mom so she can continue the interviews with Halmoni after I leave. We didn't get to the rest of Halmoni's life, the almost seventy years she lived without my grandfather—through the end of colonialism, during the Korean War or afterward, when she worked at an orphanage and became a deacon at her church in Seoul.

I tell Halmoni I will listen to what we have so far and interview her further when I return the next fall, after my fellowship in Boston is over.

I have no idea that this will be the last time I see her.

IN THE MOOD FOR LOVE

It's October 2000 and I decide to take a break—a break from family history, the atrocities of the Japanese occupation, email correspondence with the country's leading colonial history professors, my adopted family on my better-late-than-never semester abroad. I finagle a press pass from my former employer with my friend Bromley's help. Thank goodness for Bromley, whose southern English accent I used to ape, in a loving way, during our lunches together in *The Nation*'s break area.

Three days off, a long weekend to myself, away from Seoul, down the peninsula, to see my favorite director. Three whole days of watching movies. Yet-to-be-released movies. My idea of heaven.

Bromley emails me links to all the buzz of the new film festival. Tony Leung, the Bogart of Hong Kong cinema. Maggie Cheung, the Chinese Irma Vep. And the master of melancholy himself, Wong Kar-wai.

I get up early to catch the train to Pusan. To my surprise, both Hansem and Ajuma have risen early for my departure. In her simplest Korean, Ajuma explains that Hansem will accompany me to the station to make sure I get on the right train.

"An-ney-yo," I answer, shaking my head. "Ken-cha-ney-yo."

I switch to English since my head is too foggy to conjure up a foreign language at 6:00 a.m.

"I'm fine. I can go by myself. I used to live in New York, remember?" And I'm a grown woman, I think to myself.

Ajuma stares at me. Hansem translates.

Ajuma states her decree in English: "No, Hansem go."

MY MOONFACED SECOND COUSIN FALLS asleep on the subway ride to the train station. I wake her when we arrive at the appointed stop. Hansem hasn't been awake before noon since I arrived two months before. She is up long after I fall asleep to her clicks on the keyboard, since the home computer is located outside my bedroom door on the second-floor landing. She's chatting with her brother, I know. In Kyun is fourteen hours back in time and half a world away in my father's study in Houston.

I receive verbal missives about my other second cousin from my mother, who isn't used to having her nest filled.

"In Kyun drinks the orange juice out of the carton. Gallons of it."

"In Kyun stays up late on the computer and your father has to wake him up every morning so he can ride with him to school."

"In Kyun is naemse because he doesn't shower enough, which makes his skin break out. He has lots of pimples."

Mom had instated the shower-before-you-sleep rule early on in her marriage to my father. Her nose is keen, even more so after having children, and she cannot fall asleep if it is assaulted by funk of any kind.

WE WALK UP FROM THE subway to Seoul Station, and poor Hansem buys a round-trip, nonstop ticket with the money I hand her. I let her guide me to the correct track, even though I know exactly where it is, so that she feels like she has achieved her early morning assignment and can go home and report her success to Ajuma.

I arrive in Pusan at ten thirty and take the subway to the festival site. I emerge from below to balmy air with a sting of salt. The ocean is nearby.

I walk into the first yeogwan I can find. I ring the bell for service, and a disheveled man in a white wifebeater lumbers to the desk. I can see the inside of his bedroom behind the desk as he makes his way out into the light. KBS news, a woman in a spaghetti-strapped satin nightgown whose back is turned toward the door, a tangle of black hair on top.

"Two nights," I say.

"Pay up front, I give you good deal," he answers.

"Sold."

Key in hand, I walk up the steps to the third floor. The hallways are clean. There's a close to life-sized color photo of a couple kissing on the wall.

Cheesy love hotel.

I dump my bag and hurry to the multiplex in the square to catch the first screening of *In the Mood for Love.*

CHINESE RED BROCADE WITH GOLD stitching, tiny yellow song-birds against midnight blue, emerald-green ginkgo leaves showering a field of silver—a parade of gorgeous fabric expertly tailored to Maggie Cheung's lithe frame as she descends the dank stairs to the man selling steaming noodles at the bottom of a crowded boulevard. A beacon amid the steam, her face dewy from the South Asian humidity. Tony in his tailored gray sharkskin two-piece is waiting.

They both are spouseless, live at the same boarding house, and share a fondness for hot noodles on a summer night. How many times does Maggie descend the steps in the film? Four, five, always in slow motion, always dressed in a different silk cheongsam, so formfitting that she dare not sit.

I watch the movie three times—twice in a dark theater and once outside on a big screen. The ending confuses me. Tony at Angkor Wat, a silent scream through a round hole in the wall. Maggie in a new apartment, her spouse not present still, but a toddler boy at her side looking up at his mother with wide, adoring eyes.

He's Tony's son, I decide.

Or maybe she just pretends he is.

In person, Tony is tiny and perfect in his white dinner jacket and pressed dark jeans. Full lips, mournful eyes, he might be the most beautiful man I have ever seen, and I'm not even attracted to Asian men, since the only Asian men I encountered until I was an adult were members of my own family or my father's friends.

"Toe-nee, Toe-nee," scream the girls behind the thick yellow rope.

There are hundreds of them, red-faced and ecstatic, as I make my way to the press section at the front. I spot my Korean film source Scott in his flip-flops and tattered blazer. He convinced me to attend the festival when we met at a restaurant a couple of weeks before. I had contacted him the previous summer for an article I was writing on censorship in Korean cinema, since he's the unofficial, English-speaking expert on the subject.

I meet the whole of Korean cinephilia at the press party after the screening. The film critic from Toronto with the shiny head who tells me scores of Korean high school kids mobbed him that afternoon, thinking he was Michael Jordan. The shifty-eyed Asian film fanatic from San Francisco who spends the evening plotting how to ask out the best player of a Thai transgender volleyball team, the star of my second-favorite film at the festival. The earnest young film production assistant who recommends recent Korean films concerning the colonial period that might help me with my book.

I quickly befriend the Canadian film critic's publicist girlfriend and make a date with her for the following morning to explore a jjimjilbang super spa complex with different scented stations of fir and sandalwood. She opts for the full body scrub and wash. I know better, remembering the sandpaper-textured cloth my mother scrubbed me with when I was little to slough off all of the tdae, the dead skin. The result: raw pink skin and tears of pain.

I converse the longest with the Dutch Korean festival organizer who asks for my business card, which I don't have because I'm a free agent now and am not tied to an organization. I give her my email address. She's interested in my story. I'm interested in hers. She's a Korean orphan who was adopted by a Dutch couple in the late 1970s. She asks where I am staying and suggests I stay at a hotel after I tell her.

"You shouldn't stay in a yeogwan."

I leave the party warm and happy. I walk past three drunk men eating spicy tteokbokki rice cakes at the food cart at the end of the square. After midnight, deserted streets, ocean breeze ruffling my hair. I turn the corner and an insistent bass beat rolls through my insides. Smoking youngsters wearing tight black pants gather in front of a neon sign. DIS-KO.

The "dis-ko" is located directly underneath my room for the next two nights.

"Shit," I say to myself.

I climb the narrow stairway next to the pulsing den. The lumbering proprietor is nowhere to be seen. I know he wouldn't give me a refund anyway, that's why he asked for two nights up front. I consider gathering my bags and jumping ship. The logistics of finding a cab and figuring out a new hotel stops me. Plus, I already spent most of my money on the room. I curse some more as I climb another narrow stairway to my room. The walls shake.

I take a shower to drown out the noise. My mood lifts after I realize that if I were ten years younger, I'd be down at the Disko myself, dancing my ass off. I fall asleep in my towel. When I awake at 4:30 a.m., the pulsing has stopped.

IN THE MOVIE, MAGGIE'S TODDLER son places his small paw in his mother's outstretched porcelain hand. The bowl-headed boy is dressed in linen short overalls. Maggie has traded in her cheongsams for a subdued skirt and jacket, an outfit more befitting a mother. Her son looks up at her with eyes full of love. His whole being is transmitted with his gaze. She returns his look and smiles knowingly. They are living in a new apartment, mother and son, one more spacious and well-appointed than Maggie's room in the boarding house. As usual, Maggie's spouse is nowhere to be seen. His absence doesn't matter anymore. She has her son, and that is enough.

I realize, tucked two-thirds of the way up a mostly empty theater, scrunched deep down into my plush seat, that I have sat through this movie three times for that one scene.

I yearn for the look on the boy's face. I want it imprinted on my brain.

I HAVE BEEN TOO BUSY since I arrived in Korea, too immersed in my quest, to revisit the feeling that once caused me to lunge after baby carriages on Haight Street. Maggie and her son at the end of *In the Mood for Love* cause it to stir once more.

I feel so removed from the lives of mothers here and only glimpse at their existence while on the way somewhere else. I see them walking the streets with their babies on their backs on my late morning rushes to the bus. More well-heeled ones in the basement of the Lotte department store scavenging for clearance items while their toddlers run up and down the aisles. They are all younger than me, I know that for sure. I am past the breeding age here.

I know I want a baby, a child of my own. The feeling has preoccupied me the entire year I spent in Boston.

But how?

A freelance journalist in her midthirties with a nomadic lifestyle and no steady income. No home. No viable romantic prospects. No real plan except to write a book about her search for information on her grandfather and a half-baked intention to return to San Francisco since there seems to be a second gold rush happening there, according to friends, and a well-paying job might be easy to come by.

Then there is the Question—from relatives, family friends, acquaintances, even complete strangers.

"Why aren't you married?"

Which really means, "What's wrong with you?"

I try out different answers, depending on my mood.

In the U.S., women get married later.

I haven't found the right guy yet.

I'm still looking.

And finally, the real answer.

I don't want to be married.

AND THAT ANSWER IS TRUEST, if I am feeling realistic. I don't want to be married to any of my ex-boyfriends. Or any of my future ex-boyfriends. My taste in men is questionable. I have a predilection for the unsuitable.

"You like trouble," more than one girlfriend has said.

HERO

It's October 2000. Maybe we have packed too much into one day. The two-and-a-half-hour drive down from Seoul in an autumn haze that never quite morphs into rain. A quick stop in the mountains on the western edge of Taejon to visit my grandparents' graves at the National Cemetery. We linger long enough to see the green grass sprinkled over Halmoni's side of the burial mound to match that of her husband's. "Kum Soon Min" has been incised next to "Lee Chul Ha" on the pointed obelisk grave marker. The wife buried next to her husband for the rest of eternity.

Now, our last stop in the city of Taejon to visit the only other living member of the family who knew my grandfather. Great-uncle Wan, my grandfather's cousin.

Ajeossi tells us Taejon is the home of over a million people. I had no idea this interior city was so large. Mom reminds me that it is also the ancestral home of her branch of the Lee family, before her father moved to Seoul to make his fortune in the paper business at the turn of the last century. Snaking down the mountain highway from the cemetery, we are soon ensnarled in late afternoon traffic.

Ajeossi makes his way to the center of the city where the grid of the outlying boulevards gives way to a mass of overlapping circular streets. After we pass the same 7-Eleven three times, he calls Great-uncle Wan on his hand phone to get directions.

My only other living great-uncle lives in a nondescript apartment building maybe eight stories high. Ajeossi finds easy parking outside, and I unfold myself from the cramped back seat of the faux Jeep Cherokee. The small lobby of the building smells slightly rancid, like old kimchi. A swirling, muddy pattern of mop strings decorates the cramped space like wide brushstrokes on an Abstract Expressionist canvas—my attempt to prettify the scene.

Uncle Wan greets us at his apartment door with a wide grin. He has been waiting. Even though he has attended the myriad of momentous family events in the past five years that surrounded the rehabilitation of my grandfather's reputation, as well as Halmoni's funeral three months before, I have never interacted with him.

A small, wiry man, Great-uncle Wan bears little resemblance to his cousin Choong and my father, with their wide foreheads and stillness of demeanor. The deep crevices that traverse his deeply tanned face reveal many decades of a regular smoking habit. In true elderly Korean man fashion, his baggy brown pants are cinched high above his waist like a paper bag. Hair suspiciously jet-black, like fresh shoe polish, makes me wonder if he, like the current president of Korea, dyes his hair.

Wan is a widower—his wife died years ago, and he lives alone in this tiny one-bedroom apartment in the middle of the city. Well into his eighties, he keeps busy overseeing real estate dealings with his son.

A polite bachelor, he has already laid out a low table with coffee and a few of the round rice cakes filled with sweet red beans my mother loves so much. I am not a fan. I have not inherited my mother's love of sweets.

I turn on my tape recorder and ask him what he remembers of my grandfather. He sidesteps the question entirely and waves his bony skeleton hands in the air.

> *Your grandmother is the real hero of the family, you know. She was such a strong woman, that's what I admired about her. She was more honorable and respectable than your grandpa.*

He pauses for effect. He has an agenda.

> *Your grandfather, he did something for the country, but he was just a young man when he died. His short life can't compare with Halmoni's long one. A dead person doesn't suffer. The one who suffered*

was Halmoni, not him. She's the one who raised two successful sons.
She's the one who had to survive.

Wan is excitable, Dad warned me beforehand on the phone. My father also doesn't quite trust the veracity of what he says.

Your grandmother, she was a strong woman, she knew what she
was doing. She became the head of the family, you know, after your
grandfather died, and his father died the year after. She took over
the management of the family's finances. She was the matriarch.
She's the one we went to see when we had questions about family
matters, about whether or not we should sell family land. She was
the wise one.

Uncle Wan halts his monologue just long enough to take a sip of his now-cold coffee. I pretend to take a sip of mine—why does everyone in Korea serve instant coffee instead of drip? In her decorous way, my mother veers the conversation back to the past, to Wan's childhood, to his relationship with my long-dead grandfather.

He was my cousin and a lot older than me, more than ten years, so
I didn't know him that well. I never had a one-on-one conversa-
tion with him. He was close to my father, though, and they got
along very well. Your grandfather wasn't very talkative. He was
very quiet and very, very smart. Maybe that's why your father is
so smart.
    I remember his face. Your grandfather looked almost exactly like
your uncle Eun Suk. Your father looks more like Halmoni.

Uncle Wan retells the story Choong related in Kongju, the one about how my grandfather brought Wan's father books from Seoul—the books written in Japanese whose offending pages ended up on the walls of his childhood home as insulation and almost caused his father's arrest. The only difference in their stories is that Wan clings to the childhood explanation of the event, of why the Japanese police came to search the house in the first place.

My grandmother, Kum Soon Min, ca. 1960

*In the country at that time, we didn't live that clean. The police
came to check on the family's cleanliness, since country people didn't
know how to clean during that time. That's when the police discovered the pages of the books and asked my father where he had gotten
them. He told the police that he had found them somewhere; he
couldn't remember. He didn't tell them that your grandfather sent
them to him for safekeeping.*

My mind drifts as Uncle Wan babbles on about the state of his childhood home, to unanswered emails and the *New York Times* crossword puzzle that I hadn't had the time to attempt that morning, until I hear him
mention my grandfather's chicken hatchery. The mysterious chicken hatchery in Chongju, Halmoni's hometown. How did a student revolutionary
in Seoul end up running a chicken hatchery so far from the center of the
movement? I never quite swallowed Dad's explanation of his father returning to the countryside because the business opportunity was too good to
pass up. Halmoni's father took care of all the starting costs of the operation.
He bought the land, equipment from Japan, baby chicks, coops, everything.
He just needed someone to run it. Why did my grandfather agree to do so?

*Your grandmother, your grandmother, she was the reason why your
grandfather returned.*

Wan is clearly relishing the telling of the story of how my grandfather
returned to the countryside from Seoul. He licks his lips and pauses, glad
to have my full attention again.

The story unfolds like a movie; I imagine young Halmoni transposed
in the past.

Gravestone of my grandparents, Lee Chul Ha
and Kum Soon Min, Taejon National Cemetery

SURVIVAL

I t's fall, 1933, and Halmoni is twenty-five years old. She has to put her hair up again. The thick tines of her ebony comb, a wedding gift from her mother-in-law, get stuck at chin level. She wrestles them out and picks at the snarls until the comb runs free. A straight-down-the-center part splits her skull in two perfect halves. Three tries to form a bun at the nape of her neck. She is out of practice. She hasn't worn her hair up for two-and-a-half years, since she moved to Seoul in 1931 to be closer to her husband while he served his prison sentence.

Halmoni hated coming home to Kongju, for home is her husband's family's compound, not her father's house in Chongju. She is expected by her in-laws to resume her many duties—to oversee the preparation of all the meals according to her mother-in-law's exact specifications, keep track of the servants' comings and goings, perform the mending for the entirety of an eleven-person household. Back to a life of servitude after she tasted freedom in the capital city.

She had to come home, but her husband didn't. He remains in Seoul with his comrades. He should come home, though. He's ill, coughing all the time. His face white as rice paper.

Her sister is still in Seoul, too. Studying at a university, the best women's university in the country. Married to a local Chongju boy attending the agricultural college.

But Halmoni must return to the countryside, to her husband's family.

Her husband, he is the one, the one who urged her to take classes in Seoul and get an education. He told her this on her visits to the prison. He urged her to learn to read and write Chinese characters, but what good are these skills to a wife in the country? Maybe she shouldn't have even gone to Seoul in the first place. Then she wouldn't be so devastated at returning home.

HALMONI SEES THE LETTER FIRST, since she's in charge of distributing the mail. A letter from Seoul, addressed in her husband's fine hand. Addressed to her mother-in-law.

Halmoni looks around. She is alone. The cook and maids off to market. She tucks the letter in the high waistband of her billowing skirt.

And there it stays. Through the unloading of vegetables and dried fish, through the rinsing of precious white rice grains and the addition of barley and corn kernels in the large iron pot over the kitchen fire, through the scrubbing of muslin futon covers over the porous volcanic rocks at the far end of the courtyard. Once, twice, three times, then hung up to dry in the October sun.

The rosewood table in the main dining room is set for the men. A smaller one in the adjoining alcove for the ladies. A rickety pine bench in the kitchen for Halmoni and the servants. They eat after everyone else in the household.

Halmoni waits until all the servants leave the kitchen and go off to bed. She boils water in the brass teakettle. A last cup of boricha before heading back to her room. It's ten o'clock at night.

She fishes the letter from her skirt. Slightly damp from her body's heat, but not warm enough to melt away the adhesive that keeps it closed. Halmoni holds the envelope up to the steam of the kettle.

Halmoni waits until she arrives safely at her room, down the hallway in the women's section of the house. Her room is located at the end of the hall, past her mother-in-law's, her grandmother-in-law's, across from the space used for ancestor worship.

She holds the letter up to the kerosene lamp on the dresser so she can read.

Her husband wishes to remain in Seoul. Wants to start a business there. Wants to start a business with money from a woman. A woman's family. A woman in Seoul whom he wants to take as a concubine.

"No," Halmoni says aloud, surprising herself.

No, I will not let this happen.

IT ISN'T QUITE A COMMON story, but common enough. Firstborn son gets married in the countryside at age fourteen or fifteen, then attends high school in the big city for a proper education. He finds another girl, an educated one, and lives his life there, leaving his first wife with his family back home, for she is their property now. They can do with her what they like. He has no use for her now.

Halmoni knows the story well, for her sister is an educated girl in Seoul who met a firstborn son from her hometown in the provinces. He was attending college in the big city, too. They got engaged and returned home to get married. They planned a big wedding, but the morning of the ceremony the Presbyterian minister got word of the groom's first marriage and refused to perform the union. A couple of weeks later, they did get married at a much smaller church, by a pastor who turned the other cheek.

HALMONI GRABS A CHANGE OF clothing and wraps it in a pink bojagi cloth. She doesn't sleep that night. She doesn't even bother to pull her futon out of the linen chest. She waits until the birds start to sing, until she hears the cook rustling in the kitchen.

She tiptoes down the hall with her bundle, out into the courtyard, and to the back of the house where the cook dumps the previous day's ashes into a hole. Halmoni asks him to tell her mother-in-law that she had to leave immediately for Chongju. There has been a family emergency; she will return the following day.

Halmoni walks to the town center where she knows she can find a ride with one of the farmers dropping off fruits and vegetables at the market.

She must see her father right away.

HER FATHER IS SURPRISED TO see her.

"Have they not been treating you well?" is his first question. The Lee clan in Kongju, who were educated folk from good yangban stock, could they be prone to violence?

Halmoni tells him the whole story. Her husband's reluctance in returning home. How she intercepted a letter from him to his mother. Halmoni hands her father the letter so he can read it for himself. She doesn't have to explain how its contents could impact her future.

Her father shakes his head.

"This is big trouble."

"It doesn't have to be," Halmoni replies.

Halmoni devised a plan while she sat awake in her room the night before. She honed the details on the ride on the mule cart to her hometown that morning.

"It doesn't have to be big trouble. You could put up the money for a business for my husband to run. It's about money, he wants money. He doesn't hate me or want to get away from me, he just wants an opportunity to start a business for himself."

Her father raises an eyebrow.

Halmoni calmly looks him in the eye. "If you do not do this, if you do not put up the money, I will be forced to kill myself."

Halmoni's father understands fully his eldest daughter's character. He knows she will do as she says.

He will front the money under one condition: her husband must set up business in Chongju, not Seoul.

"If I give him money, I need to see how he manages it. Otherwise, the money might disappear. If he does business in Seoul, he might ask for more and more, and I won't know where it is going. So he has to do business in Chongju."

HALMONI RETURNS TO KONGJU ON another mule cart. She hands the now slightly crumpled letter to her mother-in-law and doesn't bother to explain why it has already been opened.

"Please write your son and ask him to return to Kongju as soon as possible," she says.

Her mother-in-law does as she is told, and a couple of days later, Halmoni's husband returns. He slaps the backs of his brothers, bows to his mother and father, then asks why he has been summoned home.

His mother answers, "Go ask your wife."

He finds his wife, whom he barely knows, under a pear tree in the courtyard where she has been waiting.

She asks if it is true he plans to take a concubine.

He answers, it's just for money.

She says the concubine isn't the only one with money.

MOURNING ROOM

I get the call while driving down Mass Ave. with Sabina and her family in my roommate's Saturn. On our way back from a goodbye lunch at a Greek restaurant in Boston. My adopted family for the year is headed out on a red-eye that night to Switzerland, then a connecting flight to Athens, and then the ferry to the island of Sifnos for the rest of the summer of 2000. We are on our way to the drugstore to pick up some sunscreen. Sabina in back with three-year-old Nick, who can already recite the pantheon of Greek gods.

It's Dad on my cell phone.

"Juhae," he says. "She's gone. Halmoni is gone."

That's all he needs to say.

I CAN'T SPEAK, SO I drive with tears falling. Past the CITY OF ARLINGTON sign etched in fine oak. On the left, the bike path that I took each day to my office on the Radcliffe campus, since I don't own a car. It's my year of being sporty, a new role for me since I've never been sporty in my life. John in the seat next to me watching me cry, realizing it's my dad on the phone with bad news, then half shouting at me to pull over.

I keep driving.

Dad tells me the funeral is in three days. "Take a flight to San Francisco and pick up your brother. Then you can fly to Seoul together."

Some talk of bereavement fares. "Call me later when you talk to the airline."

I pull into the drugstore parking lot.

I get myself out of the car. John is flailing about—he's prone to histrionics. Sabina hands him their toddler and silently gives me a hug.

I still can't speak.

I DROP THEM OFF AT Logan Airport just as dusk settles. Three people and one enormous suitcase.

"I hate to leave you," Sabina says.

"I'll be okay."

I begin the long negotiations with United Airlines.

"No bereavement fares for international flights."

"Why?"

The representative doesn't know. That's just the way it is.

Calls to Ed in San Francisco. He can't pick me up at the airport. He has a rock show to attend. I can stay in the extra room in his rental near USF, though.

"It's where the cat sleeps," he informs me.

"I'm allergic to cats."

"Bring your allergy medicine."

SHUTTLE TO THE AIRPORT. LED Zeppelin on the radio. Young black guy driving tells me how he loves classic rock, but his passengers expect him to listen to rap.

I hate Boston drivers. Cutoffs and honks and swear words. Massholes everywhere. Two months in, I knew I couldn't live past the year in this cold, rude place with inadequate street signage and bad fashion.

Uneventful flight. Avi picks me up from SFO in the fog and takes me to her favorite Chinese restaurant in Potrero Hill. The flakiest of my friends, she is the only one around over the Fourth of July weekend. I half expect her not to show, but she comes through when she knows it's important.

Brother Ed meets up with us after the show at the Bottom of the Hill lets out. It still shocks me every time I see him. How big he is. An entire foot taller than me.

OUR FLIGHT STOPS IN OSAKA, where a team of two men in matching jumpsuits buffs the tile to a lustrous sheen. The floor is so shiny I want to lick it. Young pimply guys in high-water suits gather in the row next to us.

"Mormons," Ed whispers.

He knows because one of his college roommates missioned for two years in South America.

One especially pasty young man walks up to us.

"Are you interested in hearing about the Book of Mormon?" he asks with a Howdy Doody grin.

"No, leave us alone," I bark. "Our grandmother just died. We're on our way to the funeral."

Howdy Doody backs away with his hands up.

"That was kind of harsh," Ed says.

I almost call the guy back to apologize, then decide to forget it.

Instead, I ask Ed if he remembers our first trip to San Francisco twenty years ago, when I was in high school and he was ten.

"We took a Bay cruise from Ghirardelli Square. You ran over to the chocolate factory wanting an ice cream sundae. Dad went running after you. There was a young Korean guy who grabbed Dad's arm and started jabbering at him in Korean. Dad yelled back at him. Something about Reverend Moon, about him being a liar. Remember? It was the first time I heard Dad yell at a stranger. Mom grabbed you and led both of us away since she was embarrassed."

Ed looks at me with a dead stare. No, he doesn't remember anything.

I TAKE MY SHOES OFF at the entrance to the mourning room, a nice Italian pair with kitten heels and tiny bows. Mom immediately lays into me.

"Aye go chum neh, why you wear red toenail polish? And no hose? It's not proper." She tsk-tsks some more.

I stop listening. But her voice is still in my head. I go through the litany of ladylike entreaties that have been hurled my way since childhood.

Sit with your legs together.

Don't put your elbows on the table when you eat.

Remember to wear a sogchima. I can see through your skirt.

Don't shake your leg. Sit still.

Bewilderment. I look down at my left big toe. Chipped "Cherries in the Snow." She's lucky I managed to pack a black dress.

Yet I know this is what my mother does whenever she is nervous or upset. She fusses.

WE ARE THE FIRST TO arrive at Veterans Hospital, or, to be more precise, a small alcove at the back of the hospital where a row of mourning rooms has been erected. Huge white chrysanthemum wreaths propped up on easels line the room. I stand in my bare feet and red toenails not knowing what to do. Dad goes off to find the hospital coordinator. Some distant cousins from Dad's side arrive, which deflects my mother's attention. Ed helps one of the cousins transport the wreaths to a riser at the back of the room. Dad returns and removes an eight-by-ten photograph of Halmoni from his briefcase. An anonymous female relative places it on one of the easels, in the middle of one of the wreaths.

Dad's brother and his wife, fresh from a flight from Los Angeles, enter. Uncle Eun Suk falls to his knees in front of Halmoni's portrait.

"Eomeoni!" he wails, a little too loud, a little too shrill.

I think about what Mom tells me with a frown.

"He's faking."

More people arrive. Dad's cousins, two of Mom's sisters, wives of the cousins, children, most of whom I've met before. I can't remember their names, though, only on which side of the family they belong. Total strangers, too, whom my father says are members of Halmoni's Methodist church.

Ajeossi sits at a small table at the entrance of the room. White rice paper envelopes are passed to him and into his ledger book. Ajeossi's wife holds both of my hands and blubbers.

Forty, sixty, maybe even a hundred people file through and bow in front of Halmoni's portrait in an hour's time.

A CHARTERED BUS WAITS FOR us in the hospital parking lot. Ed sits in the front seat with white gloves holding Halmoni's portrait for the entire two-and-a-half-hour drive. Dad walks down the aisle and sits in the far back to keep watch over Halmoni's coffin. I plop down in the middle by a window and scrounge up some crackers from the bottom of my purse to stave off motion sickness. Mom's two surviving sisters sit behind.

Chong San, my divorced piano teacher aunt, found Halmoni slumped on the floor of her apartment. She checked in on Halmoni twice a week, since she lived nearby. She checked in on her even though she wasn't related. Chong San tells us she identified with Halmoni.

"She lived alone like I do. I hope someone checks in on me when I get to be in my nineties."

AT FIRST IT LOOKED LIKE Halmoni might survive the stroke.

"She's conscious but can't speak. She can move her fingers and even winked at us," my father told me when I was back in Boston.

It never occurred to me Halmoni could die. She was a survivor. Too tough to die, too set in her ways. "She will outlive us all," I told my father.

Halmoni held on for three months, seemingly getting stronger each day, my parents by her bedside through moves from the private hospital my father's friend Dr. Shin ran to the VA Hospital, which extended free care to the spouse of a South Korean Patriot. She had held on so long that my parents were in the midst of making arrangements to move her into a long-term care facility. She held on, but she still couldn't speak. Mom talked to her on her visits, telling her about her grandchildren in the United States, about various family members in Kongju, about everything she thought Halmoni might be interested in. Halmoni gestured with her hands and nodded in response.

Early on the morning of July 4, 2000, Halmoni suffered another stroke and lapsed into a coma. Desperate phone calls were made to family members. No one could locate Uncle Eun Suk since he was on vacation. Another stroke just before midnight.

IT'S THE HOTTEST DAY OF the year. Ninety-plus degrees Fahrenheit with monsoon season humidity. Thank God I didn't wear hose, I think to myself as I walk down the steps of the bus. The smart ladies bring wide-brimmed hats. I shield the noontime sun with my hand. We gather in front of what has become a familiar place, a place I visited only a year ago.

A pile of freshly tilled soil lies to the left of the granite marker. A pair of young soldiers dressed in ceremonial uniforms marches in unison, which cues us to assemble onto the grassy swath across the walkway in front of the grave. I stand in the front row and can see the sweat streaming down the soldiers' faces from underneath their helmets.

The soldiers stand at attention on opposite sides of the grave and twirl their white show rifles. Heels click, bodies turn. They march toward each other and then past, their eyes focused on some point above the other's head. They have been trained never to make eye contact with anyone.

In the months between my last visit and her death, Halmoni celebrated her ninety-first birthday with my parents at her apartment and declared her final wish. "I will let you bury me next to my husband in the National Cemetery." The husband who died in 1936 and left her with two baby boys to raise by herself. The husband she willingly forgot. She agreed to be laid to rest in a spot she had refused to visit throughout her life.

It was a gradual process, my father explained. While he was on sabbatical in Korea from 1994 to 1996, Halmoni lived with them in Ajou, and she was able to get to know her eldest son again and vice versa. She didn't dismiss him with a flick of her hand when he discussed looking for his father's records like she had before. She even asked him polite questions about what he discovered. The tight-held grip of resentment toward her husband softened.

"I felt comfortable enough to let her know that she could be buried next to my father in the National Cemetery if she wanted," Dad told me. "It was her choice."

My father and grandmother at the
Independence Museum in Seoul, 1996

"I think she talked about your grandpa with her church friends. I think they convinced her to be buried at the National Cemetery."

Fifteen years have passed since my grandfather's reburial service, the service Halmoni refused to attend. During that time Halmoni accepted her fate, even if she still refused to visit her husband's final resting place. She was the wife of a Patriot. After spending a lifetime trying to forget her husband, Halmoni would lie in eternity next to him.

THE SOLDIERS SALUTE WHILE HALMONI'S South Korean flag–wrapped coffin is lowered into the ground. They stand perfectly still. My father, uncle, and brother bow to her on their knees. My mother and I shower Halmoni with white daisies. A paper strip on the grave marker flaps in the hot breeze. On it, "Kum Soon Min" is written in Korean characters in black India ink.

We walk back to our places. The gravediggers quickly pack earth over the coffin, forming a perfect mound that will soon be covered in wispy green grass. The soldiers turn on their polished heels and salute the family. They march together toward the entrance of the cemetery.

CONTENT

December 14, 2000. Last day in Korea. I have already packed my expandable immigrant bag—unzipped to its fullest extent. The seven volumes, which contain my grandfather's interrogation records, sit at the bottom as an anchor, my clothes rolled in cylinders around them to soften the edges. Piles of papers, academic articles, notes on family history, photocopies of handwritten pages on fifteen generations of Lee family genealogy—all neatly organized in three blue plastic binders. Small Christmas gifts for my family. A silk scarf for Mom, a Cross pen set for Ed, and nothing for Dad. His present, the best present I could ever give, is contained in the seven volumes.

My father's former graduate student, Dr. Shin—the psychiatrist/hospital administrator/accomplished writer Dr. Shin, the one who wrote the poem inscribed on my grandfather's grave—has invited me out on my last day.

"Walk and lunch before you go," he stammers in staccato English over the phone. "Meet me at shop across street from hos-pi-tal."

I didn't envision spending my last day with my father's friend—one final shopping trip is what I really wanted—but I feel obligated because he feels obligated to take his former professor's daughter out before she leaves. I acquiesce to my good girl tendencies and accept his offer. I decide to enjoy myself. After all, I achieved my mission. I fulfilled my duty. I found what I was looking for.

I expect a brisk stroll in the late December mist on the streets of Seoul on the way to a fancy restaurant, maybe in Apgujeong, like the place Dr.

Shin took us after Halmoni's funeral. The place where they served live lobster sashimi.

I dress in my urban uniform. Color-block cashmere sweater, faux Prada pants, black neoprene overcoat, and my favorite stacked-heel ankle boots purchased from Otto Tootsi Plohound in Soho before I left New York.

Coffee, toast, out before anyone else in the house—as is my custom.

Last walk to the bodega.

Last canned latte.

Last bus ride to the subway.

I emerge from underneath to a thick fog mixed with the city's ever-present, exhaust-filled haze. I can't see more than three feet ahead.

Where is Dr. Shin's hospital? Luckily, its red neon letters penetrate the weather. Hos-Pi-Tal—the Korean characters mimic the English word. There's the Greenmart right across the street, just like Dr. Shin said it would be.

Dr. Shin stands at the counter with a cup of coffee in his hand. But he's not in his usual rumpled suit and tie. Instead, he's dressed in a navy-blue parka and lace-up boots.

He looks me up and down, his eyes wide with alarm.

"You wear that for hike up mountain?"

I HAVE SEEN THEM BEFORE, the hordes of the Gore-Tex clad, scattered on the mountainsides outside Seoul like densely packed confetti. It has never occurred to me that I would join them. Or agree to join them. I guess now I will.

Dr. Shin drives up to the northern perimeter of the city, whose heights afford the best views. We are meeting some friends of his, writers—a poet/art gallery owner and a novelist, a controversial one.

"He's Henry Miller of Korea," Dr. Shin exclaims in his excitable way.

I manage a smile but cringe inside. What happens if the Henry Miller of Korea starts waxing poetic about his sex life? Or he's leering? I'm still young-looking enough to be leered at. Maybe he won't speak English?

We arrive at the parking lot at the base of the mountain. Dr. Shin leads me to the restaurant at the edge, a makeshift lodge whose staff members, all women, of course, call Dr. Shin by name. He asks one of them if I can borrow a pair of hiking boots, a pair some female patron might have left behind. The waitress finds me a pink-and-purple pair. Clean, but a half size too small. They will do.

Henry Miller turns out to be a dour balding man in his late fifties. He considers me and nods in acknowledgment through Dr. Shin's introduction. The poet/art gallery owner is warmer. She smiles in that Korean lady way and takes my arm to guide me to the trail.

It's my first experience in mass hiking. Hordes of retirees or soon-to-be retirees gather at the starting line. More crowded than the busloads of tourists crammed onto the wooden walkways at Muir Woods. Way more crowded. But less packed than the Seoul subway in the off-hours.

On your mark, get set, go! I allow the group of ajumas and their consorts in matching yellow rain ponchos to pass me on the left. The fog still thick, I fix my gaze downward toward my borrowed hiking boots so I can see where I am tromping. Scrubby bushes, the trunks of pine trees, various boots, and tennis shoes pass by.

This is not fun.

HIKING IS NOT MY FORTE. I like nature—but at a distance. At a remove. From a vista or perhaps from behind a plate of glass. I inherited a sensitive immune system from my mother. I'm allergic to tree pollen, grass, mold, dust, most flowers, cats, and dust mites. My allergies got so bad in my first-floor garden apartment in San Francisco that my doctor suggested I purchase a foam mattress to avert the dust mites—they can't live in foam—and pull up the Pepto Bismol pink carpet.

I slog, keep my pace, and try to look on the bright side. At least it's December and the plants aren't blooming.

There's a fork in the road. Dr. Shin leads us up the one less traveled. I take a deep breath and pump my arms in rhythm to my quickening step. I am the lagger, like always. I keep the nice poet's white windbreaker in view so I don't get lost.

We rise above the fog—emboldened, I raise my gaze. Giant boulders ahead on the right. A clear ellipse of sky on the opposite side of the valley, where Seoul resides. How they pack ten million people in a mountain valley is a mystery to me.

My nylon-blend pants stick to my sweaty thighs. I am actually exerting myself. I unbutton my car coat and loosen my scarf.

Dr. Shin motions me over to the boulders on the side of the path. He's holding court. Madame Poet removes a white sun visor from her baby backpack. Henry Miller sheds his parka and sits in the sunlight that has emerged from the clouds. Dr. Shin is telling jokes. About what, I'm not quite sure, but I laugh along after seeing Henry Miller's crooked smile and craggy teeth.

We hike up past the tree line where the clay-packed earth turns to silt. I march with the group and even have a nice conversation with the poet, who has become my mother for the day. A tiny breeze blows my bangs off my forehead. It occurs to me I am having a good time.

Dr. Shin points out his hospital down below. There's Seoul Tower and the Hyatt Hotel on a hill in the middle of the city. Insadong, with all the art galleries and wedding hanbok shops, where my mother grew up. The Han River snaking its way through the middle of the city. The southern skyscrapers and high-rise apartment buildings of the financial district.

It's time to head back. The descent is quick, for it has started to sprinkle. I half run down the trail with my arms floating behind. I'm a kid again, catching raindrops on my tongue.

THE LADIES AT THE LODGE greet us with clay cups of hot boricha. I pry my boots off. My socks are damp so I peel them off, too. One of the ladies points to my feet. A chain of mismatched blisters across my heel and on the tops of my toes. I had been so engrossed in the hike I didn't feel them. Exposed to air, the blisters begin to throb.

Dr. Shin treats us to doenjang jigae to warm our bodies from the inside. I eat quickly, not tasting anything. I can't taste Korean food anymore.

Madame Poet takes her leave. Dr. Shin is not ready to go home to his wife and son and suggests a trip to visit another friend, a film director, who is building a restaurant that specializes in dishes made with cactus.

Henry Miller is game and so am I. Nopales in Korea? Sure, why not? I've tired of Korean food after four months and am eager to try something, anything, new. Ajuma's overspiced fish stew, which had excited me when I arrived, felt like wet chewy cardboard in my mouth the night before, as did her innards soup and mixed vegetables. Her dishes all hit the same note—lots of red pepper and soy sauce but nothing else to lend depth.

During the past month, I've snuck in some solo lunches at McDonald's and Burger King. Fried fish filet sandwich and fries, my childhood favorite. Flame-broiled quarter pound patty with cheese.

God, I must be homesick.

THE FILM DIRECTOR LIVES CLOSE by. In the foothills somewhere, Dr. Shin assures us. It takes an hour to get there. The men sit up front, smoking and guffawing. I peer out the back window, which I crack so a trickle of cold air can penetrate the cloud inside the car.

Somehow, Dr. Shin manages to simultaneously smoke, drive, and talk into his hand phone. Uh oh, wrong turn off the highway to Incheon.

We arrive in the billowing dusk to a four-story white building, a pagoda of sorts composed entirely of isosceles triangles. The cactus restaurant, still under construction.

Dr. Shin drives down a winding road through a small grove of trees and unkempt bushes. A long-haired bearded man stands waving below. He looks like a California hipster in his jeans and T-shirt and flip-flops—a true bohemian in a land where everyone strives to look the same. Even the teenagers all rebel in the same way. Not one but half a dozen high school students with dyed punk haircuts on the bus to the subway this morning.

Mr. Bohemian Film Director gives Dr. Shin a bear hug. He introduces his tiny wife, similarly attired, who trots out of the house with their toddler son. She's a famous film actress, Dr. Shin informs me as she bows to each of us.

The film director's home is all concrete floors and rolling metal doors. He leads us into the main room, where I spy a stack of screenplays on the kitchen table. Scorsese's *Raging Bull*, Coppola, John Huston.

SNIFTERS OF COGNAC FOR EVERYONE!

I decline and opt for something a little less potent.

The men grow red cheeked. I pretend to listen to whatever they are talking about.

I'm more interested in something else.

The Director's wife is silently feeding her son some rice and soup across the room. She is smiling. He is docile and stares into her eyes. They make no mind of the increasing volume of warmed male voices. Last spoonful. She dabs at the sides of her son's rosebud lips with a cloth napkin. Mother and son rise in unison. She takes her son's paw in her own. It's time for bed.

I watch them walk hand in hand down the hallway to the bedrooms.

I wish I were her. Holding the hand of my son.

THE FILM DIRECTOR TURNS HIS attention to me. "So, how old are you?"

"I'm thirty-four."

"Why aren't you married?"

I had hoped that perhaps, just perhaps, I had escaped the Question on this, my last day in Korea.

"I don't want to be," I answer.

The film director stares at me, his eyes narrowing to coffee bean slits. Then he laughs, a deep belly laugh.

"Good answer."

He proceeds to tell me that I'm cute, which I accept in my good mood. Maybe he could introduce me to someone, a single friend in his thirties. I nod and say sure. I'll be gone tomorrow so it doesn't matter.

Dr. Shin interrupts us. "It's time to go outside now. Our host has something to show us."

THE MEN HALF STUMBLE OUT the sliding glass door. Outside, the stars are bright in the cloudless sky away from the pulsing glow of the city. A giant greenhouse, the size of a football field, covered in white tentlike material to protect its contents from the wind and wildlife, is nestled between the house and a steep incline.

We walk inside. The Director hits the lights. Henry Miller is so excited at the sight of the tent's contents he starts running the gravel paths between the plants. Up and down, back and across.

Long-armed Saguaros, flowering pincushions, prickly pears—the multi-spined and the spineless populate the greenhouse. The Director has amassed the largest cactus collection in all of Korea.

He tells us about his most recent cactus escapade down the Baja peninsula, where he and a friend spied the desired species on the side of the highway. They stopped and dug the six-footer up. It barely fit in the trunk of the rental.

The specifics of how they got it across the border are lost to me. My Korean is better but not that good. I do know it involved a couple of bottles of good tequila and perhaps a wad of American bills.

I crouch and finger a magenta blossom. The Christmas cacti are in bloom. I used to have a Christmas cactus. Was it in Austin or St. Paul? Wherever it was, I'm sure I killed it. Even a cactus needs a little water.

CHRISTMAS IS ONLY TWO WEEKS away, and I will spend it at home in Houston with my family. The thought is comforting, although it hasn't always been. Then what? Back to Boston to gather my belongings, write a book proposal, and drive cross-country to the Bay Area and begin my life again. That's what I have come up with for now.

I take in a deep breath. There's time to plan the rest of my life later.

Okay, breathe out.

I walk slowly through the crowded desert landscape. Our host must love American westerns, I think to myself, trying to take the scene in. Or not quite American westerns. Spaghetti westerns. Like those of

Sergio Leone. The westerns I liked best as a kid, the ones with the eerie soundtracks and dirty cowboys. The westerns made by foreigners, filmed in Europe and not the United States. A foreigner's view of what the American West must have been.

I feel at peace here. Content. Content to find myself surrounded by cacti in a transported desert on the outskirts of Seoul. Content to be among people who appreciate its whimsy. Content in the fact I will return to the U.S. tomorrow and present my father with evidence of the father he never knew.

It doesn't really matter what's contained in those seven volumes. At least to me. I'm curious, of course, but I've stopped looking for clues. For it's already been established who my grandfather was. A revolutionary, an intellectual, who didn't believe the Japanese should be in Korea. A young man who put ideals before family, who left grieving parents and a wife and two baby boys to fend for themselves after his death in 1936.

It's taken four months and a distance of almost six thousand miles for me to realize why I decided to embark on this journey. Not to advance my career and write a book. Not exactly.

A MEMORY POPS INTO MY head, my own little thought bubble, self-contained and churning with velocity.

Years ago, my parents visited Anza-Borrego Desert Park outside of San Diego on the way back to Texas from a visit to California. Dad accidentally squatted on a group of low-lying cactus mounds while trying to get a closer look at a butterfly. He was attacked by spines. Dozens of them. Mom pulled out each one with care and a light hand, behind the restrooms where no one could see my father bent over in his boxers.

The spines just jumped into his bomboom, Mom told me later.

They were just protecting themselves, I replied, which I guess was true. That's how cacti protect themselves.

But how did my parents protect themselves? So far away from home with no family around. For so long. My father never did take that job in Seoul after we visited in 1976. When he told his dean about the verbal job offer he received from the Korean Development Institute, the dean recommended he stay in Houston and promised tenure instead. Anyway, the dean told him, you should never accept a job without a written offer.

What would have happened if my father had resigned and told the Koreans he was coming? The answer came from my last meeting with a colonial era history PhD student, one who coincidentally shared the surname of my grandfather: Chul Ha. He assumed that my father spent his academic career in the United States because of the taint of my grandfather's past. Any Korean university or governmental agency, especially during Park Chung Hee's rule, would have never hired the son of an avowed Communist, even one who protested Japanese rule. Communism was equated with North Korea, which meant my grandfather was the enemy. The Korean Development Institute would have most likely rescinded the job offer after delving more deeply into my father's past, and then my father would have been left with nothing. No job in Korea and no job in Houston.

My parents never moved back to Korea and remain in the United States. Even after almost forty years, it still doesn't feel like home, even though they are naturalized citizens. They are still treated like foreigners on a daily basis, just like me.

Can you speak English?

Are you one of those Vietnamese boat people?

Why don't you go back to where you came from?

They planned on retiring in Korea, eventually. But they stayed away too long. The Korea they remember doesn't exist anymore. It's changed so much during their time away; it's become unrecognizable.

I BEGIN TO SHIVER. THE temperature drops quickly away from the city. There's no heat in the greenhouse, and my coat hangs by the front door inside. Dr. Shin notices my discomfort and guides the group back into the house. The cacti are used to cold nights. Even in Korea.

It's time to go back inside and take our leave.

It's time for me to go home.

HEIR

In 2000, I fulfilled my search for history and found what I was looking for—my grandfather's police and interrogation records. I brought home the seven bound volumes for my father as the ultimate Christmas present. I resumed my life soon after, starting anew in San Francisco for the second time. I returned to the friends I left behind when I moved to New York, to my brother Ed and therapy. Craigslist provided a part-time job as an afternoon receptionist for a boutique investment bank to pay the bills and mismatched furnishings from refugees of the dot-com boom that went bust.

Back in San Francisco, I worked on my book about the search for information on my grandfather in the mornings, took on some freelance editing gigs, and joined a writing group. I wrote the chapter on Choong and tried to instill mystery into the narrative of my search. I read dozens of novels to help guide me. But I had trouble inserting myself as a character in my own story. Why did I make the trek to Korea to find my grandfather? And now that I'd found him, what did it all mean?

With the therapist's help I continue trying to parse out how to work toward those things I really want, those things I articulated to Kind Bob in New York—I want to be a writer and start a family. We painstakingly go over my previous relationships: romantic and platonic. Find patterns in my behavior—conflict avoidance, feelings of overresponsibility, fear of letting go, a knack for choosing alcoholics as boyfriends. She suggests Match.com. I resist. I agree to be set up by a new best friend who offers to pick a boyfriend for me since I have difficulty choosing for myself. She suggests her husband's former suitemate from Cal Berkeley, a freelance writer for gaming companies who pens history books for kids on the side. Who loves to scuba dive and always wears shorts and Chuck Taylors.

At a housewarming party in North Berkeley in the fall of 2001, I meet Scuba Steve, who is indeed wearing frayed khaki shorts with black, low-top Chuck Taylors. My wingman Anne nudges me at the bagel table: "Margaret, he's cute and has nice legs." He does. I discover he played soccer as a teen, just like my high school crush Patrick. We chat about what books we have on our nightstands: John McPhee and Neil Gaiman for him, Ian McEwan and Paula Fox for me.

FAST FORWARD TO 2007.

The setting is familiar. The rolling hills outside of Taejon about an hour and a half south of Seoul. Stepped clearings amid pine trees. Giant steps up the ladder toward the heavens.

Instead of Ajeossi driving us in his trusty Hyundai jeep, he has rented a van for the day in order to fit all of us. For the family has grown in the intervening fifteen years since we first visited the National Cemetery for my grandfather's reburial service. Mom had made me a royal purple suit for the ceremony out of Italian nubby silk she had snatched from the remnant bin at Gallery Fabrics in the 1980s. I think I wore the matching pants, not the short, pleated skirt, in a nod to comfort and modernity. I need to check the photographs from the event to know for sure. That day turned warm, like all the days we have visited—four times . . . no five, counting today.

Humidity clings to my skin. Vestige of a late monsoon season. Fall is supposed to be the best time to visit Korea, but it still feels like summer compared to home in California. A light rain is falling. Dad in the front seat talking to Ajeossi about family matters. Mom next to me in the middle row. The large white man in the back is sweating profusely, like he always does. He's not made for the heat, he has told me dozens of times.

My first trip back to Korea since my so-called semester abroad is a gift from my parents. They have gone all out—renting a suite at an expat high-rise hotel in Insadong, my favorite neighborhood, with my cousin Mina's help since she used to be a concierge there. Oesamchun, Mina's father, greets us at the hotel after waiting for two hours. We are late. The flight delayed, the puzzle finally solved of how to fit all of our luggage into an SUV taxi.

The trip to Korea is a belated wedding present. For the sweaty man in the back of the van is my husband. Scuba Steve, the native Californian I met the year after I returned from Korea in 2000. To whom a man in baggage claim at Incheon airport asked, "You G.I.?"

"No," Steve replied, pointing to his shiny head. "I just have the G.I. haircut."

My parents had originally planned to take us to Korea the spring after our June 2005 wedding. To show off their eldest child's husband to all the relatives who couldn't travel to the States for the ceremony.

Look, Juhae's finally married at age thirty-nine! Better late than never.
Circumstances intervened.

STEVE SNOOZES AND LETS OUT periodic snorts—jet lag has hit him the hardest. He's still turned around after almost a week, and there's only a couple more days before we head back home. His mother Carol dozes next to him. My parents' generosity extends to the mother of the groom, for she occupies an exalted position in Korean society. I joke to her on the flight over that she is free to boss me around in Korea—it's her privilege as mother-in-law. I tell her I draw the line at running her household, like Halmoni was forced to do for her in-laws. Carol's head bobs up and down in time to the potholes in the highway, next to Steve's—their matching slate-blue eyes hidden away.

The guest of honor stirs beside me in his Britex throne. He wakes. I grab the orange canvas bag at my feet and extract some goldfish crackers I brought from home. I am ready for him. Cracker in hand, I smile as he blinks awake. He sees my smile, he sees the cracker. He returns my smile with a grin, the grin of his father, which extends the width of his face, showing off his tiny front teeth. "Cwack-rrr!" he yells with enthusiasm, now fully awake. He embodies his every emotion to its fullest extent, until it is brimming, until it overflows. A trait he has exhibited since birth.

Once the guest of honor awakes, everyone else does. He is our alarm clock. Just as Ajeossi veers off the main highway to Taejon. Fifteen minutes more to the cemetery. The boy king stares out through the droplets and points his chubby index finger toward something outside. He shouts his favorite word—"Bu-sssss!" He's a fan of all motor vehicles. Well-practiced after a year of riding to work with me to San Francisco from Oakland. Most of his growing vocabulary has been gathered on those morning drives: "Bww-idge," "Ahm-ord twuck," "John Len-non."

My parents smile. They are enamored. The most treasured grandson in all of Korea—and the United States—is sitting in the car with them. He is their heir. The only member of the next generation. The future. After they have waited so long. Finally, finally, they are blessed with a grandchild in their seventies.

Owen Sung Ya Lee Olson. Born June 2006 via C-section, a year minus one week after Steve and I got married in the Oakland Rose Garden. Half Korean, half Northern European mutt, 100 percent Californian.

IT WASN'T MY IDEA TO name our progeny after my grandfather, although it should have been. The husband of a friend thought it was a fait accompli after learning that I was pregnant.

Of course, you will name him after your grandfather if it's a boy.
Yes, of course.

I had been too preoccupied with my ticking clock to think about names. With taking my temperature every morning and recording the result on the pocket calendar by the bed. With brewing Chinese pregnancy-enhancing herbs my acupuncturist gave me as a wedding present. With spitting onto a round glass lens on a microscope contraption that came in a purple velvet pouch to see if the arrangement of saliva molecules indicated ripeness. And eating right and exercising and trying to be healthy.

I was worried. I feared I had waited too long.

Are my eggs still viable? Am I fertile? I asked my ob-gyn.
You won't know unless you try, he replied.

Joel, my acupuncturist, assured me I wouldn't have any problems. I wasn't sure how he knew, but he did. Joel's always right. I got pregnant without any high-tech interventions.

OWEN'S STUBBY ARMS ARE SPREAD wide. He wants his mommy. Sorry, honey, I can't get you out of your seat while the car is moving. I offer him my finger, which he immediately smothers with his juicy paw. For some reason Owen is the only one who doesn't suffer from the time difference. He refused to sleep on the thirteen-hour flight over and insisted on walking up and down the aisles on his unsteady legs with an adult escort to guide his narrow course. His first steps at the Verizon store at fifteen months—now he must practice all the time. He howled his displeasure when we tried to tether him to his seat. Exhausted servicemen and women glared at us from underneath their camouflage caps.

At the hotel, Steve graciously offered to take the floor since there wasn't room for all of us on the Asian double. Our little despot refused the white iron crib the hotel provided. I awoke that first night in Seoul with Owen's large melon nestled into my belly. He wants to go back in, I told Steve. That's where he feels safest.

WE ARRIVE AT THE NATIONAL Cemetery in a fine mist. We stop at the main parking lot and buy soy milk for the youngster, fruity soft drinks for the adults, and a couple of bunches of white daisies, their stems wrapped in aluminum foil, at the visitors' center. Owen tears across the empty dining room at full speed. The adults all praise his energy. The mood is joyous, unlike the other times we have visited.

Ajeossi drives us up the road toward my grandparents' shared grave. It is no longer at the top tier of gravestones. Many more have been added in the intervening years. More Patriots to honor. More patriarchs and matriarchs to bury. I unlock our boy from his seat and hoist him onto my right hip. Mom hands him a couple of daisies and holds an umbrella over our heads. Dad beams at the sight of his beautiful, multiracial, American grandchild, the first member of the next generation.

Owen and I
at the Taejon
National
Cemetery,
2007

My grandmother
and father, 1934

WITH MY FATHER'S HELP, I have created a new history for my family. A history previously characterized by forgetting the past has been transformed into one of reclamation and renewal. The search, which began with my father's sabbatical in 1992, continued as part of my journey. Maybe my journey is best described as a late coming-of-age story. As part of the first generation born in a new country, I began to look toward my family's tumultuous past only as an adult. On the plane to Korea in 2000, I didn't fully understand why I was embarking on this search. Now, I realize that confronting my family's forgotten past was an essential step in paving the way to the future— and having a child of my own.

I finally feel at home. Not in a particular place—the Bay Area, where I live, feels transitory, even with a baby, and Korea is more familiar but still foreign. Home isn't a place for me. It's a state of being.

I feel at home with Owen in my arms placing daisies on my grandparents' grave, with my parents, husband, and mother-in-law surrounding us. Owen will grow up knowing that his forgotten great-grandfather was finally recognized as a Patriot of South Korea and Halmoni lies in rest beside him, a decision she made during the final year of her long life. We'll never know if her decision was motivated by duty and custom or forgiveness of the husband who wanted to leave her behind in the countryside so long ago.

What we do know is that Halmoni is the figure who fought for the survival of the family into the next generation and beyond. Like Greatuncle Wan said, she is the one who had to survive and raise two sons by herself—through the end of the colonial era, the splitting of her country in two, the Korean War, her sons emigrating to the United States, and the rebuilding of a nation. She was never interested in politics, never wondered what course her country might take. She only knew that her late husband's activities could be exploited by others—family members or whomever the ruling forces were at a particular moment. Halmoni's purpose was clear: she would do anything to protect her children, to ensure their survival.

Like Uncle Wan said, she is the real hero of the family.

OWEN SMILES, AND I KISS him on his fat cheek. He smells sweet, like baby sweat. I tell him that we are visiting Sung Ya and Halmoni's grave, the grave of his great-grandparents. He doesn't quite understand. How could he? He's only twenty months old.

But he will grow up knowing who his great-grandparents were. What they did. What they lived through. He will know from where his family came.

He nods and says "flou-ers."

Yes, sweet pea, we will put flowers on their grave.

Epilogue

HEAVENLY GARDEN

A couple of miles from the National Cemetery, where my grandparents are buried, lies Heavenly Garden, Halmoni's spiritual home. Heavenly Garden (Chun Yang Won) is the name of the orphanage where she worked after the war. Ajeossi suggests we visit after we scatter my father's ashes. He understands the importance of honoring Halmoni on this day, the last of 2019.

We arrive unannounced to a two-story white brick building off the highway. A stone marker to the left of the entrance commemorates the founder, Yu Eul Hee, whose name I recognize from the last time I spoke to Halmoni in 2000. Mrs. Yu was Halmoni's first best friend, whom she met in Kongju a couple of years after my grandfather's death. Like Halmoni, Mrs. Yu was a widow. She convinced Halmoni to convert to Christianity and join the Holiness Church, whose Kongju congregation she started.

The director is out, so one of the administrators gives us a tour of the facilities. We walk outside and spy a couple of children in the distance in front of a dormitory, but the rest of the orphanage seems mostly empty. The kids wander over to the bird coops at the edge of the property. An especially elegant pheasant ruffles its hind feathers at Kiki, the animal lover. Owen is fascinated by a pair of black, broad-plumed chickens.

I tell the kids that I first toured Heavenly Garden with my parents on my first trip to Korea in 1976, when I was ten. It looked totally different back then. I remember low slung structures made of mud and concrete. Dozens of children in threadbare clothing playing in the courtyard. Brown dust soiling the backs of my white knee-high socks. But what became most seared into my brain was the enormous wire chicken coop whose squawking inhabitants were so tightly packed that the ground beneath them disappeared. The undulating sea of chickens made such a racket that we were forced to yell at each other to be heard. And the smell—naemse. I gagged and covered my mouth and nose with my hand before running away.

AFTER MY GRANDFATHER DIED, HALMONI found her calling, and survival—as a mother. First to her two sons, and then to hundreds of children at the orphanage. She became a grandmother and took care of me in the U.S. for the first five years of my life and was the caretaker for my cousins back in Kongju, before they emigrated to the United States.

She became a mother to us all.

Like Halmoni, I finally became a mother, too. Which is what I wanted all along, if I am being honest with myself. What I realize now—two decades after my stay in Korea—is that I needed to go through the process of excavating my family's past in order to clear the path to begin a family of my own. That's why I went to Korea in 2000 in search of the paper remains of my grandfather, the Patriot, the hero. I needed to fill the hole at my center, the void that I was determined not to pass down to my children.

SO, KIKI AND OWEN, THE children I always wanted, I now have an end to my origin story. I inherited a loss of history, the emptiness I tried to fill with my search for the grandfather I never knew. My quest is over. The weight of not knowing about the past has been lifted, the weight of what we now call intergenerational trauma, a concept I didn't know existed when I began my search.

I wonder what you have inherited as mixed-race progeny of a Korean American new waver and a big Northern European white guy? How will you choose to tell your story?

What I hope is that you keep the Wonder Twins in mind as time goes on. I'm guessing that you will keep on bickering through your teen years until you both head off to college. One day, I hope you sit down together and reminisce—about visits to Grandma Chong and Grandpa Eun Sul's two-story in Tigard and sliding down their stairs on a piece of cardboard; about Owen's and my trip to Kongju High School to receive a posthumous graduation diploma in honor of Great-Grandpa; about our hike up Seoraksan, north of Seoul, and both of you getting yelled at for venturing off the trail; about Dad getting food poisoning on the last day of one of our Korea trips and spending the majority of the flight home in the airplane bathroom. Remember that?

Your own searches for identity will be different than mine and your father's. One day you might be a partner, a parent, a pet owner. What I want you to know is that who you are and who you become are connected to the past. That the connection is forged through your great-grandfather's idealism and your great-grandmother's grit and will to survive. Your grandparents' love and adoration. Your mother's quest and your father's dedication.

We are all here for you.

IN THE MEANTIME, HERE'S THE fairy tale I started at the beginning of this story, with the ending we, as a family, are present for:

Once upon a time there was a girl who was born in a country where she didn't feel at home. She looked different than everyone else, she ate different foods. People asked her questions like "Where are you from?" When she answered "Houston," they would ask, "No, where are you really from?"

Ten years old, the girl traveled to the country of her parents' birth—she didn't feel at home there, either. She could understand some of what people were saying, but she could only speak in phrases, like a toddler. Her grandmother had taught her the language of her forebearers when she was little, but her parents spoke English to her at home, at the advice of the pediatrician who said, "She will fall behind in school if you don't."

The girl grew up, forgot her grandmother's language, went to college, tried a couple of careers, and settled on journalism. She decided to investigate the mystery of the grandfather she never knew, the one who went to prison and died when her father was a baby. She started by asking her grandmother questions, questions her grandmother didn't want to answer.

The girl decided to visit the country of her parents' birth again, this time alone. She wanted to solve the mystery of who her grandfather was by finding the police and interrogation records her grandmother burned during the Korean War. The records that branded him as a teenage Communist revolutionary who protested Japanese rule. After years of classes, the girl could now read and speak a bit of her parents' language. However, she realized that she needed to hire a translator and speak English to be taken seriously by the men who could help her find her grandfather's records.

The girl eventually found her grandfather's records, even though they were not where they were supposed to be. She brought them back to her father in the United States. They were the best present she could ever give him—except for grandchildren. She began to write a book about her search for lost history but put it down when life intervened. She picked it up again but was unable to finish it before her parents died.

Twenty years later, the girl, now a middle-aged woman, returned to the country of her parents' birth. She visited with her husband and two children to scatter the ashes of her parents in their homeland. Her parents had never returned to live there, because that country was so different from the one they had left over fifty years before.

The woman still didn't feel at home in either of the two countries, but she did feel at home with her family. Unlike her, her children would grow up knowing about the past and who their ancestors were. What the woman really wanted was for her children to feel at home with themselves, wherever they choose to live.

BIBLIOGRAPHY

INTERVIEWS

Lee, Choong Ha. Interview by author. Transcript. Kongju, South Korea. October 9, 2000.

Lee, Eun Sul. Email interviews and correspondence with author. 1998–2004.

Lee, Wan Ha. Interview by author. Transcript. Taejon, South Korea. October 9, 2000.

Min, Kum Soon. First interview by author. Recording and transcript. Seoul, South Korea. March 8, 1999.

Min, Kum Soon. Second interview by author. Recording and transcript. Seoul, South Korea. March 10, 1999.

Min, Kum Soon. Third interview by author. Recording and transcript. Seoul, South Korea. March 13, 1999.

Min, Kum Soon. Interview by Chong Mahn Lee. Transcript. Seoul, South Korea. July 1999.

KOREAN SOURCES

"Choego Jingyeok Yuknyeon Guhyeong" 最高懲役六年求刑 [Prosecutor Demands Up to Six Years Imprisonment]. *The Chosun Ilbo* (Seoul), April 20, 1930.

Doknipundongsa Jaryojip 독립운동사자료집 [Source Material for History of Korean Independence], Volume 13: Student Independence Movement, December 1977: 602–607.

"Gakseoga Hwaldong Haksaengeul Geomgeo" 各□가 活動 學生을 檢擧 [All Police Stations in Action: Students are Arrested]. *The Dong-a Ilbo* (Seoul), November 10, 1928.

"Gongjuseo Kinjang Gobosaeng Geomgeo" 公州署緊張 高普生檢擧 [Kongju Police Interrogating Several Students]. *The Dong-a Ilbo* (Seoul), December 26, 1928.

"Gumyeongeun Giso" 九名은 起訴 [Nine Students Indicted]. *The Dong-a Ilbo* (Seoul), December 20, 1928.

"Haksaeng Bimil Gyeolsa Sageon Jinsang Sageoneun Uioero Jungdae" 學生□密結社事件眞相 事件은 意外로 重大 [Case of Student Secret Organization Revealed: Case Bigger Than Expected]. *The Dong-a Ilbo* (Seoul), December 7, 1928.

"Haksaeng Gwahak Yeonguhoe Jeonggi Daehoe Gaechoe" 學生科學研究會 定期大會開催 [Student Association for Scientific Research Meet]. *The Dong-a Ilbo* (Seoul), April 17, 1928.

Jeong, Se Hyeon 鄭世鉉. "Chapter 6: Resistance to Colonial Education Section 7: Activities of Students in Kongju." In *Hangil Haksaeng Minjokundongsa Yeongu* 抗日學生民族運動史研究 [History of the Anti-Japanese National Student Movement]. Seoul: Iljisa, 1975.

Jeonjuissichampangongpabo Dan 全州李氏參判公派譜 單 [Geneology of the Jeonju Lee Clan Champangong Faction One book]. 1969. Collection of the author, also available at Kongjuhak Archive, Kongju, Republic of Korea.

Ji, Su Geol 지수걸. Yeolheolcheongnyeon Leecheolhaui Salmgwa Tujaeng 熱血靑年 李哲夏의 삶과 투쟁 [The Life and Struggles of Lee Cheol Ha, the Hot-Blooded Young Man]. Kongjuhak Archive, Gongju, Republic of Korea. 2000. kjha.kongju.ac.kr.

Kim, Ho Il 金鎬逸. "Iljeha Haksaengdancheui Jojikgwa Hwaldong" 日帝下 學生團體의 組織과 活動 [Student Organizations and their Activities During Japanese Colonial Rule]. *Journal of History Studies* 22, 1973: 115–161.

Lee, Byeong In 이병인. "Hangildoglibungdongga Lee Cheol Ha Seonsaeng Jaejomyeong" 항일독립운동가 이철하 선생 재조명 [Revisiting Mr. Lee, Cheol Ha, Independence Movement Fighter against Japanese Imperialism]. *Jungbu Maeil* 중부매일 (Cheongju). June 22, 2022. jbnews.com.

"Man Inyeoneul Kkeuleoodeun Haksaeng K Dangui Gongpan" 滿二年을 끄—러어오든 學生ㄱ黨의 公判 [Trial Case of Student K Organization Going On for Two Years]. *The Chosun Ilbo* (Seoul), April 16, 1930.

"Seoseo Daehwaldong Mojungbeom Chepo" 西署大活動 某重犯逮捕 [West Gate Police Investigating Big Case: Arrest of Several Youths]. *The Dong-a Ilbo* (Seoul), November 16, 1928.

"Seoseo Dolyeonhwaldong Haksaeng Imyeong Geomgeo" 西署突然活動 學生二名檢擧 [West Gate Police Station in Action: Two Students Detained]. *The Dong-a Ilbo* (Seoul), October 5, 1928.

"Seoseo Haksaeng Sageon Ilbu Jinsang Jeungineuro Haksaeng Dasu Chwijo" 西
署學生事件一部眞相 證人으로 學生多數取調 [West Gate Police Complete
Preliminary Investigation of Student Case: Many Students Taken as Witnesses].
The Dong-a Ilbo (Seoul), December 5, 1928.

"Sibsammyeongui Pangyeol Eondo" 十三名의 判決言渡 [Thirteen Students
Sentenced]. *The Chosun Ilbo* (Seoul), April 26, 1930.

Yun Kyŏngno, "Yi Hyŏnsang kwa 1928 nyŏn ŭi haksaeng kongsandang sagŏn"
[Lee Hyun Sang and the Student Communist Case of 1928], *Yŏksa pip'yŏng* 5,
1988: 346–369.

JAPANESE SOURCES

Below is list of documents pertaining to my grandfather Lee Chul Ha contained
in the seven volumes titled "Lee Hyun Sang" which I purchased in Seoul in 2000.
They are copies of original documents which were housed in the basement of the
Seoul Municipal Court. All documents are written in classical Japanese and date
from 1928–1930. These documents have since been archived and are now housed
at the National Institute of Korean History.

Volume 1
[Police summary of participants: Kang Byung Do, Lee Chul Ha, Choi
Sung Hwan, Oh Jae Hyun, Ahn Sam Won, Lee Hyun Sang, Kim
Bok Chin], Seoul, Korea, Sept. 13, 1928.
[Search warrant: Office of Haksaeng Kwahak Yonguhoe (Student
Association for Scientific Research)]. Seoul, Korea. Sept. 13, 1928.
[Police Interrogation Report of Lee Chul Ha]. Seodaemun Hyeongmuso,
Seoul, Korea, September 18, 1928. Translation by Chong Mahn Lee.
[Prison order for Lee Chul Ha], Seoul, Korea. Sept. 18, 1928.
Volume 2
[Interrogation of witness: Han Byung Sun, against Lee Chul Ha]. Seoul,
Korea. Sept. 21, 1928.
[District Attorney interrogation: Lee Chul Ha]. Seoul, Korea, Oct. 4,
1928.
Volume 3
[Preliminary trial request: Lee Chul Ha]. Seoul, Korea. Dec. 19, 1928.
Volume 4
[First Interrogation of Lee Chul Ha by Pretrial Judge], Seoul District
Court, Seoul, Korea, December 23, 1929.
[Second Interrogation of Lee Chul Ha by Pretrial Judge], Seoul District
Court, Seoul, Korea, December 24, 1929.

Volume 5
    [Prison Warden's Observational Report of Lee Chul Ha], Seodaemun
        Hyeongmuso, Seoul, Korea, January 22, 1930.
Volume 6
    [Third Interrogation of Lee Chul Ha by Pretrial Judge], Seodaemun
        Hyeongmuso, Seoul, Korea, January 21, 1930.
Volume 7
    [Police Assessment of Suspect's Behavior: Lee Chul Ha], Seodaemun
        Hyeongmuso, Seoul, Korea, October 12, 1928.

ENGLISH LANGUAGE SOURCES

Appleman, Roy E. *United States Army in the Korean War: South to the Naktong, North to the Yalu (June–November 1950)*. Washington, D.C.: Office of the Chief of Military History, Department of the Army, 1961.

"Attempted Assassination of President Park Chung Hee." National Archives Video Collection, YouTube. Aug. 15, 1974. Accessed at youtube.com.

Buñuel, Luis, director, *Un Chien Andalou* [An Andalusian Dog], 1929.

Chapin, Emerson. "Korean Women's Leader Criticizes Ford Plan for Visit." *New York Times*, Oct. 20, 1974: 12. nytimes.com.

Choi, Hyaeweol. *Gender and Mission Encounters in Korea: New Women, Old Ways*. Berkeley: University of California Press, 2009. escholarship.org.

Cumings, Bruce. *The Korean War: A History*. New York: Random House, 2010.

Cumings, Bruce. *Korea's Place in the Sun: A Modern History*. Updated edition. New York: W.W. Norton & Company, 2005. [1997].

Cumings, Bruce. *North Korea*. New York: New Press. 2004.

Eckert, Carter J. *Offspring of Empire: The Koch'ang Kims and the Colonial Origins of Korean Capitalism 1876–1945*. Seattle: University of Washington Press. 1991.

Effron, Sonni. "North Korea fires ballistic missile into the Sea of Japan." *Los Angeles Times*. August 31, 1998. Accessed at latimes.com.

Ewha Womans University Archives. *Ewha Old and New*. Seoul: Ewha Womans University Press. 2005.

Haggard, Stephan, et.al. "Japanese colonialism and Korean development: A critique." *World Development*. Vol. 25, issue 6, June 1997: 867–881.

Halberstam, David. *The Coldest Winter: America and the Korean War*. New York: Hyperion. 2007.

Halloran, Richard. "Assassin's Bullet Kills Mrs. Park." *The New York Times*, Aug. 15, 1974: 1. Accessed at nytimes.com.

Han, Bae-Ho and Lew, Yong Ick. "Armistice and Aid: Korea since c. 1400." Encyclopedia Brittanica website. britannica.com.

Han, Soongju. "South Korea in 1974: The 'Korean Democracy' on Trial." *Asian Survey*. Vol. 15, No. 1, Jan.1975: 35–42.

Han, Young Woo. *A Review of Korean History*, Vol. 3: Modern Contemporary Era. Trans. by Hahm Chaibong. Seoul, Korea: Kyongsaewon. 2010.

Hardy, Thomas. *Tess of D'Urbervilles*, New York: Penguin Books. 1998.

Hwang, Kyung Moon. *Beyond Birth: Social Status in Early Modern Korea*. Cambridge: Harvard University Press. 2005.

Hwang, Sung Kyu. *The Life and Theology of Changgong, Kim Chai Choon*. Translated by Lee Yeong Mee. Seoul: Hanshin University Press. 2005. doam.org

The Japanese Colonial Empire, 1895–1945. Edited by Myers and Peattie, Princeton: Princeton University Press, 1987.

Kallander, George. *Salvation through Dissent: Tonghak Heterodoxy and Early Modern Korea*. Honolulu: University of Hawai'i Press, 2013. jstor.org

Kim, Young-Sun. "Rethinking Historical-Comparative Methodology for Understanding the Gender Structure of Korean Colonial Modernity." *Asian Journal of Women's Studies*. Vol. 15, no. 3, 2009: 7–33.

"Korean Armistice Agreement, July 27, 1953." U.S. Department of State Archive website. released Jan. 20, 2009. 2001–2009.state.gov.

Lankov, Andrei. "A Short History of Korean Stamps." Korea Stamp Society website. July 9, 2018. koreastampsociety.org.

Lee, Eun Sul. *Dreaming with One Eye Open: A Memoir*. Oakland, CA: Stories to Last, 2012.

Lee, Eun Sul and Forthofer, Ron. *Introduction to Biostatistics: A Guide to Analysis, Design and Discovery*. Cambridge, MA: Academic Press. 1995.

Lee, Ki-baik. *A New History of Korea*. Translated by Edward W. Wagner with Edward J. Shultz. Seoul, Korea: Ilchokak Publishers, 1984.

Lee, Margaret Juhae. "Seoul's Celluloid Soul." *The Nation*. November 29, 1999: 30.

Lim, Timothy C. "The Origins of Societal Power in South Korea: Understanding the Physical and Human Legacies of Japanese Colonialism." *Modern Asian Studies*, Vol. 33. no. 33: 603–633.

MacDonald, Callum A. *Korea: The War before Vietnam*. New York: The Free Press, 1986.

Malcom, Andrew H. "Tighter Controls Imposed by Seoul." *The New York Times*. Sept. 20, 1976: 11. Accessed at nytimes.com

"Obituaries for June 2018: Eun Sul Lee." AMSTAT News. June 2018. Accessed at magazine.amstat.org.

Oh, John K. C. "South Korea 1976: The Continuing Uncertainties." *Asian Survey* 17, no. 1, 1977: 71–80. jstor.org.

Orwell, George. *1984*. New York: Harcourt Brace, 1983.

Osgood, Charles. "Keith Haring Was Here." *CBS Evening News*. Aired October 20, 1982. Accessed at youtube.com.

Pang, Kie-Chung, and Michael D. Shin, eds. *Landlords, Peasants, and Intellectuals in Modern Korea*. Ithaca: Cornell East Asia Series, 2005.

Park, Kyung Ae, "Women and Social Change in South and North Korea: Marxist and Liberal Perspectives." *Women in International Development Publication Series*. Michigan State University. Working Paper 231, June 1992.

Park, Myung Soo. "The 20th Century Holiness Movement and Korean Holiness Groups." *The Asbury Journal*, Vol. 62, No. 2, 2007: 81–108. place.asburyseminary.edu.

Park, Sunyoung. *The Proletarian Wave: Literature and Leftist Culture in Colonial Korea 1910–1945*. Cambridge: Harvard University Press, 2015.

The Place of Independence and Democracy: Seodaemun Prison History Hall. Seoul: Seodaemun Management Corporation, 2018.

"Prosecution Urges Jail for 15 in Seoul." *New York Times*. Aug. 4, 1976: 31. nytimes.com

"Resistance in Tokyo encouraged the March 1 Movement." *Korea Joongang Daily*. Feb. 17, 2019. koreajoongangdaily.joins.com

Robinson, Michael. *Cultural Nationalism in Colonial Korea, 1920–1925*. Seattle: University of Washington Press, 1988.

Robinson, Michael. *Korea's Twentieth Century Odyssey*. Honolulu: University of Hawaii Press, 2007.

"S. Korea tears down ex-Japanese building." United Press International. Aug. 7, 1995. Accessed at upi.com

Scalapino, Robert A. and Chong-sik Lee. *Communism in Korea*. 2 vols., Berkeley: University of California Press, 1972.

Shin, Gi-Wook and Michael Robinson, eds. *Colonial Modernity in Korea*.

Cambridge: Harvard University Press, 1999.

Shin, Gi-Wook. *Peasant Protest and Social Change in Colonial Korea.* Seattle: University of Washington Press, 1996. jstor.org

Shin, Gi-Wook and Rennie Moon. "1919 in Korea: National Resistance and Contending Legacies." Special Issue. *The Journal of Asian Studies.* Cambridge University Press. May 2019.

Shin, Kyung-Sook, and Helen J. S. Lee. "Living as a Colonial Girl: The Sonyŏ (少女) Discourse of School Curriculum and Newspapers in 1930s Korea." *International Journal of Asian Studies* Vol. 18, no. 1, 2021: 119–134.

Song J.H., Huh K., and Chung D.R. "Modern History of Tuberculosis in Korea." *Infection & Chemotherapy.* December 2019. 51(4):414–426. doi: 10.3947/ ic.2019.51.4.414. Epub 2019 Nov 28. Erratum in: Infect Chemother. 2020 Jun;52(2):305–306. PMID: 31782276; PMCID: PMC6940379. ncbi.nlm.nih.gov.

Sorenson, Clark W. "The Value and the Meaning of the Korean Family." Korea Society website, accessed 2021. asiasociety.org.

Spencer, Sherman. "South Korean student protests: Don't always believe your eyes." *UPI.* Sept. 18, 1988. Retrieved at upi.com.

Strom, Stephanie. "50 Years Later, Reunions Bring Joy to Koreans." *New York Times.* Aug. 16, 2000: 1. nytimes.com

Suh, Dae-sook. *Documents of Korean Communism, 1918-1948.* Princeton: Princeton University Press, 1970

Suh, Dae-sook, *The Korean Communist Movement, 1918-1948.* Princeton: Princeton University Press, 1967

Tolstoy, Leo. *War and Peace.* Translated by Rosemary Edmonds. New York: Penguin Books, 1982.

Underwood, L.H. *Fifteen Years among the Top-Knots.* Boston: American Tract Society, 1904. See gutenberg.org.

Valenzuela, Diana. "Have You Been the Victim of Eldest Daughter Syndrome?" Katie Couric Media. Nov. 16, 2022. katiecouric.com.

Wong, Kar-wai, director. *In the Mood for Love*, Jet Tone Production and Pardis Films, 2000. 98 mins. Viewed at the Pusan Film Festival, 2000.

Yoo, Theodore Jun. *The Politics of Gender in Colonial Korea: Education, Labor and Health*, 1910–1945. Berkeley: University of California Press, 2008.

Yoo, Theodore Jun. *The Koreas: The Birth of Two Nations Divided.* Berkeley: University of California Press, 2020.

ACKNOWLEDGMENTS

STARRY FIELD IS A FAMILY memoir, a true collaboration between my parents, grandmother, and relatives from both sides. To my Halmoni, Kum Soon Min (1908–2000), thank you for telling me your story, even though you were reluctant to do so at first, and teaching me what it means to be a mother. To my parents, Eun Sul Lee (1934–2018) and Chong Mahn Lee (1934–2019), whom I wish were still alive to see this book published—Dad, I am so thankful I was able to participate in your reclamation of family history and that you wrote your own memoir since mine was taking so long; and Mom, without you this book wouldn't have been written—you were the facilitator, the translator, the heart that kept us all going. And to my brother Ed, thank you for your ongoing support and answering my questions at all hours of the day.

I want to acknowledge my writing mentors, Ellen Willis (1941–2006) and John Leonard (1939–2008), for believing in me and giving me the confidence to write this book. Thanks to the students and teachers at New York University's Cultural Reporting & Criticism Program and my colleagues at *The Nation* magazine, without you, I wouldn't have become a journalist. Thanks to the Radcliffe Institute for Advanced Study for providing me the space and time I needed to begin research and to my NYC roommate Barbara Broughel for suggesting I apply for a Bunting Fellowship.

Thanks to the Korea Foundation for funding my research trip to Korea in 2000 and to my father's cousin Oh Byung Yoon and his wife Kim Sook Jin for hosting me for the four months I spent in Seoul. Thanks to my Korea Foundation sponsor Professor Chung Chin Sung and research assistant Ayoung Moon at Seoul National University. To my trusted translator, Jungmin Kuk, whose companionship and research skills were invaluable—I couldn't have found my grandfather's records without you. Much appreciation to the numerous scholars in Korea who helped guide me to my grandfather's records, especially Shin Yong Ha, Chi Soo Gul, Yun Kyung Rho, Lew Young Ik, Suh Dae Suk, Park Chul Ha, and Shim Han Bo. I want to acknowledge my great uncles Lee Choong Ha and Lee Wan Ha, now deceased, for speaking to me and providing clues to what transpired in the past. Special thanks to my late Oesamchun, Lee Chong Sae, for his translation and diplomacy skills and unflagging support.

I found my writer's voice through the Temescal Writers and Lakeshore Writers generative writing workshops—thanks to leaders Joan Marie Wood and Teresa Burns Gunther and the amazing writers with whom I had the privilege of writing. I workshopped portions of *Starry Field* at Tin House, Lit Camp, the Writer's Hotel, and the Belize Writers Conference. I appreciate the input of all my workshop leaders and fellow participants, but most of all, thank you for providing the roots of my writing community. I couldn't have written this book without the Mesa Refuge (twice), Mineral School (twice), and Anderson Center writing residencies, which allowed me to take time off from busy family life to focus on my book. Thanks to Corporeal Writing and to the writers in their virtual hours, where I wrote the introduction and epilogue of the book.

Thank you to the dozens of people who have read portions or the entirety my manuscript over the decades, including the members of the Bay Area Manuscript Group, Sabina Murray, Catherine Hollis, Joey Garcia, Rose Andersen, and Luc Walhain. I wish I had room to name everyone. Special shout out to Shanna McNair and Scott Wolven at the Writer's Hotel, for helping me polish my manuscript and introducing me to my lovely agent.

Thanks to my champion, Ayla Zuraw-Friedland, the best agent I could ask for and a hell of a good editor. None of this could have happened without you. Thanks also to the kind folks at the Frances Goldin Agency for their support. I'm so happy to be reunited with my editor Carl Bromley at Melville House, my *Nation* magazine lunch buddy from long ago. I can think of no better editor to bring this book to life. Thanks to everyone at Melville House who helped make *Starry Field* an object I can hold in my hands—Beste Doğan, Mike Lindgren, Sofia Demopolos, Michelle

Capone, Dennis Johnson, Valerie Merians, Justin DeCarlo, Madeleine Letellier, Pia Mulleady, Ariel Palmer-Collins, and Sammi Sontag.

For recent research, thanks again to Ayoung Moon for your translation skills and for introducing me to your Seoul National University colleague, Jung Joon Young, who provided essential materials, and to Juan Kim in Seoul and Minyoung Lee in Oakland for their help. Thanks to Sunyoung Park, Joy Kim, and Jungeun Hong at USC for their interest in my research materials and answering my questions. I also wanted to acknowledge my grandfather and father's alma mater, Kongju High School, for helping to keep Lee Chul Ha's legacy alive through a planned scholarship fund in his name.

I couldn't have finished this book without the support of my writing community, including my 2019 Writer's Hotel cohort, the Depressing Memoir Group, numerous Binders online groups who taught me about the publishing industry, and all the writers I met at residencies and conferences, including my soul sisters, the Lakefeeders. Thanks to all my friends, you know who you are, especially the Gang who know me best and remember the shy, bespeckled girl who got locked in the airplane bathroom. And thanks to all the people who I've encountered through this long journey that I might have overlooked.

Finally, thank you to my husband and children. You are the reason I wrote this book, even though I didn't know it when I began. This book is for you.